Stop
Burning
Your
Money

Random House

New York

STOP BURNING YOUR MONEY

The Intelligent

Homeowner's Guide

to Household

Energy Savings

JOHN ROTHCHILD

With a
Preface and
Final Word by
Daniel Yergin

Library of Congress Cataloging in Publication Data
Rothchild, John.
Stop burning your money.
1. Dwellings—Energy conservation. I. Title.
TJ163.5.D86R69   696   80-5271
ISBN 0-394-51366-5   AACR2

Manufactured in the United States of America
9 8 7 6 5 4 3 2

First Edition

To Tom,
Barbara, Eleanor,
Melanie and
Lee

Preface

This is the right book at the right time.

Its premise is very simple. Being energy-efficient in your home is not something you do for its own sake, but because keeping household energy costs to a minimum means that less of your money ends up going into your utility bill and more of it stays in your own pocket or bank account. In other words, you're efficient out of economic self-interest. As you read this book, you will learn that investing some of your time and money in home energy conservation can result in very substantial returns—often more predictable and quicker returns than you will find in money market funds or T-bills or Swiss bank accounts or works of art.

In other words, *Stop Burning Your Money* is about making money in today's inflation-ridden economy.

Home energy costs are moving in one direction—up. And it is going to get increasingly more expensive *not* to act, for prices may increase even more swiftly in the next few years than in the last. In the past, when energy was cheap, it made good economic sense to disregard energy costs when running your home. But times have changed with a vengeance, bringing about a shift in attitudes. Everyone now wants to save energy, but wanting to is not enough.

The real questions are what to do and how to do it. And here the American public faces a huge and pervasive knowledge gap. This is what makes *Stop Burning Your Money* so important. *It puts almost a decade's worth of national learning and information on home energy use into practical, usable terms between the covers of one book.* Up to now, reliable information was very hard to come by, and available information was often less than solid and sometimes contradictory. Some experts have urged you to add storm windows and more insulation, while others have advised you not to bother. You have been told to button up your house, but not too much. You have been pushed to buy a woodstove or a solar water heater, but you have also been warned to stay away from both.

How do you evaluate all the advice that currently exists? What investment in time and money will bring you the best financial returns? Should you consider buying the highly promoted big-ticket conservation items? What can you do yourself in your home? Whom do you turn to for help, and how do you evaluate the work done? How do you analyze the energy characteristics of the house you might buy? In general, how do you know that you are not making the wrong choices and wasting money?

John Rothchild is specially qualified to address those questions and answer them. For a considerable part of the last five years, he has devoted himself to researching the best available knowledge and information in home energy use. The five-year odyssey has taken him back and forth across the country many times: To Princeton University, to observe the revolutionary work of the "house doctor." To Massachusetts, to audit a utility's energy auditors. To Lawrence Laboratory at the University of California at Berkeley, to confer with people doing advanced work on energy-efficient buildings and appliances and indoor air quality. To Colorado, to meet with experts on utility financing and to obtain the best information on the intricacies of window design at the Solar Energy Research Institute. To Santa Cruz, California, to take part in a landmark symposium sponsored by the American Council for an Energy Efficient Economy. And to Washington, D.C., and the offices of the Department of Energy to pull together the entire concept of low cost/no cost energy saving.

John Rothchild is as familiar with the ongoing strands of research and experimentation on home energy use as anyone in the country. He also possesses hands-on knowledge of the principles of energy conservation, having built an energy-efficient home in Florida and a passive solar house in Georgia. But John knows that most people who will turn to this book are not likely to build, repair, or retrofit their own homes. So he has written a book aimed at busy people who simply want to make sure that their present home energy bills are economic and cost-effective, and then get back to other pursuits.

So *Stop Burning Your Money* is a first: the first book on home energy conservation organized strictly around cost-effective household investment priorities. The book, in short, is informed throughout by a healthy and necessary sense of skepticism. John Rothchild, in the face of existing conventional opinion and advice, usually plunks for the low cost/no cost technique or product first, and then asks some pretty tough, searching questions of the more costly big-ticket purchases. Just because something is expensive, highly promoted, and perceived as fashionable does not make it something to buy.

It must also be remembered, however, that a house is not like an automobile, a car being a highly standardized and mass-produced machine. One can confidently say that a Ford Mustang or a Toyota Corolla gets so many miles per gallon of gasoline consumed. But the American housing stock—numbering some 80 million residences—is very diverse in terms of construction and use. Thus no single formula can guarantee the same results for every house in the country, or even on the same block. Still, a rough rule of thumb—one based on many, many observations—is that a 30 to 40 percent reduction in home energy consumption, without reducing your accustomed level of physical comfort, represents a reasonable goal if you choose to pursue a modest strategy of energy efficiency.

Meanwhile, innovation in the building industry spreads at a snail's pace, and the housing stock turns over very slowly—even more slowly than usual at present, since high interest rates have crimped new construction. So if we want to behave in an economic manner and manage our household budgets wisely, we have to make our present homes more energy-efficient, something John Rothchild tells us how to do in precise terms. He also explains how to evaluate the energy characteristics of a home before you buy it, which is very important in the United States, since the average family moves every five years.

Professor Robert Stobaugh and I observed two things in our book, *Energy Future: Report of the Energy Project at the Harvard Business School.* First, that conservation is really a source of energy for our country; and second, that effective energy conservation depends on individual decisions made by millions and millions of people. For my money, the best decisions to be made in home energy conservation —decisions good for the nation and for the individual—will be based on John Rothchild's thoroughly sensible, practical and understandable book.

The word "economics" originally derives from the Greek word meaning "household management." The sudden rise in energy costs means that millions and millions of Americans are today no longer behaving in an economic sense insofar as their houses are concerned —neither in the modern sense, nor in the classical sense of managing our households wisely. With this book, we can regain control over utility bills, and so can once again manage our households wisely, and have more dollars available for other purposes.

Stop Burning Your Money will show you in convincing fashion that with some time and attention, along with a relatively small investment of dollars, all homeowners can receive a very substantial monetary return in the months and years ahead.

—DANIEL YERGIN

Acknowledgments

The Department of Energy, and especially Howard Ross and Susan Wells.

Lawrence Berkeley Laboratory, and especially Arthur Rosenfeld, Steve Selkowitz, Robert Sonderegger, Peter Cleary, Craig Hollowell, Mark Levine, Jim Berk, Rick Diamond, and Mark Modera.

Princeton University's Center for Energy and Environmental Studies, and especially Gautam Dutt, Ken Gadsby, Robert Socolow, David Harrje, Harvey Sachs.

Brookhaven Laboratory and Gerald Dennehy.

Pacific Gas and Electric and John Hailey.

Southern California Gas Company, John C. Abram, and Larry Asch.

Fafco, Inc., solar manufacturers, and John O'Lear.

The Florida Solar Energy Center and Marvin Yarosh.

The American Gas Association, Rich Ittelaig, Ann Roland, and Mark Menzer.

The Solar Energy Research Institute and Rebecca Vorhees.

Jay Shelton, Frank Tenney, Cheryl Merser, Trudy Smith, Ham Mattoon, Molly Berns, Joette and Michael Lorion, and the Keystone Center for Continuing Education.

Consumer Energy Council of America, Ellen Berman and Mark Cooper.

The Alliance to Save Energy, Linda Schuck and Lynn Collins.

The Tennessee Valley Authority and Robert Hemphill, Jr.

Meenan Oil Company and William F. Kenny, III.

Robert Bernstein, president of Random House, who thought this book needed to be written; Elizabeth Darhansoff, who ushered it along.

Jason Epstein, editorial director of Random House, and Grant Ujifusa, for their conscientious editing, which made this a better book.

Energy Project at the Harvard Business School and Robert Stobaugh.

Energy and Environmental Policy Center at the Kennedy School of Government at Harvard, and William Hogan, Henry Lee, Jane Shorall, and Al Alm.

California Public Utilities Commission, John Bryson and George Amaroli.

Contents

Introduction

T his book is about the money side of home energy use. I will try to clear up some confusion that exists: whether, among other things, you should invest your money reinsulating your house or spend it replacing your furnace, whether you should convert to natural gas or buy a solar water heater, or whether you should do nothing at all and simply put your money into Treasury bills and the stock market. You should know that I am not moved by the joys of woodburning or the moral virtues of a solar greenhouse, to name two ways to conserve energy that are often more a matter of fashion than they are of economics. To me, the only worthy energy conservation decision is one that pays off.

I am convinced that certain energy-saving investments do pay off, at a higher rate of return and with more reliability than many of the opportunities that tempt us from the business section of the newspaper. Some of us expend considerable effort trying to find the right moment to buy a Treasury bill, gaining perhaps an extra percentage point, while we ignore the old oil furnace, which wastes 40 percent of the fuel oil we buy. If we can make that furnace operate more economically, the oil we don't burn becomes a kind of invisible commodity. It appreciates in a mythical account that is enriched with every fuel price increase. Because we pay our fuel and electric bills in after-tax dollars, all the profits in the energy-saving "account" are tax-free. Where else can we find tax-free dividends, that get automatically larger every time the energy prices go up?

On the other hand, energy-saving investments can also be sucker investments, and more sucker money is spent every day as people consider the next round of retrofits, to use that inelegant word for modifying a house to use less fuel. I have friends who bought a woodstove, not realizing that the wood they burned was more expensive than the natural gas it replaced. I count myself as one of the misguided consumers who purchased a $2,000 solar water heater without first installing a 10¢ device that could have saved me at least half the money at a fraction of the big-ticket cost. Many people have dutifully reinsulated their attics when the same money invested in other parts of the house could have produced double the return.

Homeowners cannot be blamed for making the wrong choices. Reliable information is still in short supply, even though we now get advice from the oil company, the electric company, woodstove experts, solar experts, furnace experts, appliance salesmen, insulation contractors, heating contractors, and neighborhood solons, all of whom swear by one strategy or another. Exaggerations are inevitable as business enterprises exhort us to buy something more so we can burn something less. Such exaggerations are allowed to stand because there is no easy way to say with any certainty which product actually saved what in the monthly energy bill. People who make the biggest claims have the advantage that Thorstein Veblen saw in the early church—salvation could always be promised because failure to deliver could never be proven.

In the recent past, the affluent among us could afford to buy certain status-symbol conservation products because the payoffs were not yet critical to the family budget. This book is for people who can no longer tolerate an ineffective cure. Many of you have already passed the disturbing milestone when the monthly payment to the utility company exceeded the amount of the mortgage payment. You need to find the right investments, which will be lucrative only to the degree that not making them is going to be extremely expensive.

How can you pick the bargains out of the clamorous energy bazaar? The first step is to learn to judge energy-saving investments by their rates of return. Many of these products and devices have been advertised on their paybacks—that is, on how many years it takes to recover the purchase price in the fuel savings. Solar water heaters were once said to have a ten-year payback in most regions, attic insulation was supposed to have a three- to five-year payback, and so forth. The idea is straightforward enough, but it isn't very useful, because dividends from other kinds of investments are not calculated on payback. Rate of return, on the other hand, enables you to buy insulation on the same basis you buy Treasury bills. You can also use the method to pick out the best opportunities from the long and confusing conservation shopping list.

There are various ways to derive rates of return, but the one I suggest is a simple comparison between the value of the fuel saved and the purchase price of the device that saved it. For instance, an additional layer of attic insulation that cuts the heating bill by $50 a year and costs $600 will have a rate of return of $50/$600, or 8.3 percent. That's a tax-free return, remember, so if you are in the 50 percent tax bracket, it would take a competing investment with roughly a 16 percent yield to equal the dividend from the attic insulation.

This kind of computation will not satisfy some economists, who will say that it leaves out the discount rate and the future value of money. But most consumers don't enjoy much of a discount rate, so for the purpose of picking the best energy investments, the simple comparison works quite well. It was developed by the Consumer Energy Council of America to help homeowners decide whether conversion to gas was more or less profitable than adding more insulation or taking other conservation actions on the house. We can apply it to all the energy-saving options.

When you look at your house as a physical portfolio, a series of opportunities with different rates of return, some surprising conclusions result. The heavily publicized purchases often give smaller dividends than the more obscure purchases. The chart on pages xviii–xxi shows some generic rates of return for a theoretical house with a $1,200 annual heating bill and a $250 annual water heating bill. I don't claim that these numbers are definitive, but they are based on research done by a variety of organizations on a variety of houses, and thus are legitimate rough estimates.

You can see that there is a wide range of payoffs.

Furthermore, you might get more profit out of plugging air leaks into the house than you get from certain expensive modifications like storm windows or wall insulation. I'm not saying you can solve your energy problems with a caulking gun or a few rags to stuff in the fireplace damper, but these low-cost measures get less attention than they deserve. Many of us hoped to buy our way out of the energy dilemma with one or two big purchases, but it is precisely this

RATES OF RETURN AND RISK RATING ON VARIOUS
ENERGY-SAVING INVESTMENTS TO THEORETICAL HOUSE WITH
$1,200 HEATING BILL AND $250 WATER HEATING BILL

Investment	Cost	Percent of Heating Bill Saved	Annual Payback
1. Investments to the Shell of the House:			
Attic insulation where none now exists	$600	20	$240
Attic insulation added where five inches now exists	$400	5	$60
Wall insulation	$800	5–10	$60–120
Storm windows	$640	10	$120
Plugging the air leaks	$100	5–10	$60–120
Duct insulation	$100	5	$60
Basement insulation (low-cost technique)	$50	5	$60
Clock thermostat	$100	5–10	$60–120
Passive solar greenhouse	$3,000	5–20	$60–240
2. Furnace Modifications for Oil-Burning Equipment:			
Replace the burner	$340	10–15	$120–180
Vent damper	$200	2–14	$24–168
Aquastat to control boiler temperature	$600	5–15	$60–180
Nozzle change on burner	$2	5	$60

Rate of Return (percent)	*Risk Rating*	*Pitfalls*
40	A	Attic must be sealed from air leaks before insulation put down
15	B	Diminishing returns: leaks harder to seal beneath existing coverage
7–15	B	Work hidden from view; voids sometimes left in wall cavities
18	B	Returns are hard to predict
60–120	A	Caulking must be systematic and thorough
60	A	Return depends on location of ducts in house
120	A	Heat loss in basement varies from house to house
60–120	A	Must be used for night setback
2–8	B	Demands careful design, including heat storage
35–50	A	Works best with old, leaky furnaces and boilers
12–84	B	Savings depend on location of furnace, also on flue temperatures
10–30	B	Savings reduced on equipment with good burner
300	A	Service people usually won't do it unless in conjunction with new burner

Investment	Cost	Percent of Heating Bill Saved	Annual Payback
Replace the entire furnace or boiler	$2,500	25	$300
Convert to gas by switching burners	$800	30	$360
Convert to gas by installing new high-efficiency gas boiler or furnace	$2,500	50	$600
3. Furnace Modifications for Gas-Burning Equipment:			
Vent damper	$200	5–10	$60–120
Pilotless ignition	$100	5	$60
Replacing gas boiler or furnace with new, high-efficiency equipment	$2,500	30	$360
4. Water Heating Modifications:			
Solar water heater	$2,000	30–70	$75–175
Heat pump water heater	$800	30–60	$75–150
Water heater blanket	$20	5	$12.50
Showerhead flow controller	$1	30	$75

Rate of Return (percent)	Risk Rating	Pitfalls
12	A	Expensive strategy
45	B	You are gambling that gas will continue to be cheaper than oil
24	A	Expensive strategy, but with two possible payoffs—one for better efficiency, another for cheaper fuel
30–60	B	Savings depend on high flue temperatures and location of furnace
60	B	Heat from pilot may be beneficial in winter
15	A	Expensive strategy
4–9	C	Installation problems abound; savings unpredictable
9–19	A	Savings vary with climate, greatest in warm areas
62	A	Do-it-yourself installation
7500	A	Investor must have conserving attitude

passion for the big fix that can lead to fanciful miscalculation. One can see the folly in purchasing a solar water heater (with a 4 to 9 percent rate of return) without first at least trying to reduce the hot-water bill with showerhead flow controllers and an extra layer of insulation around the tank (for up to a 7500 percent rate of return).

This chart still doesn't indicate the specific rates of return you will get in your own house, and the only way to get a moderately accurate analysis is with an on-site audit. Fortunately, many utility companies are now providing audits to any ratepayer who requests one, and you might as well take them up on the offer. The audit will estimate annual dollar savings from various purchases like insulation and storm windows, and you can compute the rates of return by dividing the cost of the retrofit into the predicted savings.

If the audit represented the final word on energy-saving techniques, there would be no need for this book. But it doesn't. Not by any means. For one thing, there may be several weaknesses in the audits that distort the numbers, so before you call the auditor you should read Part 4, "Auditing the Auditors." For another thing, many audits don't reveal how one investment can affect the profita-

REJECT LIST

You can save hundreds of dollars by simply avoiding a few products that don't deserve their fuel-bill-cutting reputation.

Attic ventilators	These are great for airing out the attic and keeping it free of moisture. But according to the Department of Energy, they don't produce lower air conditioning bills, as sometimes promised.
Timers for electric water heaters	They have an insignificant effect on hot water bills, according to researchers at Oak Ridge national labs.
Combustion air humidifiers	The claim is that these devices increase furnace efficiency by putting water vapor into the combustion air. According to Brookhaven, they don't.
Storm doors	More cost-effective to weatherstrip existing door.

bility of another, and this is a crucial point. When you buy a more efficient furnace, you cut the fuel bill and therefore reduce the rate of return on other investments like insulation or storm windows. Or if you reinsulate first, you may conserve your way out of the need for a more efficient furnace. So how do you decide what to do first? The most profitable way to get through the quagmire is to make the investment with the highest rate of return, then move to the investment with the next best rate of return, and so on. You may find that a series of small purchases, coupled with a little conserving behavior, will give you the highest dividend on your energy-saving dollar.

But there is one other factor to consider besides economics. Even the most intelligent strategy can be undone by poor installation or by the idiosyncrasies of your particular house, and it is in this physical arena where energy savings are frequently sabotaged. Attic insulation may lose up to 30 percent of its value because a few subtle air leaks allow heat to bypass the coverage. Certain types of wall insulation tend to shrink inside the wall cavities, where heat can escape right along with some of your savings. Part of this book is devoted to these spoilers, and how you can either correct them or avoid them, because the effectiveness of energy-saving devices is surprisingly dependent on the quality of installation. Since the chance of partial failure is greater with some products than with others, I have given the various purchases a risk rating, similar to a bond rating, as shown on the chart. You are more likely to get the predicted dividends from an A-rated purchase than from a B-rated purchase.

When the risk factors are connected to the rates of return, a clearer picture emerges. Low-cost efforts are often the most profitable, and in some cases these small adjustments must be made before a big-ticket product like insulation will produce a high return. Because of air leaks and other factors, the riskiest purchases often involve the shell of the house, which is where homeowners have put most of their money and attention. Some of the most reliable investments are found in furnaces and appliances, and these investments have been given less publicity than they deserve. Appliance energy labels are as important to the household budget as the EPA mileage ratings for cars. Some of my friends in Florida have spent hundreds of dollars to reinsulate their attics at the same time they have bought inefficient air conditioners, putting them into a deeper financial hole than if they had forgotten the insulation and purchased high-mileage air conditioners.

Not every section of this book will apply to your house, so the best way to use this book is to skip around. If you are wondering whether to buy electric or gas appliances, or whether to convert from oil to gas as your primary heating fuel, I suggest that you read the section on prices. Otherwise, you can move right to the furnace section. I am convinced that furnaces and boilers offer superior opportunities to save money, either through modification of the existing equipment or through total replacement. While there is no across-the-board answer as to which of these options is the most profitable, I have explained how to make the evaluation and how to ask the right questions of the furnace technician.

If you already have an efficient furnace, then you can concentrate on winning the shell game with more insulation or better window treatments or more caulking and weatherstripping. The shell of the house is where you find many of the spoilers, and also many low-cost techniques to remedy them and retrieve the savings that you should have been getting.

Part 4 describes the auditing procedure and tells you how to judge the quality of the audit and apply fudge factors to the savings calculations that the auditor makes. Read it before calling in the auditor. Part 5 looks at the buying and maintaining of appliances; next to furnaces, this is where the biggest returns can be gained, and sometimes from purchases that have to be made anyway.

The section on fashionable alternatives appears quite far back in the book, and its placement reflects my conviction that woodstoves, solar water heaters, solar greenhouses, and other such products can make less-than-desirable investments. There is a long discussion on the demerits of woodburning, which concludes that the way to get the most out of your fireplace is to plug it up and forget about it.

Beyond the fashionable alternatives, there is a section on how to rate a house for its energy efficiency and how to compare the energy economy of one house against another. This is an important new procedure, especially for prospective home buyers who don't want to learn in February that the house they purchased the previous June is too expensive to support.

At the end of the book, there is a list of side effects, the unfortunate consequences of caulking or insulating in the wrong places. Such consequences can be very costly, and in some instances even hazardous to health, but they all can be avoided. Finally, there is a short description of some Canadian houses that have heating bills of less than $10 a month. These houses are conventional in most respects, which indicates that you don't need to live in a yurt or a cave to conquer the energy bills. With the right techniques, conventional houses can be built in most areas of this country that require little or no artificial heating or cooling.

Throughout the book, I rely on the extensive work done at four large energy laboratories—Lawrence Berkeley in California, Oak Ridge in Tennessee, Brookhaven on Long Island, and Princeton in New Jersey. Scientists at all these places have spent several years learning how energy is consumed in real houses, and some of the best information has gotten scant dissemination. The Reagan Administration's antipathy to both consumer information programs and energy conservation research insures that we won't be hearing much from these people in the near future. But we can all benefit from what they have found out so far.

I also rely on the experiences of my friends and acquaintances who have both succeeded and failed in attempts to reduce energy bills. You will meet some of them in this book, either as real people or as fictional composites. The practical problems they faced deserve full notice. I want you to profit from their mistakes.

Part One

FUTURE SHOCK: THOSE 1990 PRICES

The weather—how cold the winter, how hot the summer—and the future price of energy present the two great uncertainties surrounding any energy conservation investment. If a winter is cold, your insulation of course becomes more valuable to you. Nature's whim is one thing, but what you decide to do on your side of the electric and gas meter also depends on what the cartels, sheikhs, and energy companies do, what happens to overall costs, political upheavals in the Middle East, and the balance between supply and demand. Before you can figure how much money to invest and where, you have to make an intelligent estimate about where prices may go.

Some electric utilities, in particular, are now perhaps more eager for their customers to conserve than the customers are themselves. And this leads me to consider the unforeseen benefits of doing nothing to your house. A friend of mine, an energy laggard from the Pacific Northwest, scoffed at neighbors who were insulating their houses and bought a hot tub instead. I imagined a "Three Little Pigs" ending to this, with the laggard hastily buying insulation in 1980, which he could have gotten much cheaper in 1973.

But my friend's utility, Pacific Power and Light, upset my expectations. Recently, the utility offered the laggard a full insulation and retrofit package to be financed by a no-interest PP and L loan. And my friend doesn't have to pay back the principal until he sells the house. Moreover, PP and L's insulation program possesses more stringent quality control than the random jobs previously done in my friend's neighborhood. So the man with the hot tub is rewarded for his indifference. He spent nothing for something his neighbors had to pay for—although this way his neighbors were able to avoid having to pay their share of the cost of building a new electric generating plant.

Not all utilities are as helpful as Pacific Power and Light, but many are moving in that direction. Meanwhile, the federal and state governments have upped the tax benefits to homeowners who invest to save energy. So, in communities where utilities have not yet established such a program, the longer one waits, the less one may have to pay out-of-pocket for such things as insulation or clock thermostats or water heater devices. At the same time, energy prices continue to create pressure to invest now. When to wait and when to buy, whether to stick with an old electric appliance and an oil furnace or convert one or both to gas, are decisions that depend on a very complex price and regulatory structure. But the trend is clear.

Home Heating Oil

The $1.30-a-gallon mark has been passed in many areas of the country. Compare that to the 18¢ a gallon in 1970. Attempts to predict what happens next are risky, but home heating oil already costs more than forecasters of a few years ago predicted we would be paying in the year 2000. Oil prices are still tied to the whims of the producing countries and political "accidents" like the fall of the Shah of Iran, but it is safe to assume that those prices will continue to rise faster than the rate of inflation. Fuel oil dealers will probably not offer the kind of conservation financing that PP and L does, although some dealers are installing more economical burners to keep their customers from switching to natural gas.

If you heat with oil, you can bet that any conservation purchase recommended in this book will make money for you. Future prices virtually guarantee that.

Natural Gas

Natural gas has been an energy bargain. People who heat with gas pay less than what their neighbors pay for the same amount of heat from oil, and one-half of what most people pay to heat with electricity. Many homeowners have seen the ratios and have converted to gas. They haven't saved much energy that way, but they have saved money. In 1979, at least 225,000 people switched out of oil, according to the American Gas Association. More than 300,000 converted to gas in 1980, and 200,000 more will likely switch by the end of 1981. The exodus is the result of a quirk in the energy marketplace that has made conversion profitable.

The gas suppliers welcome the new customers for two reasons. First, they have lost some industrial business to other fuels, which they want to cover with an expanded residential market. Second, the residential market itself is getting much stingier with the gas it uses. Pacific Gas and Electric reports that energy-saving efforts in its service area during 1979 alone freed up enough natural gas to supply 75,000 new homes for ten years.

The AGA says that improving household energy "mileage" saves enough gas to meet the demand for any and all new residential customers in the country, including the converts from oil. If supply shortages ever occur, the AGA argues, they will affect the industrial users of 15 trillion cubic feet of gas, not the residential users of 5 trillion cubic feet. Federal law requires that the residential customers be the last to have their gas cut off. Not to worry, AGA concludes.

So assuming that gas is available in your area, and that future supply is no problem, is it still smart to convert? The benefits are best calculated by determining how much it costs to produce 1 million BTUs of heat with the standard competing energy sources—gas, oil, and electricity. The BTU, or British thermal unit, is an energy yardstick representing the amount of heat it takes to raise one pound of water by one degree Fahrenheit. The science isn't important here, but the term is. You can hardly converse with local energy experts without throwing around some BTUs.

It takes 293 kilowatt-hours of electricity, 7.2 gallons of home heating oil, and 10 therms of natural gas to make 1 million BTUs of heat. With that benchmark, it is easy enough to compare prices and decide whether to buy oil or gas furnaces, or electric or gas appliances. You call the local gas company and ask them what 10 therms is costing these days, and then do same with the electric company for 293 kilowatt-hours and the oil dealer for 7.2 gallons. Let's take a typical case. I pay 6¢ per kilowatt-hour for electricity, so it costs me $17.58 to get the 1 million BTUs from my outlets. I pay 50¢ a therm for natural gas, so it costs only $5.00 to get an equal amount of energy from the gas line. I don't buy oil, but at regional prices of $1.30 a gallon, it would cost me $9.36 to produce the same amount of heat from oil. Similar ratios are common, but not universal, throughout the country. You have to make a local determination.

Propane or bottled gas should not be confused with natural gas, the kind that is piped into the house. Bottled gas is generally more expensive than natural gas, and it is therefore in relative terms not a bargain. Bottled gas is sold in gallons, and it takes 10.9 of those gallons to make 1 million BTUs. You can use this number, plus a phone call to the bottled gas dealer, to derive the cost of 1 million BTUs of energy from this fuel.

The advantages of natural gas are apparent. All other things being equal (and we will determine later if they are), a gas stove is a better buy than an electric stove; a gas water heater better than an electric water heater; and a gas furnace better than an oil or electric furnace. It may even pay to replace certain electric appliances with gas appliances, depending on the cost of the new appliance and how much you are going to use it. We'll read more about this later.

The hitch is that you can be certain about the price advantage only for a short time. There is no telling whether gas users will continue to pocket the difference next year and the year after that. The American Gas Association, eager to woo more converts, says that gas will be cheaper right through 1995. In this, they are supported by an independent analysis of the Energy Information Agency, a statistical arm of the Department of Energy.

If EIA is right, we should all pay less attention to how much energy we burn and more attention to what kind we burn, especially if gas is available in the neighborhood. Again, if EIA is right, conversion will be the premier money-saving home energy investment into the twenty-first century.

However, there is growing skepticism in some quarters about this assumption. For instance, the Consumers Energy Council of America has declared that such studies "overstate the future differences between oil and gas, substantially ignoring the likely upward pressure on gas prices resulting from recently enacted legislation to deregulate natural gas in 1985." The present system of natural gas pricing is the result of a bloody year-and-a-half congressional battle that resulted in the Natural Gas Policy Act of 1978, which is supposed to decontrol "new" natural gas completely by 1985. The idea was that the price would rise to the equivalent price of oil. It was generally thought in 1978 that the equivalent price of oil would be about $15 a barrel in 1985. But it is already over $35 a barrel today. So natural gas will move up in very big steps between now and 1985, and the amount of "old gas," still controlled, will be much less.

But there is a further twist. A lot of people want to decontrol natural gas faster. Some politicians are fearful of an angry public reaction when natural gas prices take the last great leap to world levels in 1985. The Department of Energy has estimated that interstate residential natural gas prices might increase 30 percent in one year, and intrastate natural gas prices for homeowners might increase by 90 percent in just one year! So these worried politicians want to smooth out the jumps—meaning bigger increases sooner. Natural gas producers—though not necessarily gas utilities—want decontrol sooner because it will mean higher incomes for them. As the *Wall Street Journal* reports, the Reagan administration "philosophically supports total decontrol of natural gas" as soon as possible. So, decontrol of natural gas could come very quickly, which would wipe out the current price advantage. Thus, there is a very wide range of reasonable predictions that can be made for natural gas prices for the next few years.

Natural gas is just as valuable as oil. Some would say even more. The supposition has to be that it will have an equivalent price to oil in the marketplace sometime in the next few years. Nobody knows for sure when or exactly how this will happen. But conversion from oil to gas, which was a sure bet two years ago, now looks more and more like quite a gamble.

Electricity

We can be more certain that gas and oil will always be a bargain relative to electricity. Electricity is the worst buy in energy, as shown

THE UPWARD MARCH OF RESIDENTIAL ENERGY PRICES
(AVERAGE UNITED STATES—CURRENT DOLLARS)

	1970	1979	1981 (March)	1985 (estimated)
Home heating oil (dollars per gallon)	18¢	66¢	$1.25	$1.80–$2.20
Natural gas (dollars per thousand cubic feet)	89¢	$3.23	$4.17	$10.00–$15.00
Electricity (cents per kilowatt-hour)	2.1¢	4.6¢	5.8¢	8.0¢–10.0¢

SOURCES: Lawrence Berkeley Laboratory; Department of Energy; Energy Information Agency; Robert Stobaugh; American Gas Association. Estimates assume real price increases and inflation.

DOING IT IN BTUS: NATIONAL AVERAGE RESIDENTIAL PRICES
(CURRENT DOLLARS PER MILLION BTUS)

	1981 (March)	1985 (estimated)
Home heating oil	$9.28	$13.00–$16.00
Natural gas	$4.17	$10.00–$15.00
Electricity	$16.88	$24.00–$29.00

in the EIA projections. Not a natural resource itself, it has to be generated from other natural resources, and that step makes it less economical, for the same reason meat is less economical than grain. Two-thirds of the energy value of the fuel used to make electricity is lost by the time the power reaches the customer. The customer pays for the loss, which explains why electricity is usually the most expensive way to heat a house, water, or food.

The reason that owners of all-electric homes haven't been priced into oblivion is that all-electric homes tend to be newer, smaller, better insulated, and therefore require less heat. Also, electricity does enjoy one advantage over natural gas or home heating oil. Once it gets to the house, it can be 100 percent useful, while about 30 percent of the heat value of gas or oil is lost up chimneys or flues. A development, however, may reverse the advantage—new gas- and oil-burning furnaces can now reach 80 percent efficiency levels. But yet another development may extend the advantage—the wider use of the electric heat pump, a device that uses roughly half the energy as standard electric heating equipment to produce the same amount of heat. I'll explain how this works later.

Electric rates vary from as little as 2¢ per kilowatt-hour in the region served by the Tennessee Valley Authority to more than 10¢ per kilowatt-hour in parts of New York. But the costs all over the country share one disturbing characteristic: they have been kept artificially low. We moan about our electric bills, but so far we haven't seen the worst of it. The heavy electric user is in for a big fiscal shock in the near future—price increases may be as large or larger as those predicted for oil or natural gas.

The reasons are to be found in the peculiar character of utility company finance, and the concept of marginal costing.

Any new power the utility company generates tomorrow is going to be more costly to produce than the power it now sells. Electricity generated in a new plant is much more expensive to produce than energy that comes from a hydroelectric plant built in 1940, partly because the new plant was much more expensive to build than the old. As its old generating capacity deteriorates or as its customers demand more energy, a utility must meet its commitments with higher-priced energy from new, expensive plants. The marginal cost of electricity is the cost of this new or replacement energy.

Utility customers, however, don't pay the marginal cost. When we buy electricity, we pay a kind of compromise price, one that includes some bargain energy from the old plants and expensive energy from the new ones. Utility executives complain, with some justification, that their product is underpriced, because they are not allowed to charge for the full replacement value of their plant and equipment. If utilities were allowed to charge at the margins, the economic signals would be harsh—prices would double or perhaps triple overnight. Marginal costs are moving up spectacularly as the price tag for new equipment reaches the budgetary stratosphere.

Some conservationists propose marginal pricing as a way to get the energy-saving message out to the rest of us, but public utility commissions could not allow such increases without facing lynch mobs. So the seller-buyer relationship gets rather mixed up. A few utilities, which after all are in the power-selling business, are practically paying their customers to use less of their product. Pacific Power and Light, as we have seen, finds it more profitable to offer no-interest loans on insulation and storm windows than to install new capacity to generate electricity and meet higher demand. PP and L isn't doing this out of the goodness of its electric heart, but to maximize profits for the company and its stockholders. To invest 30¢ to save a kilowatt is smart, when an extra kilowatt costs them 40¢ to produce for which the company is allowed to charge only 10¢.

This economic pressure on the utility is creating a conservation bonanza for people like my hot-tub friend, but the windfall is by no means universal. Some utilities embrace the energy-saving idea; others shun it as the work of no-growth dreamers. Demand for electric power has been growing nationwide, but at a much slower rate than was assumed back in 1973. Utilities that didn't anticipate a much slower growth rate put their chips heavily on the growth table, notably in nuclear plants. Such utilities likely will want to keep demand high enough, and prices high enough, to pay for this new construction.

To find out whether your utility will finance your insulation or other retrofits, you have to ask them about their future conservation plans. Before you spend your own conservation money, call the electric and/or the gas company (depending on which is your principal source of energy), and find out what programs are on the drawing board. The local utility manager's office is usually the best place to call. I discovered, for example, that my own utility, Florida Power and Light, will be giving its customers $300 rebates on ceiling insulation and similar rebates on sun-control film as soon as its $600 million conservation proposal is approved by the Florida Public Service Commission. So I may wait until then to get my insulation, and spend my own money elsewhere. The first rule of energy-saving is: it is always better if somebody else pays for it.

You can also receive some financial help from the federal government, although some of its programs have become victims of Reagan budget-cutting. The feds have expanded the residential energy tax credits, so your purchases may get a bigger break from the IRS. Unfortunately, the increased benefits do not reflect the new understanding of which energy-saving devices and products work best— the subject of this book. The list of devices that qualify for the 15 percent tax credit on purchases up to $2,000 (for a maximum annual write-off of $300) looks about the same as it did when the credits were established in 1978: insulation, replacement oil or gas burners (not conversion burners from oil *to* gas), flue dampers, electric or mechanical burner ignition systems (to eliminate pilot lights), thermal windows, storm doors, clock thermostats, caulking and weatherstripping, and energy meters (which work like taxi meters and display one's daily usage). Notably absent from the credits are money-saving items like indoor storm windows, heat pumps, replacement furnaces, and passive solar additions.

The solar energy tax credit for active equipment, such as rooftop solar water heaters, has been increased from a maximum of $2,200 to a maximum of $4,000, even though a solar purchase is a real risk and often uneconomic. In this instance, the government provides the most lucrative incentive to a product that is least attractive financially.

By way of summary: there is some current advantage in buying gas-burning furnaces and appliances. If you heat or cool with electricity, there is a chance that the utility will pay for modifications to the shell of your house. If you heat with oil, there is a chance that the oil dealer will help you fix the equipment to get improved fuel economy.

So don't spend your money without calling the people who sell you the fuel. Utilities were once thought to be the enemies of conservation, but because of their capacity and pricing problems, they are becoming our unlikely allies in the energy-saving struggle. This private-sector alliance is especially important, since the government is cutting back on its support of efforts to conserve energy.

Part Two

THE HIGH MILEAGE FURNACE

Gordon Greenspan lives in a large two-story house on the New Jersey commuter belt—lots of windows, a fireplace, a view of the ocean. He bought the house ten years ago on aesthetic grounds, not for its BTU rating, and he and his wife paid more attention to their two children's dental bills than to mail from the local utility. The priorities began to change when home heating oil hit 50¢ a gallon, and gasoline went to 75¢.

These early warnings caused Greenspan to put a Toyota in the garage and to use bicycles for neighborhood forays. He then made his first energy-saving investment in the house—six inches of insulation in the attic plus storm windows for every pane of glass—at a total cost of $1,800.

In 1980, Greenspan got stuck with a $1,200 fuel oil bill, not to mention a succession of $50-a-month electric bills, and he suspected that his insulation and storm windows weren't doing enough. Greenspan wanted to put more insulation in his attic, but I pulled him down to the basement. Here, behind the ice skates and the old rug, was the greatest—although the sootiest—investment opportunity in the house, a 150,000 BTU oil burner, vintage 1965.

My friend hadn't looked at the thing twice since he moved in. He certainly hadn't thought of replacing it. Greenspan had sacked his old car for guzzling but still believed that furnaces are forever.

It's an expensive belief. Energy-efficient furnaces are now on the market, the household equivalent of small cars. The fuel economy of both gas- and oil-burning furnaces and boilers has increased dramatically, with the new units providing an equivalent amount of heat on 20 to 40 percent less fuel. A process called pulse combustion has brought gas units beyond 90 percent efficiency, a level that approaches full utilization of the fuel. This breakthrough means that many homeowners can cut one-third off their heat bills by switching to pulse combustion. It represents the single most drastic reduction in energy costs that can be made from any one investment.

There are also replacement opportunities for electric heating systems, now that better heat pumps are available. In certain climates, a heat pump can bring the costs of electric warmth down to the level of burning oil or gas.

So your furnace room is the first place I'd look for the next big-ticket investment. The returns here can be more predictable than those on the shell of the house because fewer extraneous factors are involved. For that reason, I'd give several types of furnace and furnace-related purchases the A rating.

Total replacement is only one of the choices. If you have a boiler (the kind of heating system that makes hot water or steam and sends it to the house via radiators), you can stretch the "mileage" in a number of ways. You can stop some of the heat from leaking up the flue pipe, or chimney, with a vent damper. You can lower the temperature in the boiler. You can cut the fuel flow into the system. You can replace the burner, the place where the fuel is mixed with air and ignited. If what you burn happens to be oil, you could also convert to gas.

Or if you have a hot-air furnace (the kind that heats the air and sends it to the house through ducts), the choices are slightly more limited, but no less promising. You can install a vent damper. You can fix the fan so it pushes more heat from the ducts. With oil-burning hot-air furnaces, you can replace the burner or cut the fuel flow.

These interim steps all have to be measured against the ultimate one: someday it's going to pay you to junk the old unit and get one that throws out a lot of BTUs per gallon.

You can't make a decision to buy a new unit on your own, and neither could Greenspan. Somebody had to help him figure out the costs and benefits in his own case. He needed an expert to look at the furnace (when I say "furnace" throughout this section, I also mean "boiler." If I am talking just about boilers I will say so), to estimate its efficiency and to compute the relative savings from the three possible strategies—replacement, conversion to gas, or modification. If you already have gas equipment, of course, the choices are narrowed to two: replacement or modification.

The Revealing House Call

Can Greenspan get good advice? And why hasn't he gotten it earlier? The answer explains in part why conservation efforts in the basement have been somewhat half-heartedly pursued. The local guardians of furnaces, the people who tune them and check them and tell us what to do with them, are often the same people who sell us the fuel. They are not always anxious to teach us how to use less of their product, although more of them are moving in that direction.

Greenspan has been contacted by a succession of New Jersey salesmen hustling a variety of devices, but his oil dealer never asked him if he wanted a tune-up or an efficiency check or a new fuel-stingy burner. In parts of New England, some oil dealers have decided the only way to keep customers from defecting to natural gas is to adorn their furnaces with these new burners—called high-speed or flame-retention head—that cut oil consumption. So if Greenspan lived in parts of Massachusetts, or even in another part of New Jersey, he would know all about them. But in other service areas, where dealers are traditionally resistant to improving furnaces, the health of the burner is still a big secret.

Gas utilities exhibit the same extremes of enthusiasm and indifference to energy-saving assistance. In parts of California, gas utilities tell their customers about economical new furnaces and show the same customers how to save some money now by turning off pilot lights during the nonwinter months. Other utilities are silent on these matters, so the efficiency of your furnace is largely dependent on geographical accident.

Whenever you have to seek advice (meaning the oil dealer or gas utility hasn't *volunteered* it), you have to wonder about the objectivity of what is said. Any expert can easily scare a customer off by saying that such and such an adjustment will clog the nozzle or damage the fire chamber, and that you are better off leaving poor enough alone. If you hear that kind of thing, get a second opinion from somebody else in the business. Your potential returns here are too important to be scuttled.

As you follow Greenspan's technician through the tune-up and the house call, you will learn what a good evaluation entails. I'm hoping what I am about to outline will help you get a good evaluation from your own local service people. The procedure involved is similar for oil and gas equipment, except in certain cases where it is impossible for the gas technician to get access to the flue pipe to take the measurements. The gas efficiency ratings differ somewhat from the oil efficiency ratings, so separate charts are provided below.

Greenspan's local fuel technician, Jerry Craig, brought the right equipment, which is always a positive sign. He took out a flue gas

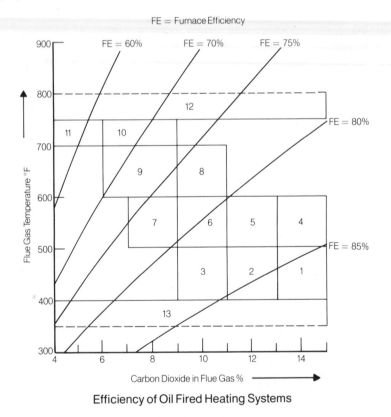

Efficiency of Oil Fired Heating Systems

SOURCE: Department of Energy, Mines and Resources, Canada

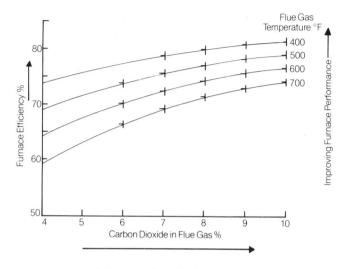

Efficiency of Gas Fired Systems

SOURCE: Department of Energy, Mines and Resources, Canada

thermometer, which looks vaguely like a meat thermometer; a combustion efficiency analyzer, or gas analyzer; and a smoke spot tester, which looks like a small tire pump. Craig fired the furnace and let it heat up for a few minutes before making readings that would determine Greenspan's furnace "mileage." Two readings are crucial here. The first is the temperature of the gases as they are exhausted up the chimney or flue. Flue temperatures vary from as low as 200 degrees to as high as 800 degrees; and in the high range, too much heat is escaping and fuel is wasted.

The second reading is a measurement of how much air the burner needs to completely ignite all the fuel without smoke. The ratio of oxygen to carbon dioxide in the exhaust gases tells you that. Poor burners use more air, which in turn sends more heat up the chimney.

Greenspan's flue temperature was running at a hot 650 degrees, and the carbon dioxide rating was 7 percent. That put his furnace in zone 9 on the chart on page 20, a chart you can review with your own furnace technician. Craig then announced that Greenspan's furnace was operating at 70 percent efficiency, steady-state.

Steady-state is like the EPA rating for highway driving. Greenspan had an outmoded burner and his oil boiler was probably too big

EFFICIENCY OF OIL-FIRED HEATING SYSTEMS

Zone Number	Quality of Performance Furnace	Burner	Efficiency Range (percent)	Commentary
1	Excellent	Excellent	90–83	Rarely if ever achieved.
2	Excellent	Good	87–82	Uncommon: only achieved by the best of new (less than five years old) equipment.
3	Excellent	Typical	85–80	Common to new (less than five years old) equipment, retention head burners.
4	Typical	Excellent	85–82	Rare.
5	Typical	Good	84–80	Uncommon, except in good retention head burners.
6	Typical	Typical	82–76	Common to new (less than five years old) equipment, retention head burners.
7	Typical	Poor	80–72	Unfortunately common in new equipment where it is evidence of a poor burner; in old equipment (more than five years old) (with standard head burners) this is a good performance.
8	Poor	Typical	80–74	Common; in new equipment it is evidence of poor heat-exchanger design or overfiring.
9	Poor	Poor	76–65	Common in old systems, where again it may be evidence of overfiring or inadequate heat-exchanger design.

10	Bad	Poor	74–61	Both categories are uncommon except in the oldest of systems. This performance is very poor.
11	Bad	Bad	Below 61	
12	Completely unacceptable. Flue-gas temperatures above 750°F constitute a materials problem and a fire hazard.			Unsafe operation from the point of view of fire hazard.
13	Completely unacceptable. Flue-gas temperatures below 400°F can constitute a corrosion hazard.			Unsafe operation from the point of view of the structural stability of the chimney.

SOURCE: Department of Energy, Mines and Resources, Canada

for the house. So he was losing 30 percent of the oil he bought, even while his furnace was giving its most favorable performance. Most of the time, as we shall see, his equipment doesn't even work that well.

After these measurements are taken, an adept technician can often make small adjustments to upgrade the efficiency right on the spot. Craig, for instance, was able to clean Greenspan's furnace and reset the air intakes, which brought the steady-state level up to 74 percent. Greenspan was still in zone 9, but a simple tune-up had saved him 4 percent, or about $50 over a heating season, which was at least enough to pay for the service call.

While you've got the expert in the house, there are a couple of other things you can ask him to do that will cut at least a few dollars off your fuel bill. The adjustments are different for furnaces (hot-air equipment) and boilers (hot-water equipment), so I take them separately.

Small Adjustments with Big Payoffs

There is a secondary thermostat that controls the fan pushing the air through the furnace ducts. The fan often comes on too late and cuts off too soon, so some of the heat left in the furnace itself is not extracted and blown into the house, where it could do some good.

Once the furnace adviser shows you where these fan thermostats are located, it is easy to reset them so the fan turns on and off at a lower temperature. There is no danger in doing this. The adviser may object, claiming that cold air might come through the ducts at certain intervals as the furnace cycles on and off. Tell him you are willing to take the chance, and that you will return the thermostats to their original position if the adjustment causes any discomfort. That will relieve him of the fear of consumer complaint, which is what usually stops technicians from suggesting the move, even though the odds are good that you won't notice any ill effects and that you'll save $10 or more a year at no cost.

BOILERS

A corresponding adjustment can be made on the aquastat, the device that sets the water temperature before the water is sent into the radiators. During the milder parts of the winter, radiator water doesn't need to be as hot as it does during the cold spells. When you reduce the water temperatures in the boiler system by 35 degrees, you can save as much as 5 percent of a total annual heating bill, although you may have to adjust the setting back and forth a couple of times during the winter. Ask how to do it.

An equally profitable adjustment is called a nozzle reduction, and this one is even better because it's a once-and-for-all proposition. Fuel oil flows into the burner at a fixed and constant rate, predetermined by the size of a nozzle located inside the burner. Many furnaces are too big for the houses they service, a problem that can be partially rectified by inserting a smaller nozzle and cutting oil flow. It's like sending less water to the garden by crimping the hose. Nozzle reduction involves a $2-to-$3 part and a few minutes' labor.

Sometimes the firing chamber on the furnace has to be relined to accommodate such an adjustment, but usually not. With a smaller nozzle, you can achieve an annual fuel saving of from 5 to 10 percent, according to the Brookhaven lab. The trouble is that people like Jerry Craig don't like to do it.

If you heat with gas, forget even suggesting nozzle reduction: gas technicians say it isn't usually a worthwhile adjustment. But oil technicians are more sanguine about it, and the issue is worth discussion with your adviser. He might say that nozzle tightening will cause fuel lines to clog, but that should not be a concern, Brookhaven says, as long as the flow rate is better than 1 gallon per hour. Or he might say that nozzle tightening will leave you with no hot water, which might be true if your hot-water source is the boiler itself. But according to some savvy furnace people I know, the objections to nozzle tampering have mostly to do with oil-dealer economics—no money in it and a slight chance of consumer dissatisfaction.

Gerald Dennehy of the Brookhaven lab offers these general guidelines: "For a well-insulated home of average size, a nozzle as small as .75 gallon per hour is now common. It may have to be more than that if the family gets its hot water from the tankless coil in the furnace. In a typical home that is modestly insulated, a 1-gallon-per-hour flow is usually acceptable. The old doctrine was not to go below 1.5 gallons per hour. But many dealers are finding no problem reducing that to 1 gallon."

Try to get the oil dealer to cut the nozzle to at least 1 gallon per hour. He may do it only if you buy a new burner, which, as you will see, may be a sensible compromise.

SEASONAL EFFICIENCY: CITY DRIVING FOR THE FURNACE

You've squeezed as much as you can out of the cheap adjustments, but it may not be enough. Craig raised the steady-state efficiency of Greenspan's furnace to 74 percent. That wouldn't be bad, except that real fuel economy is measured by the seasonal efficiency rating, which falls far below the steady-state performance. Seasonal economy is lower here, for the same reason that EPA city auto mileage isn't as good as EPA highway mileage. A furnace wastes fuel when it cycles, or stops and starts. The bigger the furnace, the more it cycles, and the more wasteful it is. Oversizing may not add much to the fuel bill of gas furnaces, but it can have a costly effect on oil and gas boilers.

Most furnaces, perhaps yours included, are more powerful than they need to be, because the home builders who ordered them never thought about energy efficiency. They wanted to provide heat to spare on the coldest day in recorded history—the same kind of thinking that put a V-8 in the family garage. The result is also the same: furnace owners pay for oomph they don't need.

Greenspan thought that because his furnace stayed off a good part of the time during the winter, he had an economical unit. In fact, if a furnace does a lot of stopping and starting on a cold day, it is evidence that money is being squandered.

There is no precise way to pin down seasonal efficiency on installed oil or gas equipment, but the experts can guess. Craig figured Greenspan's seasonal rating at about 60 percent. Many oil boilers, especially the old ones converted from coal, do much worse than that, hovering in the 40 percent efficiency range. Standard gas furnaces with no vent dampers and conventional atmospheric burners don't exceed 65 percent seasonal efficiency. A seasonal efficiency of 60 percent means that Greenspan is getting only $60 worth of usable heat for every $100 worth of oil he has to buy.

Greenspan now had all the information he needed to make a choice of one of three major courses of action. He had an estimate of seasonal efficiency. He knew how much it cost him to heat the house with the existing boiler. (Heating costs may be harder to define with gas, especially if the house also has other gas appliances. But you can get ball-park accuracy by comparing gas bills in the winter months to gas bills in the nonwinter months.) Even if Greenspan gave himself a $200 credit for the low-cost adjustments, he was still left with a $1,000 fuel bill that could still be lowered by a substantial margin.

Because the available options are different for oil and gas furnaces and boilers, I will treat them separately.

The Case for Conversion: Oil to Gas

There are two ways to convert. The simpler way is to switch the burner on the furnace or boiler so it burns gas instead of oil and leave the rest of the unit alone. This method possesses a substantial limitation: it doesn't make your heating plant any more efficient. The fuel trade-off—oil for gas—has a very uncertain future rate of return, because the return depends entirely on the price differential between oil and gas holding up indefinitely.

I talked to Jim Gilroy of Brooklyn Union Gas about this simple procedure. He said that standard oil-to-gas conversions run about $800 in most places. Conversions that require bringing a gas line from the street to the house are a little higher, perhaps $1,200. It's not a big job, in either case.

The important thing is to get an estimate for the complete transaction, including the furnace work, the gas pipes, and any electrical modifications that may be required. Gilroy suggests getting two or more bids on the project from contractors on the gas company's approved list. If you can help it, don't let the contractors include oil-burner or oil-tank removal as part of the job. You can keep the old equipment and have it reinstalled if the prices revert again in favor of oil.

After you pin down the costs of conversion, the short-term benefits unfold in some simple mathematics. The equivalency is 7.2 gallons of home heating oil to 10 therms of natural gas. After making the low-cost adjustments, Greenspan would use 1,000 gallons of home heating oil next winter, so by multiplying by 10 and dividing by 7.2, he finds that he would need 1,390 therms of natural gas to provide the same amount of heat. Natural gas in his area is selling for 50¢ a therm; home heating oil is around $1.20 a gallon. Greenspan can therefore project that his converted furnace would burn $695 worth of gas, while his existing furnace would burn $1,200 worth of oil.

The question is how long the price advantage will hold up, and nobody can predict that with any assurance.

The less chancy, and more complicated, conversion is to replace the entire boiler or furnace with a gas unit possessing 90 percent efficiency or better. Even if gas prices catch up with oil, you still save 30 percent and perhaps even 40 percent on fuel bills because you have cut consumption by that amount. And if gas prices stay lower than oil prices, you have saved yourself that much more.

There are two kinds of super-efficient gas heating techniques, pulse combustion and the recuperative furnace. In pulse combustion, the gas is ignited in a series of short bursts, the way fuel is ignited in a rocket engine. The spark-plug effect enables the furnace to extract more heat from the fuel. And instead of the by-products of combustion going up the chimney as hot air, which causes a tremendous loss in efficiency, the by-products are cooled or condensed. A pulse furnace doesn't need a chimney or flue pipe, and can be vented like a clothes dryer.

The recuperative furnace burns fuel in the traditional way, but it also pulls more heat out of the exhaust gases to reach high efficiencies.

At least three domestic manufacturers—HydroTherm, Inc., of Northvale, New Jersey; Lennox Industries of Marshalltown, Iowa;

SOME HIGH-EFFICIENCY OIL FURNACES

BTUs per Hour	Make	Number	Size	Seasonal Efficiency (percent)
65,000–75,000	Blueray	BF-60	69,000	82.60
	Thermo Products	OC3-72	72,000	80.70
80,000–85,000	Blueray	BF series	several	82.00 or better
	Thermo Products	OC1-80	80,000	80.70
	XXth Century	OZ-CEK series	81,000	81.00
85,000–90,000	Williamson	1454 series	93,000	82.60
	Thermo Products	OC5-85	85,000	80.70
	Blueray	BF 75 series	86,000	82.57
90,000–100,000	Williamson	1277 series	100,000	80.50

SOME HIGH-EFFICIENCY OIL BOILERS
(HOT-WATER RADIATOR OR STEAM SYSTEMS)

BTUs per Hour	Make	Number	Size	Seasonal Efficiency (percent)
45,000–50,000	Ultimate Engineering	K4040D	49,000	87.10
60,000–70,000	Ultimate Engineering	K3T050D	60,000	85.62
	Ultimate Engineering	K4T050D	61,000	87.10
	Ultimate Engineering	K5T050D	62,000	87.90
	Blueray	BF60	69,000	82.60
70,000–75,000	Blueray	BR-60	73,000	86.10
	Ultimate Engineering	K5060D	74,000	87.60
75,000–90,000	Ultimate Engineering	K4065D	78,000	85.80
	Blueray	HBF75	87,000	82.70
	Burnham	V-13D	87,000	82.50
90,000–95,000	Blueray	BR-75	90,000	84.20
	Ultimate Engineering	K6T075D	92,000	87.20
	Dunkirk Radiator	PS-42	93,000	81.30
95,000–100,000	Burnham	BBCA-109 FRD	97,000	81.70
	Belcher	FR-98-W	98,000	82.80
	New Yorker Steel	FR-98-W	98,000	82.80

100,000–105,000	Ultimate Engineering	K4T085D	100,000	84.10
	Ultimate Engineering	K5T085D	102,000	85.80
	Ultimate Engineering	K7085D	104,000	86.30
105,000–120,000	Burnham	HE-22FRD	106,000	83.70
	Ultimate Engineering	K3T100D	112,000	80.50
	Dunkirk Radiator	134-2D	116,000	82.80
	Ultimate Engineering	K5100D	118,000	83.90
120,000–125,000	Burnham	BBCA-111-FRD	120,000	81.19
	Belcher	FR-122-W	120,000	81.00
	New Yorker Steel	FR-122-W	120,000	81.00
	Ultimate Engineering	K8T100D	121,000	85.90
	Ultimate Engineering	K5100D	118,000	83.90

SOME HIGH-EFFICIENCY GAS FURNACES

BTUs per Hour	Make	Number	Size	Seasonal Efficiency (percent)
40,000–60,000	Lennox	G14 series	40,000	95.00 (pulse combustion)
			60,000	95.00
	Tappan (also Frigiking, Janitrol)	DR or UR series	40,000	87.00
			60,000	87.00
75,000–85,000	SJC	DI100D16EI	75,000	80.70
	Rheem	RGBG-10K	78,000	79.10
	Ruud	UGBC-10K	78,000	79.10
	Tappan (also Frigiking, Janitrol)	DR or UR series	80,000	87.00
	Lennox	G14 series	80,000	95.00
	Heil Quaker	Energy Marshall	various	80.10
	Whirlpool	Tight Fist	various	80.10
85,000–90,000	GE	BAY series	85,000	80.50
	Lennox	G12RQ3E-110	85,000	78.90
90,000–100,000	Thermo Products	GL11-125-V5	94,000	80.30
	Sears	963240	94,000	81.32
	Lennox	G14 series	100,000	95.00 (pulse combustion)
	Tappan (also Frigiking, Janitrol)	DR or UR series	100,000	87.00

100,000–110,000			
Heil Quaker	Energy Marshall	various	80.10
Whirlpool	Tight Fist	various	80.10
Thermo Products	GL13-133-V5	100,000	79.40
SJC	UL38D15	108,000	82.20
GE	BAY series	various	80.50

SOME HIGH-EFFICIENCY GAS BOILERS

BTUs per Hour	Make	Number	Size	Seasonal Efficiency (percent)
50,000–65,000	HydroTherm	Hydro-Pulse	50,000 BTUs/hr.	91–94
	Columbia Boiler	CEG-75ASID	60,000	81.40
	Utica Radiator	PEG-75AID	60,000	81.40
	Blueray	BG-75D	65,000	84.40
	Weil-McLain	EG series	various	80.70
90,000–105,000	Dunkirk	PS-42	94,000	81.32
	Crown	JS42EI	94,000	81.32
	HydroTherm	Hydro-Pulse	100,000	91–94
	Blueray	BG-125D	103,000	82.70
120,000–130,000	Weil-McLain	EG-45-PID	122,000	80.70
	Blueray	BG-150D	124,000	82.40
	Crown	JS52EI	124,000	81.12
	Dunkirk	PS-52	124,000	81.12
	Pennco	1605ID	124,000	81.12
140,000–160,000	Weil-McLain	EG50-PID	142,000	80.70
	Utica Radiator	PEG187AID	151,000	80.20
	Columbia Boiler	CEG187ASID	151,000	80.20
	Crown	JS62EI	154,000	80.95
	Dunkirk	PS-62	154,000	80.95
	Pennco	1606SID	154,000	80.95

and Tappan of Mansfield, Ohio—are developing the new units. HydroTherm's version is a gas-fired boiler. It has already sold several thousand of these pulse combustion models in the 100,000 BTU/hour size class and is now developing a 50,000 BTU/hour version. Lennox makes a pulse combustion gas furnace, with seasonal efficiencies of 95 percent. Tappan will market a recuperative furnace in the fall of 1981 under the name Tappan, Frigiking, or Janitrol. The unit gets 87 percent seasonal efficiency.

It may take a year or two for the manufacturers to install enough of these furnaces to establish a full network of distributors and service people. But the equipment has already gotten good reviews. The big issue is whether the condensed gases, which form a type of acid, will corrode or damage the exhaust pipes, but HydroTherm's Dick Prusha tells me that problem has been solved. Noise might also be another drawback. Pulse furnaces give off what Prusha calls a "60-cycle hum." I suggest that you go listen to a pulse furnace before you buy one.

But minor admonitions aside, these high-rated boilers and furnaces are the preferred technology because they achieve high efficiency numbers and don't require chimneys. The boilers, Prusha tells me, cost about $1,000 more than standard equipment, or $3,000 rather than $2,000. The additional investment makes sense, provided that you burn enough fuel to benefit from the added efficiency. Price lists on the furnaces were not available as this was written.

The Case for Replacement: Oil to Oil

Two developments at the appliance store give the furnace buyer tremendous advantage. First, furnaces and boilers now carry fact sheets showing the seasonal efficiency of every new model. So to shop for fuel economy, Greenspan doesn't have to know a thing about the chemistry of combustion or even what a burner looks like. All he needs to do is glance at the fact sheets to find the high-efficiency units. Manufacturers, by the way, still make some guzzlers along with those economical furnaces, so Greenspan can't assume that any new furnace is an improvement over the old. In case your appliance store doesn't carry the top of the line in efficiency, I have included a list of some of the highest-mileage models now sold in America. The list is not comprehensive, but it does give you an idea of what's available.

The second advantage is the upgraded efficiency itself. The best new oil equipment reaches levels of 80, and in some cases, over 85 percent. That doesn't quite match pulse combustion, but it gets close.

The costs and benefits can be worked out on page 35. In Greenspan's case, the 1,000 gallons of oil he burns in his existing 60 percenter would diminish to 706 gallons in a new 85 percenter, even if nothing else were done to the shell of the house. The new furnace would cost him $2,500, which produces a first-year savings of $354, for a tax-free return of 14 percent.

It would take a few years to make back the purchase price, but we are talking about a long-term investment that gets increasingly lucrative as time goes on. If Greenspan can justify replacement in 1981, he can't fail to benefit in 1990. The only reason to wait would be the chance that even more economical furnaces will be out on the market any time within the next few years. But experts tell me that with oil equipment, at least, existing 85 percent seasonal efficiencies are not likely to be improved upon in the foreseeable future.

So if the furnace or boiler is in poor condition and cannot be effectively modified, there is no reason to delay replacing it. The longer you delay, the more expensive oil you will have in the interim. If the furnace or boiler is in relatively good condition, however, you might find better rates of return in some of the modification devices we will discuss in a minute.

When you do decide to get another furnace, there is absolutely no percentage in settling for less than the most economical units available. That also means a unit of the proper size. If a salesperson cavalierly says that the new furnace should be "about 150,000 BTUs," or simply "the same size you had," then go elsewhere for advice and take your business with you. Formulas for determining correct furnace size are too arcane to be laid out here, but the salesman should at least go through the formulas before recommending a size. The old practice, as I say, was to provide enough heating capacity for the coldest day ever, plus 10 percent for good measure. More enlightened furnace designers have changed the prescription to the coldest day in an average year, and forget the 10 percent. Since appliance heat and sunlight can account for 20 percent of the heat in an average house, anyway, they figure smaller furnaces can handle matters.

HOW TO CALCULATE THE BENEFITS OF
REPLACING THE FURNACE (OIL OR GAS)

1. Last year's fuel use (in therms of natural gas or gallons of home heating oil) _____

2. Estimated seasonal efficiency of existing furnace _____

3. Seasonal efficiency of new furnace _____

4. Fuel use for new furnace ($1 \times 2 \div 3$) _____

5. Cost of new furnace, including installation _____

6. Fuel saved by purchase ($1 - 4$) _____

7. First year's savings ($6 \times$ current cost of fuel) _____

8. Return on investment ($5 \div 7$) _____

(The same analysis can be applied to air conditioners. Extra power does not mean better fuel economy. In fact, the reverse is true, as we shall see later in the book.).

The Case for Replacement: Gas to Gas

Most gas furnaces are the forced-air kind. These furnaces are somewhat cheaper to buy and install than the oil boilers: the job can be done for perhaps $1,500 instead of $2,500.

Traditional gas furnaces—the kind with pilot lights, no vent dampers, and what are called atmospheric burners—don't get better than 65 percent seasonal efficiency, and in many cases, less. As the list on page 30 shows, the new generation of gas furnaces has reached 90 percent seasonal efficiencies. What you have to decide is whether the 15 to 20 percent boost in fuel economy is attractive when measured against the cost of replacement. Gas is cheaper to burn, so the savings will probably not be as great as they were for oil-fired Greenspan. (The worksheet on page 35 can be used to derive a rate of return here, just as we used it for the Greenspan decision.)

Pulse combustion and recuperative furnaces, as previously described, make the economics of replacement look quite favorable. If I had to buy a new furnace, I would give first consideration to one of these new super-efficient models. Their first costs are higher, but the long-term savings may more than cover the extra investment.

The Case for Modification: Oil

Several add-on devices—special burners and vent dampers and so forth—cost in the $200-to-$600 range and will give you modest boosts in seasonal efficiency. Buying one of these devices is like fiddling with your Cadillac to pull out a little extra mileage because you aren't ready to trade it in for a VW Rabbit.

People often invest in add-on devices without considering the long-term furnace strategy, which is silly. Even in the best of conditions, an add-on device like a vent damper can only nudge consumption down by 10 percent. So there is no reason to buy one if you plan to go to the 85 percent new furnace in the near future. But a few of these devices are sensible if you have decided not to replace for three or four years, and if the rate of return from modification exceeds the rate of return from replacement.

There are cases where spending $300 to use 10 percent less fuel is preferable to spending $2,500 to use 30 percent less. The costs and benefits of the various devices described here can be analyzed in precisely the same manner as furnace replacement.

As we have seen, the prime modification for the oil furnace is burner replacement. Conventional burners do an inadequate job of mixing fuel and air (usually too much air and not enough combustion). The high-speed burner makes for less air flow, less draft up the chimney, and thus less heat wasted.

The Brookhaven lab tested the new burners in 94 homes in Long Island and reported an average fuel saving of 13 percent. The Better Home Heat Council, an association of New England heating oil dealers, has been installing the burners, and they claim savings in the 10 to 15 percent range.

The burners cost about $400 installed, but since they qualify for the 15 percent federal tax credit, the real cost is reduced to about $340. When the switch is made, the nozzle size may also be changed, so it is hard to separate the benefits of this $340 outlay from the benefits of the $2 part discussed earlier. The experts seem to agree that replacement burners work better than nozzle crimping alone. A practical advantage of the $340 solution is that many oil dealers are happy to sell burners, while they resist replacing nozzles.

Brookhaven also finds that the new oil burner is a superior overall purchase to the more publicized device, the vent damper. In what seems to be a typical characteristic of energy advice, the preferred investment is often the one you may have heard the least about.

Vent dampers are metal flaps installed in the flue pipe to stop some of the heat from going up the chimney during the off cycle. The dampers operate either electrically or mechanically to close off the flue when the furnace is not firing. This solves part of the problem created by an oversized furnace.

A few years ago, vent dampers were the subject of a raging safety controversy. The American Gas Association was reluctant to endorse them because a malfunctioning damper might cause volatile or poisonous fumes and gases to back up in the furnace or into the house. The fears turned out to be exaggerated, and after some testing, the AGA began to certify certain types of dampers. Underwriter's Laboratories also certifies electrically operated dampers. If you buy one, get a damper that carries either UL or AGA approval.

Brookhaven didn't address the safety issue of dampers for oil furnaces. But the lab found another reason to prefer the replacement burners. Dampers save money only when the furnace is not firing, by cutting down the draft. The burners do that, too, by reducing the amount of air that goes into the other end of the furnace. And burners also save money when the furnace is in active operation. In no event, Brookhaven says, should you buy both a new burner and a vent damper. The burner renders the damper almost irrelevant.

The two devices cost about the same, but the new burner gives you a better return across a wider variety of circumstances. Vent dampers can save up to 10 percent on heating bills—provided that flue temperatures are very high, and provided that the furnace is located in the house. When a furnace is located in an unheated basement the vent dampers don't do any good.

A third modification is the flue economizer, which uses the extra heat in the flue pipe or chimney to warm the water before it passes through the boiler into the radiators. This preheating can cut fuel consumption by as much as 20 percent. But again, if you install a new burner, the returns from flue economizers drop to 9 to 12 percent, not always enough to warrant the purchase of a $600 device.

So go with the high-speed burner first.

The Case for Modification: Gas

Gas technicians say you shouldn't change the nozzle size on gas furnaces, so that cuts out the low-cost adjustment. No burner replacements are commonly available, so that cuts out the middle-cost adjustment. The only other choices available are vent dampers and electronic ignition kits that douse pilot lights.

Vent dampers have been shown to produce a 5 to 10 percent fuel savings on gas equipment. They cost between $150 and $250 depending on the type—simple thermal or the more complicated electric version. When you think about spending $250 here, remember that a replacement furnace might not cost more than $1,000.

Vent dampers on gas furnaces have the same limitations as they do on oil furnaces. They pay off only if the furnace is inside the heated perimeter of the house, and if the furnace cycles on and off frequently.

You can eliminate the pilot light for $100 to $150, and that may make sense, depending on natural gas prices. When gas was cheap, burning the eternal flame hardly mattered. But with gas at 40¢ a therm or better, it costs $4 and up for the flame's monthly support. The furnace technician should be able to pin the cost down exactly and tell you if electronic ignition pays. Pilot lights can help warm the house in winter, as long as the heat gets to the right places. But they also add to the burden on an air conditioner in the summer, making the pilot light a double loser in the warm season.

It is possible to turn off the furnace pilot manually after the winter season, although some gas utilities worry about the safety of this maneuver. At least two utilities, Pacific Gas and Electric and Southern California Gas Company, tell their customers how to put out the pilots. I suggest you call your utility and ask them what their position is. They might perform the service for a nominal fee, or show you how to do it yourself.

Greenspan's Decision

Greenspan opted for the new burner. At $1.20 a gallon for oil, he expects a $120 savings in the first year, on the adviser's estimate that the burner will cut his fuel use by 10 percent. That amounts to a 30 percent tax-free return on investment.

He thought about conversion to gas, but he decided to hold off until matters are clarified in Washington. He said he could always convert to gas later by installing a completely new gas boiler, perhaps with pulse combustion. That would give him both the higher efficiency and the price break on the cheaper fuel.

Greenspan's choice is by no means the only one to make. The summary from the experts goes as follows: (1) furnaces or boilers that are too far gone to modify with any certain success, should be replaced; (2) equipment in decent overall condition, but having an identifiable defect, should be modified; (3) modification generally looks better for expensive systems, which means boilers, since replacement costs for these units are high; (4) replacement generally looks better for gas forced-air systems, since the cost of a new unit is relatively low; (5) pulse combustion is an efficiency breakthrough that may be worth waiting for; and (6) conversion from oil to gas has been a good deal in the past but may not continue to be so.

The Heat Pump: The Way to Make Electric Heating Systems Economic

A couple of portable electric heaters won't do much harm, especially if you use them to spot-heat the bedrooms and if you turn down the furnace at night. You can get the exact cost of running the portable heaters by finding the wattage—shown somewhere on the case—dividing by 1,000, and multiplying by your per-kilowatt-hour electric rate. A 1,500-watt portable heater burns at the rate of 10¢ an hour in my area.

But if you own a central electric furnace, if you pay average-to-high electric rates, and if you live in an area with long winters, you are advised to take major corrective action.

One solution is to convert to gas. The other approach is to install a heat pump, a device already used in half of the electrically heated homes in the country. The machine looks like an air conditioner and works like an air conditioner in reverse. That is, the heat pump doesn't heat the air, it pulls heat *out* of the air. An air conditioner absorbs heat from indoor air and pumps it outside; a heat pump similarly absorbs heat from the outdoor air and pumps it inside.

Even winter air has enough heat in it to permit some to be put to good use. It takes much less electricity to extract heat out of the air than it does to generate warmth through the traditional method, called resistance heating. A resistance heater merely warms up the surrounding air the same way the coil on a stove warms up a pot.

A heat pump, meanwhile, can provide the same heat for one-half to one-third the electricity.

When heat pumps were first sold twenty years ago, they were plagued with maintenance problems and consumers rejected them. They still aren't infallible—more things can go wrong with a compressor than with a simple resistance heater—but their performance is now deemed reliable. And their energy efficiency is improving. A standard electric resistance heater converts electricity into heat for an efficiency rating (called coefficient of performance, in the case of heat pumps) of 1. Older heat pumps could bring twice as much heat into the house for the same electricity, for a coefficient of performance (COP) of 2. Newer models have COPs that approach 3, meaning that they actually pick up three times as much heat as the electricity traditionally consumed could generate.

But heat pumps only work at full efficiency when the outdoor temperature stays above 20 to 30 degrees Fahrenheit, and this is the place to be careful. When it gets colder than that, the heat pump automatically switches to standard resistance heating, and you lose the advantage. The more a heat pump operates on the standby resistance mode, the smaller the return from your investment in this device.

For this reason, heat pumps are not commonly seen above Washington, D.C., and they have become a kind of appliance divider between the middle states and the cold North. But then again, electric furnaces of any type are not commonly seen in the North, which leads to us to a general conclusion: no longer is there any reason whatever to buy central electric resistance heating. In places too cold for heat pumps, electric resistance heating is already too expensive. In places suitable for heat pumps, the energy savings demand their purchase. (There might be certain pockets of the Deep South and the Far West where electric rates are so low that central resistance heating is still economical, but this I don't think will last for long.)

To decide whether to convert to a heat pump, you need to know your annual heating costs, but that's hard to determine when all the power used runs through the same electric meter. What you use for heat alone isn't broken out on your utility bill. A simple way to figure heating costs is to look at an electric bill for a month when no artificial heating or cooling is used, such as September, and compare it to a bill from a winter month. The difference is a rough estimate of your heating cost.

Then check the furnace store to get prices on heat-pump installations. To compute the savings accurately, you have to know how much the heat pump will run on "pump" and how much it will run on standard resistance heating. A local heating contractor ought to be able to help you with this calculation, but I would also cross-check by asking a couple of heat-pump owners what their experience has been.

Heat pumps now come in all sizes, from window units to the large central installations. Most of them serve the dual function of air conditioner and heater. If you use your window air conditioning units as heaters in the winter, switch to a heat-pump unit (also called "reverse cycle") the next time you replace the machine. Stay away from the resistance heating system, or "heat strip."

If you are going to buy a central heat pump, look for equipment with a high coefficient of performance (COP) on the heating side, and a high energy efficiency ratio (EER) on the air conditioning side. You should be able to get a machine with a COP of at least 2.5, and an EER of better than 8.

Part Three

WINNING THE SHELL GAME

The Shell of the House

The connection between insulation, storm windows, and your pocketbook is not as simple and direct as you may have been led to believe. Many workbooks and charts presume to show you how to turn X amount of insulation into X number of dollars, but there are some kinks here. The Tennessee Valley Authority runs one of the most elaborate retrofit programs in the country, and TVA hired a Washington research firm, ICF Incorporated, to analyze the results. ICF said that most people did save money from insulation and storm windows, but the firm was puzzled by a lack of any pattern to the savings. "Particularly notable in our results is the large variability in the savings obtained. A significant proportion of homes achieved very little or no savings as a result of program intervention."

The Center for Energy and Environmental Studies at Princeton reached similar conclusions from its Twin Rivers energy project. Twin Rivers is to conservation what the South Pacific is to anthropology, the most metered and monitored residential area in the country. The Princeton people found little secure basis for predicting that a given layer of insulation in the attic, or a given layer of glass on the windows, results in any determined drop in the fuel bills.

The experts have pondered this anomaly, and they seem to agree on its explanation. Neither houses nor people behave as the physics textbooks would like them to. Furnace heat does not march in orderly fashion toward the insulation barrier and then politely and predictively stop there. Houses are full of secret passageways and idiosyncrasies that allow heat to escape the insulation coverage, regardless of how thick it is. Moreover, certain types of insulation shrink and lose strength when wet.

The purchasers of storm windows or insulation often do their part to lose the advantage by raising indoor temperatures, thus making it harder for the shell to hold its heat. It goes back to the earlier admonition: you can't just buy your way out.

Of course, a certain amount of insulation and a certain level of thermal protection has to be there before a house can begin to hold its own against the weather. Part of this section is devoted to an analysis of these big investments, to help you decide whether you have enough insulation and glass or whether you need more. Your economic analysis should reflect the fuel savings you have already gotten, or are planning to get, from the furnace.

Some low-cost techniques also come into play here. There are things you can do inside the house to improve the dividend from the insulation or storm windows you have already bought. And the best rate of return of all is found at the furnace thermostat.

The Setback That Gets You Ahead

When I visited my friend Greenspan for his furnace analysis, I asked him if he practiced night setback. He thought I was talking about some masochistic ritual. Some people do see it that way, but night setback of the thermostat is the mother lode of home energy savings. The practice does make the house colder, but only during the time one is in bed, and it cuts annual fuel consumption by a documented 5 to 15 percent. Honeywell, a company that sells setback devices, has estimated the savings obtainable in thirty-eight cities, and those estimates can be found on page 48. These savings will not be the same from house to house, and of course they depend on what kind of fuel you use and what your heating bill is, and Honeywell's numbers are for both day and night setback. But you get a rough idea of the benefits from the chart—they are never less than $56 and reach as high as $199, with a temperature reduction of 10 degrees.

The "thermal struggle" explains why the simple act of turning back a thermostat could have such economic impact. Consider a barrier dividing a lake. As long as there is an equal amount of water on both sides, it doesn't matter how strong or weak the wall is: a leak is impossible. But as water on one side recedes, the water pressure from the other side intensifies. When the water level on one side is half that of the other, the wall has to be extraordinarily sturdy to hold back a deluge.

In the thermal struggle featuring the walls of your house, temperature is like the levels of water. When indoor and outdoor temperatures are equal, there is no heat loss, and insulation is irrelevant. But when the outdoor temperature drops even a degree relative to that indoors, the pressure on the shell of the house intensifies. No house is as tight as a dam, so as the temperature differential widens, heat pours out through walls, windows, and cracks. The furnace therefore has to pump harder to replace interior heat, and it works hardest at night, when the exterior side of the thermal dam is at its lowest ebb.

So reducing the temperature with thermostat setback is like draining water from the high side of the lake. Some of the pressure is relieved, and heat flow is diminished from a torrent to a gurgle. Fuel, obviously, is saved. The same process works in reverse with air conditioners in the summer. A small adjustment on the thermostat can make a big difference.

People in large houses are getting noticeable savings at minimal sacrifice by lowering the night thermostat to 55 or 60, and then spot-heating the beds with electric blankets. Art Rosenfeld, a scientist at Lawrence Berkeley Laboratory who studies a baffling array of complicated products to save energy, says he favors the blanket over all of them. A quilt, which doesn't use any electricity, is even better.

On a fuel bill of $1,000, night setback of the furnace thermostat produces a personal "profit" of $50 to $150 a year, which is the same return one might expect from buying blown-in wall insulation for all the outside walls of the house. But one might easily have to buy $1,000 worth of the wall insulation to strengthen the thermal dam enough to get that $50 to $150 return. Manual night setback provides an equal level of return for nothing, or if one buys an automatic setback device, for perhaps $100. I'm not suggesting that this is an either/or situation. But many people have tried wall insulation instead of night setback, which for the former is like keeping the money in a savings account, rather than choosing first the risk-free, tax-free, 60 to 120 percent return on investment.

ANNUAL SAVINGS FOR TYPICAL HOUSEHOLD
SETTING BACK THE THERMOSTAT TEN DEGREES
FOR EIGHT DAY HOURS AND
EIGHT NIGHT HOURS

Oil Heat		*Gas Heat*	
$199	Albany, NY	$123	New York, NY
$195	Rochester, NY	$120	Rochester, NY
$195	Syracuse, NY	$115	Springfield, MA
$187	Erie, PA	$103	Albany, NY
$187	Scranton, PA	$101	Newark, NJ
$184	Harrisburg, PA	$101	Syracuse, NY
$182	Madison, WI	$100	Trenton, NJ
$181	Pittsburgh, PA	$100	Worcester, MA
$180	Buffalo, NY	$99	Camden, NJ
$180	Chicago, IL	$99	Harrisburg, PA
$180	Newark, NJ	$96	Boston, MA
$180	Sault Ste. Marie, MI	$95	Chicago, IL
$180	South Bend, IN	$91	Scranton, PA
$179	Lansing, MI	$89	Erie, PA
$178	Atlantic City, NJ	$89	Philadelphia, PA
$178	Milwaukee, WI	$88	Milwaukee, WI
$178	Springfield, MA	$87	Buffalo, NY
$178	Toledo, OH	$86	Atlantic City, NJ
$178	Trenton, NJ	$85	South Bend, IN
$178	Worcester, MA	$83	Fort Wayne, IN
$177	Grand Rapids, MI	$83	Madison, WI
$176	Camden, NJ	$80	Pittsburgh, PA
$176	Cincinnati, OH	$79	Cincinnati, OH
$176	Columbus, OH	$78	Toledo, OH
$176	Detroit, MI	$77	Green Bay, WI
$176	Fort Wayne, IN	$75	Columbus, OH
$176	Green Bay, WI	$75	Detroit, MI
$176	La Crosse, WI	$75	East St. Louis, IL
$176	Philadelphia, PA	$74	Dayton, OH
$175	Boston, MA	$74	Sault Ste. Marie, MI
$175	Cleveland, OH	$72	Grand Rapids, MI
$175	Dayton, OH	$68	Lansing, MI
$173	East St. Louis, IL	$67	Cleveland, OH
$173	Peoria, IL	$67	Indianapolis, IN
$172	Indianapolis, IN	$67	La Crosse, WI

	Oil Heat		*Gas Heat*
$172	Springfield, IL	$67	Peoria, IL
$169	Evansville, IN	$67	Springfield, IL
$167	New York, NY	$56	Evansville, IN

SOURCE: "Reducing U.S. Heating Costs with Thermostat Setback," Energy Management Information Center, Honeywell, Inc., Minneapolis, Minnesota, 1980

Insulation: How Much and Where

1. Attic Insulation. Last year Owens-Corning ran a national TV advertisement showing the Pink Panther rolling a thick carpet of new insulation over an already insulated attic. The message: energy prices have gone up again, and insulation is cheaper than oil. The extra layer, the ad asserted, would "put you in the pink."

But there is some chance that buying more insulation will put you in the red, a fate not discussed in all the advice on how to save energy. My friends who absorb energy information through a kind of consumer's osmosis still think of attic insulation as the proven choice, the safe choice, the IBM of home conservation investments. Greenspan, for instance, wanted to spend money in the attic a second time rather than buy a furnace device or insulate the ductwork. He is just the type of buyer the Pink Panther is looking for.

Insulating the attic the first time made sense for Greenspan, and for everybody else. In the early 1970s, perhaps three-quarters of American attics had no insulation at all. Where no insulation exists, adding even a little bit can cut energy consumption by sizable amounts. As much as 45 percent of the indoor heat is lost through uninsulated attics, and half of that may be recovered by a first layer. But a second layer presents a case of diminishing returns.

You have probably bought some insulation after looking at one of those charts that show recommended R-values in different climate zones. The R-value is one of the reasons that insulation has been so successful. It reduces the complexities of heat loss to a number that we can all deal with. The R-value is a measure of the resistance of any material to heat passing through it. Poor insulators like wood, concrete, or glass have very low R-values. The stuff that is sold as insulation—fiberglass, rock wool, cellulose—has much higher R-values, and the R numbers increase as the material is thickened. Companies that sell insulation for its money-saving potential often estimate dollars saved per R, and agencies that regulate the construction industry can mandate energy efficiency by requiring a certain number of Rs in each attic and wall.

The recommended levels for new construction have been increased in recent years, and this is a source of confusion for people who want to modify their existing houses. In 1975, a house with R-19 in the attic and R-7 in the walls was considered an energy saver. Now such a house barely meets the minimum requirements for new construction in areas that have adopted energy-conscious building codes. The Department of Housing and Urban Development and other agencies that subsidize home mortgages have upped their insulation standards to as much as R-30 for attics and R-11 for walls. Proposed building performance standards will require even higher levels than that.

Thicker insulation is a good investment in *new* construction. As long as the contractor is being paid to insulate the house, it doesn't cost much more to buy the extra material to boost the coverage from, say, R-19 to R-30 in the attic. The labor charge is about the same in either case. It is also easier to get an effective insulation job while the house is being built. The contractor can stop the air leaks and correct other defects that can rob insulation of its money-saving power.

But as recommended levels for new construction are increased, people in old houses are inspired to add more insulation to meet the new-house standards. This is where an overemphasis on insulation can lead you astray. The charts of insulation levels, like the ones shown below, made no distinction between existing houses and new houses. The simplified sales pitch is: "You live in Minnesota? You need R-38 in your attic." That doesn't mean it's profitable to get to R-38 if you already have R-19.

There is also a convenience factor at work here. Insulating the attic is relatively simple when compared, say, to insulating the crawl space or the walls. Many contractors like to blow stuff into the attic because they can do it quickly. You would no doubt prefer to put down another layer of fiberglass under your feet in the attic than to install it overhead in the basement. The tendency is to go back to the attic a second time, when the money and the effort might be better spent elsewhere.

The next time you get the attic insulation sales pitch, remember that the money you save on another increment of insulation depends not only on the coverage you end up with but also on the coverage you start with. The payoffs always dwindle as the coverage is thickened, and the big dividends lie between zero and four inches of attic insulation, or R-0 to R-11. Somewhere around eight or nine inches, the return per additional inch drops precipitously. As George Tsongas, an associate professor of engineering at Portland State University, concluded in a three-house energy study for Chevron: "Adding more ceiling insulation when four inches already exists can have a payback time as long as thirty to forty years." This is undoubtedly an extreme case; other paybacks have been reported in the four-to-eight-year range. But you should calculate very carefully with the auditor before you decide that this is one of your best investments.

As a point of illustration, consider this Department of Energy analysis on what happens to an electrically heated home in a moderate climate zone. The first three and a half inches of attic insulation, or R-11, save more than 5,000 kilowatt-hours of electricity a year. That's $300, with electricity at 6¢ per kilowatt-hour. Beyond R-11, returns plummet, as the savings line on this page shows. Increasing attic insulation from R-11 to R-19 saves only 700 kilowatt-hours ($35), and the next jump from R-19 to R-30 saves less than 500 kilowatt-hours ($25).

The numbers are different for every house and for every climate zone. But the rule of thumb is the same: the first four to six inches are ten times more profitable than the next four to six inches. I am not making any final case against reinsulation, because a second layer

can still make you money in certain situations. I am making a case, however, for caution.

You can figure the R-value of the existing insulation by identifying the type of insulation you have and then measuring its thickness. Three basic types of insulation are commonly used in attics—fiberglass, which has a cotton-candy look and can be red, yellow, or white; rock wool, which has the same consistency as fiberglass, but is gray; and cellulose, which is mulched newspaper soaked in a flame-retardant chemical, also usually gray. The first two materials are either fused into slabs or into long, continuous rolls, or sometimes installed loose. Cellulose is always installed loose, or even blown into the attic with pressurized equipment.

A quick examination of your existing attic insulation, and a probe with your ruler, should produce enough information to locate the R-value on the chart shown on page 53. The chart also indicates how much of each type of insulation must be added to get to higher R-levels.

So how high should you go? Department of Energy people tell me that R-19 is a reasonable cutoff point for existing houses. If you already have R-19 in the attic and you don't live in someplace like Minnesota or Maine, you can find better investment opportunities than overhead. If you have some attic insulation, but less than R-19, reinsulation becomes a judgment call—a potentially good idea in cold climates, a not-so-hot idea in moderate climates.

The Princeton energy researchers have found an excellent way for you to decide for yourself, and I think this five-minute experiment is more useful than a stack of R-value charts. Take a thermometer into your attic on a cold winter's night. Then compare the attic temperature to (1) the temperature inside the house, and (2) the temperature outdoors. If you don't want to linger in the cold attic long enough to take an accurate reading, leave the thermometer up there and come back later.

A properly insulated attic should be about 10 degrees warmer than the outside temperature, at most. If your attic is warmer than that, or if its temperature is closer to indoor levels than to outdoor levels, you know the attic needs some attention.

But before you call the insulation contractor, there is a much cheaper remedy to consider. The attic might be warm not because

NOMINAL R-VALUES FOR VARIOUS THICKNESSES OF INSULATION (IN INCHES)

R-Value	Batts or Blankets		Loose and Blown Fill		
	glass fiber	rock wool	glass fiber	rock wool	cellulose fiber
R-11	3½	3	5	4	3
R-13	4	3½	6	4½	3½
R-19	6	5	8½	6½	5
R-22	7	6	10	7½	6
R-26	8	7	12	9	7
R-30	9½	8	13½	10	8
R-33	10½	9	15	11	9
R-38	12	10½	17	13	10

the insulation is too thin, but because hot air from below is bypassing the insulation. The Princeton researchers say the attic bypass is a common affliction. Most attics, they find, are full of hidden cracks and passageways that allow heat to escape from the house below regardless of the thickness of the insulation blanket. As long as the bypasses are not attended to, blowing a few more inches of cellulose or other material into the attic may be a wasted effort.

Unfortunately, only a small number of insulation contractors are aware of the importance of attic bypasses, and few will take the time to correct them. That is why I present leak-plugging as a low-cost project, something you can learn to do yourself (see pages 66–71). Once the leaks are plugged, you can again do the thermometer test. If the attic is still too warm, it is time to reinsulate.

Or you might get lucky and find an insulation installer who has his own infrared viewing equipment to ferret out the bypasses. I would hire such a contractor even if he is more expensive than some of the others. Too much attention is paid to the *quantity* of the coverage, when the *quality* of the coverage can make or break the attic insulation investment. A contractor who is willing to take the time to seal leaks at the perimeter of the attic or around chimneys will probably be more valuable to you than a couple of extra inches of blown-in padding.

So the type of insulation you put into the attic is much less important than the skill of the person who puts it there. If you are buying loose-fill stuff, you need to check to make sure that you get enough coverage for your money. It is easy enough to fluff the material out so it reaches a certain thickness, which may mean too much air space and not enough insulating material. Density is the important factor. To obtain a given R-value, the contractor will have to use the necessary number of bags of insulation for the area to be properly covered. Make certain that he uses that number.

The minimum requirement, then, is honesty, and you are likely to get that in a high percentage of cases. But what you are really looking for is a contractor who has heard about attic bypasses and believes them to be a problem.

In summary, you can figure out if you need more attic insulation by using the R-19 cutoff point, by doing the temperature test, or by asking an energy auditor or contractor how much money you will save with the extra coverage. Make sure the auditor or contractor figures for diminishing returns in the calculation.

If you decide to buy more insulation, you can protect your investment by sealing the bypasses before the extra layer is installed. Or better yet, find a contractor with the equipment to do a thorough leak-plugging job.

2. Wall Insulation. If attic insulation savings are unpredictable, wall insulation savings are unfathomable. There is simply no way to generalize about the profitability of making the investment. Little research has been done. At Princeton, researchers are saying that frame houses that have no wall insulation are good retrofit candidates. Two-story homes that have balloon framing (ask a local builder if your house fits this category) are excellent retrofit candidates. This tentative green light does not apply to houses that already have some wall insulation or to brick or masonry houses, where insulation cannot always be blown into wall cavities.

Energy auditors, the ones that utilities will send around, will give you some cost-benefit calculations based on standard heat-loss formulas. Insulation contractors also have methods to predict the return from wall insulation investments. Are these predictions accurate? You can use your own heating bills as a very rough test for exaggeration here. Wall insulation might recover 15 percent of your heating costs.

The undoing of wall insulation is *partial coverage.* In new homes, the insulation is applied before the walls are enclosed, allowing for better quality control. Here the installer knows if he has filled all the nooks and crannies because he can see what he is doing. But in existing houses, the work is hidden from view. There is no cheap way to pull off the interior walls, position the insulation, and replace the walls. The insulation has to be forced under pressure into the wall cavities through tiny holes drilled either through the exterior siding or the interior paneling. The work, in other words, is done blind.

It would be hard enough to insulate walls if the cavities were empty. But they are not. At various points around the perimeter of the house, one finds electrical conduits, plumbing pipes, heating ducts, crossbeams, and wooden braces running across or through the inside of the walls. It is difficult for the insulation contractor to determine where these obstructions are located, presenting a chance that the blown-in material will get stuck behind the braces or hung up on the pipes, leaving unfilled gaps in the walls. Small gaps can become major escape routes for indoor heat, sabotaging both your coverage and your investment.

Even when the wall cavity is filled completely, gaps can develop later when the insulation settles or shrinks, a real problem with certain types of insulation, notably urea formaldehyde foam.

What are your chances of getting full and effective coverage? I know of only a few attempts to study walls that have been insulated as a retrofit. One was done for the Minnesota Energy Agency by John Weidt Associates. Their conclusion was that blown-in cellulose does not usually settle or shrink, but that urea formaldehyde does. The researchers also found voids at the top of a few wall cavities, suggesting that the fill jobs are not always perfect.

Another study was performed for the National Bureau of Standards on thirty-nine houses in eight states. Only one wall section out of the six examined had a gap, or void, at the top of the wall. While this study gave blown-in insulation general good marks, it also suggested that "sufficient isolated problems were seen to serve as a warning that acceptable practice should be diligently followed during the retrofitting of sidewalls." In other words, the installation has to be done right. So choose the right insulation material and the right contractor.

Four materials are commonly used to insulate wall cavities—rock wool, fiberglass, cellulose, and urea formaldehyde foam. Rock wool and fiberglass are the least controversial of the materials; these two haven't been accused of damaging walls. But these inert substances may be more expensive than cellulose, and they have slightly less insulating power per inch. For example, five inches of glass fibers give the same R-value as three inches of cellulose.

Cellulose, meanwhile, has a mixed reputation. Its advantages are lower cost and higher relative insulating value, plus its apparent ability to slide by the obstructions in the wall cavity. It is easy to make (the product consists of shredded paper and a flame-retardant chemical), and there are hundreds of manufacturers. Because there are hundreds, problems of quality control have arisen, especially in fireproofing. A few attic fires were reportedly caused by cellulose, giving the material a bad name.

But there is now a government standard for combustibility of cellulose, and it is now illegal to manufacture cellulose that doesn't meet specifications. If you want to make absolutely certain you are getting material that is safe, check the bags of cellulose that the contractor brings to the house. They should carry a certification label from either the Consumer Product Safety Commission, the General Services Administration, or the Cellulose Manufacturers Association.

Urea formaldehyde foam, the blown-in wall substance with the worst reputation, has been banned in Massachusetts because of its tendency to produce noxious formaldehyde fumes when improperly cured. The experts at the various energy labs I visited have little good to say about the stuff. It demands installer expertise, because the installer must mix various chemicals (foaming agent, catalyst, hardener) into a liquid that is squirted into the walls like so much shaving cream. If the chemicals are not combined in the right amounts, the foam will not harden and the components will continue to react with one another to produce formaldehyde gas. It doesn't happen very often, but when it does, the situation is at best unpleasant. And there are no standards to protect the consumer who buys the product.

The wall insulation studies did not find much evidence of lingering gas or of rotted walls from poorly cured formaldehyde foam. But they did discover another reason to stay away from the material— it shrinks inside the walls. According to the Minnesota study, "all foam samples exhibited shrinkage." The National Bureau of Standards also said that "shrinkage had occurred in all inspected sidewalls containing urea." The shrinkage varied from 4 to 9 percent. Even though 4 to 9 percent doesn't sound like much, it is enough to undermine the single advantage of urea—it has the highest theoretical R-value per inch of any of the options.

My friends at the labs seem to lean toward the cellulose, although they have no quibble with rock wool or fiberglass. They do not recommend the urea formaldehyde.

That brings us to the second important element—the right installer. Wall insulation is a business that anybody with a drill, a ladder, and a truck can enter, with no licensing or training required in many localities. Moreover, there is no way you can check the work even after it has been completed. Any contractor can promise a careful job when he knows you aren't going to rip out a wall to prove him wrong.

If you can find a wall insulation company that uses infrared scanners, go with that company. It is the only method by which one can actually see the heat as it leaks or escapes through the walls. A few contractors around Princeton, where so much advanced energy work has taken place, have bought their own scanners and now guarantee the work. They come back to reinsulate if the scanner reveals gaps, voids, or omissions in the coverage. Perhaps if enough customers ask about infrared equipment, more insulation installers will invest in it.

Assuming you can't find anybody with a scanner, you can sort out the contractors by quizzing them about the general procedure they follow. Do they study the framing pattern of the house, perhaps from blueprints, to discover where the holes should be drilled? A conscientious installer will anticipate problem areas and try to guess where the insulation might be impeded by cross-bracing or other obstructions in the walls. He will also examine overhangs, gables, and other hard-to-reach spots that, if not properly insulated, can subvert your investment.

Some of the places routinely overlooked include: gaps around the cross-bracing at the corners of the house; areas above or below the fire-stops, blocks of wood that separate the wall studs; walls that connect with unheated carports or garages; overhangs of porches and of second stories; gables, bay windows, and other extensions of the basic structure of the house; and the perimeter of the house at the point where the first and second stories are joined together.

You could set up a conference with the prospective insulation contractor and the builder or architect of the house to discuss the framing eccentricities and where the holes should be drilled for complete coverage. Then before you pay for the work, you can inspect the job to see that all the holes were drilled as promised. (Installers plug the holes, but the plugs are sometimes visible on close inspection.)

But the best proof of good installation will come with your fuel bills. All other things being equal, you should notice a downturn in fuel consumption after the insulation is put in place. When that doesn't happen, you have reason to suspect the installation.

3. Basement and Crawl Space Insulation. Of the big three insulation jobs—attic, walls, and basement—the last gets the least attention. Contractors don't seek the work, probably because it is so labor-intensive. They can't blow the insulated fluff under the house and beat a hasty retreat, as they often do with attics. Even homeowners with do-it-yourself tendencies seem to shun the basement, because it is an inconvenient and unpleasant place to work. When most home-owners have insulated the attic, the basement has become the repository for junk, not to mention ducts and pipes and conduit. Hence insulating the basement can look hopeless.

Moreover, the popular belief has it that since heat rises, there is nothing to gain by protecting yourself from below. Research done at Princeton and elsewhere suggests otherwise: in the Twin Rivers townhouses monitored by Princeton, 17 percent of the heat produced by the furnace was lost in the basement before it got upstairs.

In the townhouses, the furnace was located in the basement, which accounts for much of the loss. But even when the furnace is upstairs, a little insulation underfoot can also do a lot of good. Its advantage over wall insulation is that the basement job is visible; it's also cheaper, since you will probably have to insulate your own basement and you can't do your own walls.

Again, there is no honest way to generalize about the savings from basement insulation. Two natural signs that money can be made here are: (1) a cold floor above a basement; and (2) a warm basement in the wintertime. The issue is not so much what type of insulation to use as where to put it and how to install it. You need to plug some leaks first, or the rest of the job will be sabotaged.

Take a look at the perimeter of your foundation or basement wall, from inside the crawl space or basement. The key to the thermal struggle down here lies where the wood framing of the basement meets that foundation wall, a juncture that makes the longest continuous potential air leak in the house. At the top of the wall, you will probably find a board lying on its side; this is called the sill plate. Above the plate, you will notice the rib structure, or rafters, of the basement. The rafters cross the sill plate and then butt into another piece of wood, called the band joist. Between each set of rafters, you can see a section of the band joist, as shown in the illustration.

When this area is left untreated, cold air can blow into the basement from around the sill plate, or heated air can seep out through the bare wood of the band joist, which has a low R-value. Much of the cold air will find its way into the house, since the first floor sits directly above the band joist/sill plate connection.

So before you insulate the basement, caulk the sill plate all the way around the perimeter of the house with silicone or some other long-lasting caulking material. Then take small pieces of insulation and stick them in between each rafter, right up against the band-joist section, as shown in the illustration. This will ensure that the perimeter of the house is protected from infiltration.

The band-joist area is also a telling place to judge a contractor's work. A careful installer will attend to this caulking and sealing detail on his own. If your installer has already finished the basement work and neglected this effort, ask him to return and remedy the situation; if you don't, it will cost you money.

Once the band-joist area has been treated, you can proceed with the general insulating job. If the house has a crawl space and not a basement, the standard technique is to drape the fiberglass insulation from the top of the foundation wall to the ground, as shown in the illustration. The ground itself should be covered with a sheet of plastic, the kind used in the garden. Some heat from the house will get into the crawl space, but at least you will have stopped the heat from escaping and drawing more heat into the cavity of the house. The insulation should be installed here with the foil backing turned outward, or away from the installer.

If the house has a full or partial basement, you have more options.

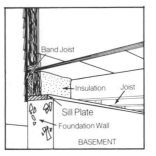

Band Joist Insulation

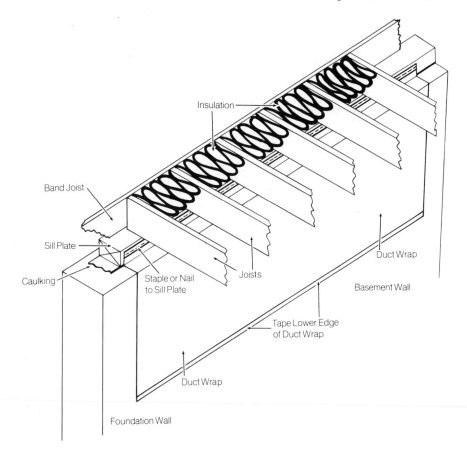

You can insulate overhead or insulate the walls from inside. The Princeton people have developed a third technique, which I describe first since it is the cheapest and the easiest way to solve the basement problem.

Imagine a typical situation. You have thought about putting insu-

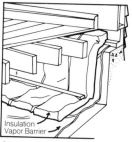

Crawl Space Insulation

lation overhead in the basement, but there are too many pipes and furnace ducts and you can't figure a way to work around them. You have considered insulating the basement walls from ground to ceiling, but that involves carpentry and a lot of money and bother.

Princeton's idea is to insulate around the top of the basement walls, only where those walls extend above the ground level. Below that point, the ground itself becomes an insulator, so you don't really need to cover the entire surface. The simplest way to do this is with air conditioning duct wrap, a rather sturdy type of insulation sold in ample widths at appliance or building supply stores. You string the duct wrap longitudinally around the perimeter of the basement, as shown in the illustration, tacking the top edge to the wood of the still plate and taping the bottom edge to the concrete or stone walls. The insulation should extend at least eighteen inches below the ground level outside the house.

It doesn't look terrific. And it doesn't make for totally effective coverage, since some heat can still bypass this insulation by moving up through the basement walls and then outside. But it can stop most of the basement heat loss.

There are still some advantages to the conventional options, which must be weighed against the Princeton approach. Insulating basement walls the regular way (you either build a new inner wall with two-by-four studs or nail vertical strips to the concrete or stone walls, apply rigid insulation between the strips, and then cover everything with paneling) can be expensive, especially if you hire a carpenter to do it. But it is also more attractive if you plan to use the basement as a workroom or a den.

If the furnace is located in the house and not in the basement, insulating the basement from overhead has extra fuel-saving potential. When you do this, you isolate the entire area from thermal contact with the house. This saves more money than insulating the basement walls, because you are then of course required to heat a smaller space. When the furnace is in the basement, it is better not to insulate overhead, because you lose the benefit of errant heat leaking from the furnace box and traveling freely to the first floor, where it can do some good.

Whatever you choose to do, a careful installation is as crucial to the energy savings here as it is in the attic.

4. Duct Insulation. People pay thousands of dollars to insulate a house and then fail to do anything about the heating and cooling ducts, which is the energy version of screening the porch and forgetting to close the door. The ducts, branches of the furnace or central air conditioner, are metallic conduits that carry hot or cold air to the various parts of the house. When the ducts traverse insulated spaces, nothing need be done to them because whatever heat they lose will remain in the house. But a duct system often passes through uninsulated areas, such as cold basements, attics, and crawl spaces. Here, the ducts can lose 20 percent of the heat from the furnace or the cooling from the air conditioner.

I'm sure you view the prospect of wrapping the ducts with the same enthusiasm as sanding the bottom of an old boat, and I don't blame you. It would be easy enough to encircle the ducts with insulation if they were located in some mercifully convenient spot, but they aren't. You may have to wiggle and crawl on your belly to reach these things, and then there may not be enough room to wrap the insulation around them. But the rewards may be as substantial as the hassle: if you do the ducts yourself, you may get a return equal to that you would get from a $500-to-$600 furnace device or from a set of storm windows. In some cases it might even be worthwhile to pay a contractor or a laborer to insulate the ducts, although there is no simple way to determine that, so the safest approach is to do it yourself.

You can buy duct wrap already measured and precut for the size ducts you have, or you can make your own wrap from a roll of foil-backed fiberglass insulation. You also need some tape to seal the cracks around the perimeter of each section of ducting where it meets the next section. One of the Princeton experts suggests long-lasting aluminized tape, because regular duct tape may lose its adhesive power in a couple of years, and you don't want to have to do the work over again.

From the roll of insulation, cut pieces long enough to encircle the entire circumference of the duct, with a little left over for fastening. Wrap the duct with the insulation, and then butt the ends of the insulation together and seal the seam with tape. You may want to cut the pieces of insulation a little long, scrape the insulation off the foil for a few inches on one end, and use that end as a tab or flap to cover the seam.

Repeat the procedure with the next piece of insulation, working your way down the duct. The seam where each wrap ends and the next begins should also be covered with tape. And the foil backing on the insulation should be kept to the outside, or visible.

This project takes more time and patience than skill. Perhaps you could lessen the burden by reviewing with the furnace serviceperson exactly which ducts are the most important to insulate, and then concentrating on those. On some furnaces, there are ducts that bring cold air to the combustion chamber from outside the house. These ducts do not require insulation.

You also need to protect yourself by wearing a mask whenever you work with insulation.

If you decide all of this is too troublesome, you might ask a contractor to throw in the duct project as part of a package that includes some larger job, like insulating the walls. Perhaps some installers would be willing to cover several of the small jobs (insulating the water tank, plugging the leaks in the attic) if a big contract were involved.

Plugging the Leaks

Air leakage, as infiltration is informally called, was hardly a matter of concern in the early energy research that first sent the nation running to the people who sell insulation. Yet field testing now shows that random leaks in, out, and through the house waste about 40 percent of the money used to heat it. In a very porous house, adding insulation is as futile as sweeping back the tide with a broom. Air leaks not only are pernicious energy drains but are also complex and subtle. Doors and windows are the least of the problem. Houses are full of hidden conduits and passageways that allow warm indoor air and cold outdoor air to mingle in the winter, or the reverse in summer.

Those of us who have bothered to caulk and weatherstrip at all have concentrated our efforts in the more accessible spots. Meanwhile, the big air leaks show up around bathtubs, behind recessed medicine cabinets, along baseboards, under recessed light fixtures, over dropped ceilings and stairwells, and even inside the walls themselves. Plugging these leaks is a great second chance to cut energy bills in a house reinsulated to little noticeable effect.

In fact, the Princeton people calculate that air leaks through attics alone—called bypasses—sabotage predicted insulation savings by 30 to 70 percent. In one experiment with thirty New Jersey townhouses, an energy team put more insulation in the attics, filled the cracks around windows and doors, insulated the furnace ducts, wrapped the water heater, and plugged some leaks in the attic. "Sealing these air leaks was the most important of the actions," according to Gautam Dutt, one of Princeton's energy gurus.

The energy cadre at Princeton developed a plan called house doctoring, in which two trained people can come into a house, sniff out and then treat all the leaks, and leave two hours later with the furnace bill cut by 10 to 20 percent. At least those are the initial results from a demonstration with eighteen houses in New Jersey.

The Princeton savings are tantalizing, because the success of house doctors won't do you any direct good. Outside the Princeton area, house doctors are as impossible to find as medical doctors who make house calls, and you can't recruit local talent without buying them some expensive equipment. The Princeton team uses a huge blower, installed in the door, to depressurize a house and intensify the leaks, which makes for easier detection. They also carry a hand-held infrared viewer, the kind lugged around Vietnam to ferret out the enemy. The viewer enables the house doctor to see heat escaping up the inside of the walls. I have taken the viewer into an attic that looked perfectly well insulated, only to discover dozens of red blotches, indications that vast quantities of heat were pouring out around the insulation.

But the Princeton routine can still do you a lot of indirect good if you are willing to handle the doctoring yourself. You can get most of that 10 to 20 percent fuel saving, house doctors argue, with the home remedy. All you need is a caulking gun and a few tubes of caulk, a part of a roll of fiberglass insulation with no foil or paper backing, and some sort of leak detector—a few sticks of incense, a cigarette, or a piece of tissue paper attached to a stick or coat hanger.

The idea is to roam the house, preferably on a windy winter day, passing the burning incense stick or the tissue paper slowly around the edges of windows, baseboards, light fixtures, electrical outlets, fireplace dampers, corners and seams where walls and ceiling join together, attic hatch covers, and any other likely leaky spots. You will see telltale variations in the smoke patterns—for example, where the smoke just hangs in the air, there is no leak; where it blows quickly to one side or another, a large one. The method can be used to find cracks and holes and to check the effectiveness of your caulking and weatherstripping.

You can set up a fancier mode of diagnosis by placing a window fan into a centrally located window, blowing out. If all the other windows and doors are shut tight, all the heating and cooling registers are closed, and the area around the fan itself is sealed with duct tape or plastic, the fan will depressurize the house. This makes the incoming drafts stronger and easier to pick up with the smoke or the tissue paper.

Amateur leak-hunting gets best results on the indoor side of the outer walls of the house. It doesn't expose the bypasses, those rivers of heat that can move up through the wall cavities and out the attic. You need an infrared viewer for the bypasses, and there is no home-made equivalent of this $5,000 piece of equipment. But the house doctors have investigated enough attics to know that the major bypasses show up in the same places again and again.

The Princeton analysis of leaks and bypasses in hand, I took a friend of mine named Dan Palmer on a tour of his drafty Victorian. We concentrated on the following areas.

1. The Attic. On windy nights, Palmer's attic was as drafty as a pup tent. It had been insulated with five inches of fiberglass by a local contractor back in 1976, and the attic was still warm in the winter. That is a sure sign of inadequate coverage or bypasses or both.

Palmer and I climbed through the crawlhole in the second-floor master bedroom to the attic. Across the floor joists lay a few boards, which made a kind of raft in a sea of fiberglass. If you undertake a like foray, be careful not to step between the rafters, and wear a mask to keep small bits of fiberglass from getting into your lungs.

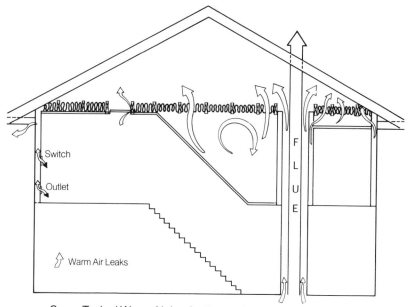

Some Typical Warm Air Leaks Bypassing the Attic Insulation

SOURCE: Center for Energy and Environmental Studies, Princeton University

Palmer's fiberglass insulation was somewhat easier to get a fix on than blown-in cellulose, which covers everything like a blizzard. We checked the following trouble spots:

The Attic Hatch or Door. Palmer had a 2,000-square-foot attic insulated to a level of R-19. But the contractor had neglected to insulate the covers on the two crawl-space holes—the one we entered through, and the other at the far end of the attic. The total area of the two bare spots was about ten square feet, and they looked like trivial omissions of effort. I had to convince Palmer that they were not as insignificant as they appeared.

The bare wood, I told him, has an R-value of 1. Ten square feet of uninsulated wood in the attic creates a heat-loss factor of 10/1, or 10. The rest of the 2,000 square feet, insulated to R-19, creates a heat-loss factor of 2,000/19, or 105. Comparing the 10 to the 105, one could see that 10 percent of the escaping heat was getting through two bare spots making up only 1/200th of the total area of the attic.

Had there been more insulation in Palmer's attic, the two bare spots would have caused much more than 10 percent of the total heat loss. In fact, up around the R-30 levels, covering the attic hatches or doors could save more energy than reinsulating the entire attic with a couple of extra inches.

In any event, insulating attic bare spots gives you one of the largest return-on-investment ratios of any single action you or Palmer could take on a house. Conversely, leaving hatches and doors uninsulated is a simple reason why attic insulation often doesn't pay off the way it is supposed to.

Palmer went downstairs and brought back the remnants of an old roll of the foil-backed fiberglass insulation, plus some scissors and a staple gun. It took only a few minutes to cut pieces of insulation the size of the two hatches, and to staple them to the hatch covers from the attic side, the foil backing facing down.

"That takes care of that," Palmer said.

It didn't quite. Warm air could still leak around the sides of the hatch covers into the attic. What Palmer did, once we finished with the attic, was to tape the edges of the hatches with duct tape from below. This should also be done to the edges of a fold-down attic door.

The Chimney or Flue Pipe. Looking through their infrared scanners, the house doctors find the brightest red blotches around the outer edges of chimneys or flue pipes where these pass through the attic. The blotches indicate intense heat escape. Of course heat also moves through the inside of the chimney, but that's not what makes for the blotches. These are created by an external draft, when heat from around the furnace below is pushed up through the walls and framing of the house, and then exits through the gaps that exist between the sides of the chimney and the attic floor. Since it is very hot around the furnace or fireplace, such a draft can be as powerful as it is expensive.

Even when insulation appears to surround the chimney or flue pipe, the heat can still escape, and it is stopped only when insulation is actually stuffed down into the gaps on all four sides of the chimney or around the flue pipe circumference. The material has to be tightly packed into either crevice.

Palmer and I edged our way carefully from one chimney to the other (his house has two). We peeled the foil backing from the fiberglass insulation and plugged the four sides of both chimneys.

Princeton says the practice poses no fire hazard as long as the insulation is applied at the attic floor level and as long as fiberglass insulation without paper or foil backing is used. Fiberglass insulation begins to char only at 800 degrees, and the flue at the attic floor never gets hotter than 200 degrees.

Carpenter's Holes. Palmer's attic was riddled with entry holes for pipes, wiring, and ducts. We couldn't see these holes below the fiberglass sea, but every time we saw evidence of a pipe or a wire, we pulled back the fiberglass to find a gaping hole, usually five to ten times larger than necessary to accommodate the pipe or wire. Palmer couldn't believe that he had spent so much time weatherstripping his doors and caulking his windows when there were holes in his house this big.

"What your contractor should have done," I said, stealing a speech from Princeton, "was to put a continuous plastic vapor barrier down on the attic floor before he rolled out the insulation. Any sheet of vinyl plastic, the kind sold at the garden stores, would have been fine. The plastic would have sealed the attic and eliminated all the leaks and bypasses at one time. Your man didn't do the job right, but he is typical. These characters think they take care of infiltration with the foil backing attached to the insulation. They can't."

So we tried to fill every hole in the attic with fiberglass; whenever a pipe or wire popped out of the floor, we stuffed the perimeter. Palmer seemed to enjoy doing this, getting overly zealous only once, when he tried to cover a metal box that was part of a recessed light fixture. These are attic protrusions that should not be covered.

Stairwells and False Ceilings. I discovered Palmer's false ceiling after pushing back some insulation in search of another carpenter's hole. I didn't find an opening an inch wide, but a deep chasm into which one of us might have fallen. Above the dropped ceiling, an attic floor falls to a lower level, continues for a few feet, and returns to the original level. At the edge of this chasm, I could actually look down into the interior walls below. They were not closed off at the top.

Palmer said I was standing over a dropped ceiling in the second-story bathroom. Instead of allowing the insulation to follow the contour of the chasm, down and back up again, the contractor had merely spanned the hole with two straight runs of fiberglass blanket.

From a cursory inspection, one would think that the attic floor was flat and level, because the insulation camouflaged the hole.

Princeton has found that heat pours out of such chasms as follows: (1) warm air from the furnace makes its way inside the walls of the house through electrical outlets and around baseboards, bathroom cabinets, and so forth; (2) the same warm air travels up through the walls until it finds an opening like the one around the dropped ceiling; and (3) since the contractor strung insulation over the top of the hole, but didn't actually seal off the passageway, the heat escapes easily. When I put my hand down into Palmer's dropped-ceiling hole, I could feel a draft.

Palmer made a trip to the hardware store, where he bought a twenty-foot roll of vinyl plastic for $5.95. If his problem was as bad as I thought it was, he would make the $5.95 investment back in one winter month.

We scrambled back into the attic and removed the insulation strung across the hole. We rolled the plastic into the hole, down one side, across the bottom, and up the other side, the same as one would cover a hole in the ground. The plastic made a continuous lining along the cavity, so no warm air could penetrate from below. Then we replaced the original insulation. The procedure would have been the same for an attic hole above a stairwell.

The Overall Coverage. I took one last look at the fiberglass sea to ensure that all the insulation fit snugly between the floor joists. In many attics, the house doctors find lumpy or uneven coverage, places where the insulation seems to puff or buckle. Such lumps provide more opportunities for heat to bypass the insulation.

Blown-in insulation, or loose-fill insulation, does not buckle. But it can drift like a snowbank, especially around the attic vents. The resulting drift can create bare spots, which is why it makes sense to check the attic every once in a while.

Palmer's attic didn't have buckles, but there were some places where the insulation didn't reach from one floor joist to the next. I stuffed these places with some extra pieces of fiberglass.

We made our exit.

If we had done the job in the winter, we could have used a thermometer to measure the payoff of our work by taking the temperature of the attic before and after our efforts. (For the test to yield meaningful results, the outdoor temperature must be the same both times.)

2. *Walls.* If filling the walls with insulation is too expensive, you can get at least some of the savings by sealing the walls so that air cannot travel as freely as before inside them. It's a replay of the attic situation, where most of the attention is paid to insulation, while air leakage around the insulation accounts for most of the money drain.

Any perforation of the surface of a wall is a potential escape hole for heat. Most houses are full of holes cut to make room for electrical outlets, light fixtures, ducts, exhaust fans, and recessed cabinets. What you want inside a wall is dead air space, and you can get that only by plugging the holes.

Electrical outlets can be sealed off with rubber gaskets, which are inexpensive hardware-store items. To install them, you pull the circuit breaker or loosen the fuse to the outlets in question, take off the faceplates, insert the gaskets, and screw the plates back on. This involves about two minutes' worth of effort for each outlet. If you don't have time to do the whole house, at least treat the outlets that feel drafty as you pass your hand in front of them on a cold, windy day.

The gaps around fans, cabinets, and other recessed fixtures tend to be quite wide, because they can always be covered up with decorative trim or with the faceplate of the fixture. When, for example, you remove the metal frame around a kitchen exhaust fan (always turn off the circuit breakers before touching any electrical equipment), you will probably find a gap of an inch or more separating the wall from the sides of the box housing the fan. Gaps such as these can be stuffed with fiberglass insulation or other fireproof material.

Of all the gaps you can plug, none is more important than the one in the fireplace damper. Even when dampers are in the closed position, they rarely close tightly, and because of the strong air flow up the chimney, a small crack here can create a substantial leak. If you don't use the fireplace, you can put a board over the damper or stuff the crack with fireproof insulation.

Now it's time to get out the caulking gun. The usual areas around windowsills and casings need to be caulked, and windows and doors should all be weatherstripped. But the caulking effort has to be extended to other key areas both inside and outside the house.

Inside the house, transparent caulk can be used around the edges of the fireplace, where it meets the walls, and anyplace else where masonry or stone abuts wood.

Outside, caulk any crack or hole possessing the remotest possibility of letting cold air into your house. There are usually numerous holes cut into outside walls allowing plumbing pipes or electrical and telephone conduits to enter the dwelling. You can also caulk the seams where any two pieces of lumber come together, especially at the vertical corners of the house. The best way to caulk is to remove the trim boards, or battens, and squiggle the stuff behind them.

If your furnace is in the basement, you might want to check for bypasses that would permit the heat to get into the wall cavities above. When the chimney or flue pipe is run inside the walls from basement to attic, the gap around the edges of the chimney at the basement level should be stuffed with insulation just as we did where the chimney came through Palmer's attic floor. Look for other places where plumbing or electrical holes are drilled into the "ceiling" of the basement, allowing pipes and wires to travel up into the house through the walls. These holes should all be stuffed or caulked.

I have been in basements where the area around the furnace itself was like a sauna bath because too much heat was being lost from the furnace box itself. Heating contractors often have useful ideas about how to cut an extra duct or hole into the floor above the furnace to divert some of that heat to the living space.

How to Caulk and Weatherstrip

Caulking is a messy operation unless you know how to squeeze the goo out of the tube so it makes a continuous, thin line. If you haven't ever tried it, I suggest you get a tube of cheap caulk and practice on a piece of scrap wood. The trick is to be able to stop and start again without leaving a big blob, and to move from one place to another without leaving a trail of taffy.

Wherever you buy your caulking gun and tubes, you can probably get some advice on how to snip the ends of the tubes and how to handle the gun. It doesn't take much caulk to seal a gap or crack, provided that the caulk adheres to the crack and doesn't droop or sag away. For this to happen, the surface to be caulked has to be clean and free of paint or old putty.

The right time to caulk? For the best coverage, you should do it in the winter, when boards are the driest and the cracks the widest. For the best application, you should caulk in summer, when the substance is warmer and flows out of the tube. I suggest a compromise—the spring or the fall.

The best kind of caulk? I would buy stuff that lasts a few years, since the labor time here is more valuable than the materials. I would also buy transparent caulk whenever possible—it is more aesthetically pleasing because it makes the blobs invisible. The tubes tend to crack and split over time, so they can't be stored indefinitely.

To aid consumers, I've reprinted a summary on caulks produced by the U.S. League of Savings Associations (see page 74).

Since that summary was published, however, a new kind of pressurized caulk has hit the market. It is foamy material that shoots out of an aerosol can like shaving cream, only it's not as friendly as shaving cream. You can't use the stuff without wearing gloves, but it has the terrific property of expanding to fill huge holes and cracks that stymie the gun-type caulks. But because of certain chemical properties of the foam, you should apply it only where it can be covered with battens or trim boards.

Weatherstripping. There are so many kinds of windows and doors and so many types of weatherstripping that I can't be comprehensive. The building supply people who sell windows and doors in your area ought to be able to tell you the best way to weatherstrip them. Or there's always that weekend oracle, the hardware-store expert.

Most varieties of weatherstripping require a little hammering and nailing and positioning of metal strips or wooden stops. There is a new lazy man's weatherstripping made of foam that you can just stick around a window or a door, but two people have complained to me that the foam stripping is easily blown out of position. The complaints don't constitute a definitive consumer report, but they're enough for me to issue an informal word of caution.

CAULKING COMPOUNDS

Type	Cost	Ease of Application	Weather Resistance	Effective Life (Years)	Paintable	Wood	Metal	Adherence to Water-Base Paint	Adherence to Oil-Base Paint	Masonry
Oil base	Low	Good	Poor	2–3	Yes	Good	Good	Good	Good	Good
Acrylic latex	Moderate	Good	Good	10	Yes	Good	Good	Good	Good	Good
Butyl	High	Good	Fair	10	Yes	Good	Excellent	Do not use over paint	Good	Good
Silicone	Very high	Good	Excellent	20	Yes—sometimes	Excellent	Excellent	Excellent	Excellent	Excellent

SOURCE: U.S. League of Savings Associations. © 1978 U.S. League of Savings Associations

Types of Weatherstripping

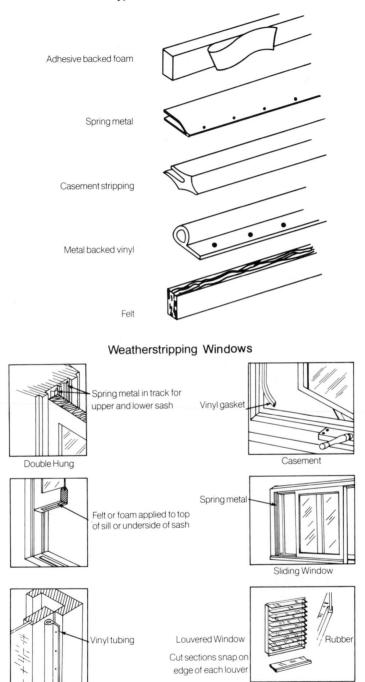

Adhesive backed foam

Spring metal

Casement stripping

Metal backed vinyl

Felt

Weatherstripping Windows

Spring metal in track for upper and lower sash

Double Hung

Vinyl gasket

Casement

Felt or foam applied to top of sill or underside of sash

Spring metal

Sliding Window

Vinyl tubing

Louvered Window

Cut sections snap on edge of each louver

Rubber

SOURCE: Center for Energy and Environmental Studies, Princeton University

What to Do with Windows

Molly Branfman has a house with a view in Golden, Colorado. The house itself is no architectural wonder, just a block-and-stucco rectangle set on a concrete slab. But whoever built it back in the 1960s didn't skimp on windows. It has 60 square feet of glass on each side, in a dwelling with 1,200 square feet of floor space.

The windows give Branfman what she calls her live-in diorama—snowcapped mountains to the north and west, prairie to the east, large park with duck pond to the south. They also, she thought, gave her some nasty energy bills. She had no basement and no easy way to insulate the concrete walls, and the attic was already cushioned to R-19. An eager contractor persuaded her that putting in storm windows would do the most for her energy balance sheet.

It is true that Branfman's single-paned windows had been losing a lot of heat. Her 240 square feet of single panes were allowing as much or more heat to escape from the house as all the wall areas combined. She thought she had been paying heavily for her wonderful views, and that once she got the storms, she would have her panorama for nothing. Like many of her neighbors, Molly believed single-paned windows to be the problem, and double-panes or storms to be the answer. So she paid $950 to get storms put on all four sides of the house, expecting her heating fuel consumption to drop about 25 percent.

It didn't, and when I visited Branfman on a trip through Denver, we got into the reasons why. Storm windows possess limitations with which Branfman was unfamiliar.

In fact, that extra pane of glass does very little to stop the march of heat out the window. Single pieces of glass have an R-value of 1, which is quite low, meaning that heat has no problem traveling through it. Adding a storm window or replacing an existing window with the double- or thermal-paned variety (either of which gives about the same benefit) increases the R-value to about 2. This is 100 percent improvement, but it isn't enough when the adjoining wall may have an R-value of 11 or even 19. The better insulated the house, the higher the percentage of indoor heat that pours out the windows, even the windows with double glass. The general rule is that a square foot of your average window, storms and all, loses five times as much heat as a square foot of the wall that surrounds it.

So when you hear people say, "This house has a lot of window area but it is no energy problem because we bought storms," you can chuckle quietly in the knowledge that they don't know what they are talking about.

Absent a single mitigating factor, homeowners in cold climates would now be forced by fuel price increases to board up their windows entirely. That factor is sunlight, which puts millions of BTUs back into a house, making up for some of the heat escaping in the other direction. Sunlight tilts the thermal balance so that windows are energy losers only during part of the day. Understanding the relationship between the sun and windows leads one to a different conclusion about the most effective treatment here.

To illustrate, I rely on some analysis done by Jay McGrew, a Colorado energy researcher who often takes maverick positions on how to save energy. McGrew has done a heat-loss profile for windows in the Denver area, and his work applies directly to Branfman's house. With two of McGrew's charts—one for a winter day, another for a summer day (see pages 78 and 79)—I could tell Branfman to what extent each of her windows was a credit or debit on her energy bill, and at what times. These charts would not be exactly the same, of course, in different climate zones, or even on different days when the sun shines for fewer hours. But they support the point I want to make: there is economic advantage to a flexible response to windows.

In February, between 12:00 A.M. and 6:00 A.M., the windows on all four sides of Branfman's house operate below the line—that is, they let more heat escape than they take in. This is when windows run up their biggest energy debts, but by sunrise some of them begin to reverse matters. The east-facing windows are first to make it into the black, followed almost immediately by the south-facing. East continues to put heat into the house until noon, when it returns the loss column. By noon, east has wiped out all of the midnight-to-six debt and has actually made Branfman a small profit. South stays in the black much longer, not going below the line until nearly 6:00 P.M. South windows are the big thermal winners, and McGrew's chart

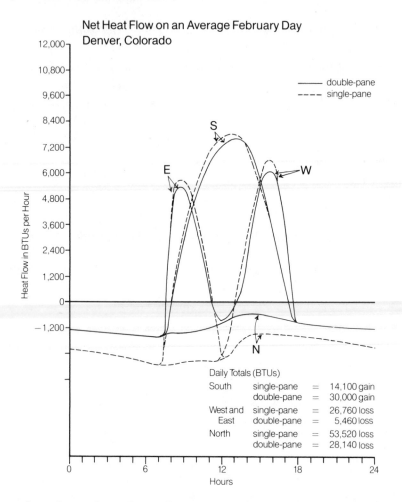

Net Heat Flow on an Average February Day
Denver, Colorado

Daily Totals (BTUs)

South	single-pane	=	14,100 gain
	double-pane	=	30,000 gain
West and	single-pane	=	26,760 loss
East	double-pane	=	5,460 loss
North	single-pane	=	53,520 loss
	double-pane	=	28,140 loss

makes clear why solar collectors are placed on the south sides of houses.

The west-facing windows don't contribute the first penny to the heating bill until noon, about the time that east starts to lose heat. West adds the same amount of heat to the house during the afternoon period as east did during the morning period. West and south drop off simultaneously, and by 6:00 P.M., Branfman is supporting all the windows out of her own pocket.

North stays in the red all day and all night, which is the reason that energy-saving houses don't have many windows on the north side in cold climates. The thermal balance sheet is altered dramatically when the window area is decreased on the north and increased on the south, but Branfman of course has an equal number of windows on all sides of her house.

The solid line on the chart on page 78 shows what double-panes or storms do for Branfman's pocketbook. They manage to cut the below-the-line losses virtually in half, so on cloudy days or at night (a performance chart for a cloudy day would be more flattering to storm windows than the one shown here) they save Branfman money. But one notices that storm windows make little difference during the times when the sun is adding heat to the house.

This doesn't mean that storms are useless. Storms are still a cost-effective purchase in many climate zones. Storm-window contractors or utility audits ought to be able to do a simple heat-loss calculation

Net Heat Flow on an Average July Day
Denver, Colorado

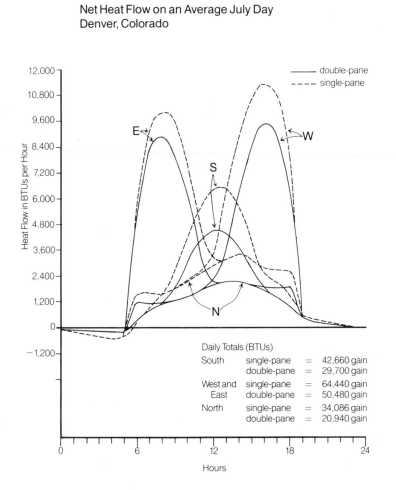

on your house and determine what the savings will be; the only thing to watch out for is whether these calculations give any thermal credit to the sunlight going in the other direction. If they don't, the savings estimates may be exaggerated. Steve Selkowitz, Lawrence Berkeley's window expert, says that a storm-window savings estimate gets suspect when it exceeds one-sixth of the annual heating bill. Storms will likely save you more money if installed on the north side of your house, where less sunlight falls, than they will if installed on the south side.

Storm windows perform another function. They stop cold air from leaking into the house from around the windows (infiltration) as well as retard heat flow through the glass (conduction). So the best storms to buy are the ones that cover the outside of the existing windows completely and make for a tight seal with the outside frame. Storm window components also possess varying degrees of leakiness, so you should buy the kinds with tight gaskets. In moderate and sunny climates, the infiltration savings from storms may be greater than the savings that come from doubling the glass. But unless a storm window is profitable on its anticonductive merits, it is an expensive way to stop leaks. Leaks around most windows, after all, can be plugged very cheaply with caulking and weatherstripping.

High energy prices, meanwhile, are making nighttime window losses so costly that homeowners need to consider other investments that will cut such losses more effectively. Branfman's storm windows cost her $4 a square foot. For the same money or less, she might have gotten equal or better R-value coverage from buying something else. One such alternative purchase can lower nighttime debit while preserving daytime credits. People who have not yet bought storms, or even people who have, would be wise to consider some of the alternative, though underpublicized, choices that have reached the marketplace.

Many of the new alternatives to storms, such as thermal drapes or multilayered shades, are installed on the inside of the windows— good for people who don't want to bother putting them up and taking them down again before and after each winter. A product like a thermal drape also provides another option for people like Branfman, who suspect that their storms have been less than effective. Even ordinary drapes and curtains, when arranged properly, can do the job of storms, or when used in conjunction with storms, can double the savings. Any drape or shade can be better than a static solution because it can be operated flexibly to catch thermal ins and outs. Some of the new products look like standard drapes and shades but have superior insulating power.

The research into window treatments is now so sophisticated that houses of the future may not have windows at all in the conventional sense. Innovations such as heat mirrors, just off the drawing board, will give fixed windows the thermal resistance of an insulated attic, yet will still permit sunlight penetration. Because of such advancements, even traditional houses can be turned into passive solar houses, which is to say that the windows will add more heat than they lose. If the windows can become thermal walls during the nighttime, and a house is well insulated in general, the house of the future can be heated in most areas of the country from a tiny furnace or from the exhaust heat from appliances.

Meanwhile, listed below are the energy-saving window products available today. Their thermal effectiveness can be compared through their R-values—the higher the R, the better the insulating qualities. A list of manufacturers begins on page 88.

1. Conventional Storm Window. R-value: 2. The window doubles the thermal resistance of a single pane of glass (which has an R-value of about 1), stops most of the window air leakage, and cuts nighttime losses in half, and does not affect window performance when sunlight strikes it. But the conventional storm window is ineffective compared to thermal resistance of ceilings and walls.

2. Conventional Drapes or Roll-Down Shades. R-value: 1.1. Loose-fitting drapes or shades keep a small amount of heat from escaping, enough to improve the R-value of a single-paned window about 10 percent. If you have drapes or shades, keep them closed at night and you'll save a little money. Loose-fitting drapes are far less than effective heat savers because the warm indoor air can usually get around them and find the window.

3. Conventional Drapes or Roll-Down Shades That Fit Tightly. R-value: 2. When regular drapes or curtains are sealed along the edges of the window casing, allowing no air to get to the window, they will provide you with the same energy savings as storm windows. If storm windows are already installed outside, the tight-fitting drapes inside can raise the total R-value of the window unit to 3.

Many people are using Velcro strips, grommets, battens, and other homemade attachments to stick their curtains and drapes to the window casings. Some companies now make interior roll-down shades with tracks, slats, and other like hardware provided. These shades are priced competitively with storm windows.

4. Exterior Roll-Down Shutters. R-value: 2. Popular in Europe for a number of years, these are now being sold in America. Their main function is to reduce heat gain in the summer, making the interior of the house cooler. They also offer the same wintertime heat-saving benefits as storm windows, but because they cost more, they are not competitive with storms in cold climates.

5. Multilayered Roll-Down Shades with Special Film. R-value: 5–14. This is where a window begins to perform like a wall. Compared to the paltry R-2 one gets from a storm window, one can double or triple the energy savings with such a shade. It works like the roll-down shades still seen in old hotels, except the shade part is constructed of a high-resistance thermal material. The shade made by Ark-tic Seal Systems, Inc., even provides a range of thermal materials that can be rolled down separately for varying summer or winter conditions.

These shades require a small amount of human effort to move up and down, and they cost more per square foot than most storm windows. But the high R-value may make them worth it, especially on north-facing windows in very cold climates. Ark-tic Seal also makes a special roll-down for sliding glass doors, which can be the biggest energy losers in the shell of the house. (Another company, Sunflake Window, makes a sliding glass unit with an advertised R-value of 14.)

If I lived in one of the colder climate zones, had several windows on the north side, and didn't want to consider the insulating panels described below, I'd consider the high-R shades. Price lists are available from the manufacturers.

6. Window Blankets or Quilts. R-value: 3–4. Old-timers in Appalachia have always insulated their windows by covering them with quilts. A company in Vermont (see the list of manufacturers) has improved on the technique by making a quilt that is better insulated and is filled with a reflective vapor barrier. The quilt is moved up and down along a track installed in the window casing, a track arrangement that reduces air leakage.

The company claims an R-rating of better than 4 for a single-paned window with a window quilt, which is twice as good as a storm window, as long as the quilt is retracted during the sunny hours when the window is a heat producer. There is of course some aesthetic advantage to the quilt versus the multilayered plastic roll-down shades.

7. Insulating Panels or Shutters. R-value: 5–8. Homemade insulating panels or shutters offer the highest return for the lowest cost. Opening and closing the shutters manually does require some effort, but that for me at least is better than chopping wood for six hours. The idea is to close off the windows with a solid, well-insulated panel every time there is negative heat flow, and even a homemade insulated panel can provide as much R-value as some of the newfangled products being developed in the research labs. This is another case where a backyard product and a bit of human exertion is much better than expensive gadgetry.

Insulating panels can be made in a multitude of ways. A piece of rigid insulation board, like styrofoam, is usually sandwiched between two pieces of paneling or decorative wood to make a reasonably attractive indoor shutter, one that fits inside a window casing or frame. The shutter can cover the whole window and operate on one hinge, or it can be divided into sections and fold back like an accordion door. People who don't like the look of indoor shutters sometimes install them behind drapes.

A local carpenter can advise you about the various ways to make and hinge these shutters so they can be easily operated. The only requirement: they must fit tightly in the window casing, so that air doesn't leak around them. Air leaks can also cause moisture problems between the shutter and the window frames, not to mention a loss in energy savings. Shutters can be sealed against the window casing with rubber gaskets, Velcro strips, foam weatherstripping, or other types of flexible edging materials.

The indoor insulating panels can be worked on the four sides of the house to correspond to the position of the sun in the sky, a technique that also applies to drapes and quilts. The north side is the first place to install panels, even if they aren't put anywhere else. The north-side returns are the greatest, and the panels here don't have to be moved quite as often.

In north-facing rooms unoccupied during the day, the insulating panels can remain closed throughout the winter. With the windows sealed off, these rooms will be a much smaller drain on the energy budget, though the actual savings depends on the severity of the winter and the size of the windows.

The insulating panels on the other three sides of the house are put to best use in conjunction with the sun's path across the sky. In the morning, the east- and south-side panels should be opened to get the first above-the-line savings. At noon, when the east windows start to lose more heat than the sunlight replaces, the east-side panels should be closed and the west-side panels opened. At sundown, west and south should be closed.

Such efforts may approach nautical compulsion, but in cold climates, the rewards are significant. Insulating panels with dedicated operators can double the energy savings of standard storm windows. Any person willing to make the morning and afternoon rounds is advised to see if the indoor panels can be made locally for the same or less money than storms.

8. Future Prospects: Heat Mirrors, Gassy Windows, Special Optics. R-values: 5 and better. Many researchers are trying to invent windows that let in sunlight, insulate like a pile of cellulose, and don't require panel-pulling dedication. There are prototypes of windows that darken or lighten like newfangled sunglasses, windows that contain heat-repelling gases, windows with thermal shutters sandwiched between two panes of glass. The trouble is, they still cost too much. A $500 window just can't save enough energy to support its gadgetry.

It is unlikely that any of these sophisticated windows will capture the retrofit market, but they may appear in new construction. I mention them because of their potential effect on the real estate market. Right now, storm windows are considered energy-saving products; in the next five years, I think that notion will be outdated, thanks to poor thermal performance.

The most promising of the new inventions is the heat mirror, a thin metallic film that can be applied to new or existing windows. Because of certain esoteric characteristics, the film lets sunlight into the room while it reflects or repels most of the heat that might otherwise escape out the window. Heat mirrors reflect only certain wavelengths of radiation and allow other wavelengths to pass through. Since heat is a form of radiation with characteristics different from light's, it is possible for a heat mirror to admit the one and repel the other. Heat mirrors combine the static advantages of storm windows (they don't have to be moved) with the flexible advantages of insulated panels. They can also be manufactured at relatively low cost, although retail prices have not yet been set.

Unfortunately the thin film is not tough enough to withstand scratches, smudges, or other scars of household use. If the surfaces were less sensitive, the film could be glued right onto existing windows, just like standard sun-control film. The inventors now plan to manufacture a window unit with the heat mirror already embedded between two panes of glass. That way the film itself can't be damaged.

The Department of Energy estimates that if a naked single-paned window loses 100 units of heat, a double-glazed window with heat mirror coating will lose only 30 units. If sold in film form, the coatings would be cheaper than storm windows or insulating shutters or any of the popular window options. In any case, because they will probably be sold as part of a manufactured window unit, they will be more suited to new construction than to retrofit.

When to Buy. As energy prices continue to rise, a point will be reached when it becomes cost-effective to purchase an indoor insulating product in addition to storm windows. There is no way to generalize when that time may arrive for you. If you have large, north-facing windows and north-facing sliding glass doors, it may already be intelligent to buy a roll-down shade or a window blanket. My advice is to get an energy audit from the local utility before deciding what to do. The auditor will measure your window area and determine how much heat is lost through all the glass during an average winter, and if your auditor is a good one, he will take window heat gains into his calculations. Ask him if the audit program factors in heat gains. If not, reduce his estimated savings by half.

From the audit, you should get an idea of the amount of heat lost per square foot of window, which you can then compare with the per-square-foot cost of improvements. The auditor may not be aware of insulating panels or window quilts, but you can show him the estimated R-values and ask him to compute the savings for these competing products as well as for storm windows.

Summer and Shade

The mass exodus from cold climates to the Sun Belt is hitting a curious snag. People who, hoping to avoid high heating bills, abandoned northern dwellings for the warmth of the South, generally bought houses that could not be kept cool in the summer months without air conditioning. The airy, porchy traditional southern architecture has been long since abandoned, replaced by stucco bunkers. The new inhabitants of the Tucson or Tampa or Houston subdivisions quickly became dependent on air conditioning, which is decidedly habit-forming, and what was a household oddity in 1950 became a necessity in the 1970s.

Now that all these people are happily ensconced in the stucco bunkers, their backyard central units whirring, the electric rates are going up. They are going up so fast that it is already as expensive to cool some houses in Houston as it is to heat some houses back in Ohio, especially if the houses in Texas have little shading and no natural ventilation. The refugees from freeze-or-go-bankrupt are now facing swelter-or-go-bankrupt.

Because Sun Belt migrants are learning that the investments made to save on heating bills in winter on paper at least save on cooling bills in summer, many are making the same investments they would have made in the North—more insulation, storm windows, caulking

R-VALUES AND COST: COMPARISON OF INTERIOR
AND EXTERIOR SHADES AND SHUTTERS WITH
TRADITIONAL STORM WINDOWS, CURTAINS, AND
BLINDS

Product and Manufacturer	Cost per Square Foot	R-Value with Single-Paned Window	R-Value with Double-Paned Window
Standard exterior storm windows	$3.00–$6.00	2.0	3.1
Conventional roll-down interior shades	$.75–$1.50	1.1	2.3
Conventional draperies		1.1	2.3
Indoor shutters or panels with insulated core	$3.00–$15.00	7.1	8.3
Window quilts or window blankets (manufactured as Window Quilt)	$4.50	4.1	5.2
Quilted draperies (manufactured by windowBlanket)	$4.00–$6.00	2.9	4.0
Multilayered roll-down shade with special plastics (manufactured as Insealshade)	$8.50	5.0	7.0
Multilayered roll-down shade with five layers of aluminized plastic (manufactured as High-R Shade)	$6.00	14.0	14.0
Exterior roll-down shutters made of plastic slats (several manufacturers)	$8.00–$18.00	2.0	3.1

Product and Manufacturer	Cost per Square Foot	R-Value with Single-Paned Window	R-Value with Double-Paned Window
Conventional venetian blinds	$5.00–$6.00	1.2	2.3
Interior roll-down slats of plastic (manufactured as Thermo-Shade)		2.5	3.3
Interior roll-down shades in tracks		2.0	3.0
Interior roll-down shades with tape to seal edges		2.0	3.0
Interior plastic storm windows		2.0	3.0
Sun-control film with extra insulating power		1.2	2.2
Special sliding-glass window panel to substitute for sliding-glass door installations (manufactured by Sunflake Windows)		14.0	14.0

ADDRESSES OF MANUFACTURERS OF
ENERGY-SAVING WINDOW EQUIPMENT

Product	Manufacturer
Insulated folding panels to be used as indoor shutters	Insulshutter Box 338 Silt, CO 81652
Window quilts with installation hardware	Appropriate Technology Corporation P.O. 975 Brattleboro, VT 05301

Product	Manufacturer
Quilted draperies	windowBlanket Company Route 1, Box 83 Lenoir City, TN 37771
Multilayered roll-down shade that installs on inside of windows	Insealshade Ark-tic Seal Systems P.O. 428 Butler, WI 53007
Multilayered roll-down shade similar to above	High-R Shade Insulating Shade Company P.O. 282 Branford, CT 06405
Exterior roll-down shutters made from plastic or wooden slats	American German Industries 14611 North Scottsdale Road Scottsdale, AZ 85260
	Abox Corporation 629-3 Terminal Way Costa Mesa, CA 92627
	Rolsekur Corporation Fowler's Mill Road Tamworth, NH 03886
	Pease Company Ever-Strait Division 7100 Dixie Highway Fairfield, OH 45023
	Serrande of Italy P.O. 1034 West Sacramento, CA 95691
	Solex 244 San Lorenzo Ave. Coral Gables, FL 33134
Interior roll-down shades made from plastic slats	Thermoshade Solar Energy Construction Company P.O. 718 Valley Forge, PA 19481

Product	Manufacturer
Interior roll-down shades in tracks	NRG Shade 288 Willow Drive Levittown, PA 19054
Interior roll-down shades that seal to window casing with tape	Minute Man 305 West Walker Street East Flat Rock, NC 28726
Interior plastic storm windows	In-Sider Storms Plaskolite P.O. 1497 Columbus, OH 43216
	Flexigard Storms 3M Building 223-2 3M Center St. Paul, MN 55101
	Window Film Thermotech 410 Pine Street Burlington, VT 05401
	Insulite Northeast Energy Corporation 11 Beacon Street Boston, MA 02108
	Vinyl Therm Insulated Pane Industries 2227A Heybourne Road Minden, NV 89423
	Thermatrol Perkasie Industries 50 East Spruce Street Perkasie, PA 18944
Sun-control film with extra insulating power	3M Company Energy Control Products 3M Center St. Paul, MN 55101

Product	Manufacturer
Sun-control film with extra insulating power	Solar-X Corporation 25 Needham Street Newton, MA 02161
	Madico 64 New Industrial Parkway Woburn, MA 01801
	Solar Control Products Standard Packaging Corporation Cranbury, NJ 08512
Special sliding-glass window panel to substitute for conventional sliding-glass door	Sunflake Window 625 Goddard Avenue Ignacio, CO 81137
Adhesive gasket to enable drapes to seal with sides of window	Fluff Gasket Russell and Associates 110 Riverside Drive Jacksonville, FL 32202

and weatherstripping. Unfortunately, such investments provide even less certain returns in summer heat than in winter cold. Most modifications to the shell of a house stop heat from flowing through the walls, ceiling, and windows by conduction. Conduction, the energy version of osmosis, is more pronounced in winter than it is in summer.

During the winter, a house is struggling to contain heat against an outdoors that may be 60 degrees colder. Since the rate of heat loss by conduction is determined by the temperature difference between inside and outside, conductive barriers like insulation and double-paned windows have the most energy-saving effect during extremely cold weather. During the summer, a house has to hold its coolness against an outside only 10 degrees warmer. With the smaller summer temperature differentials, the conductive savings are more limited.

So how does one save money and still keep cool? In some ways the summer does offer a greater opportunity for savings than the winter. Furnaces and heaters, after all, cannot be turned off in cold climates or people will freeze; one can only hope to save energy by making the furnace more efficient. But air conditioners can be turned off in warm weather. In fact, while heating is a universal phenomenon in northern climates, one can drive the streets of Houston or Tucson or Atlanta on a hot day and find half the houses with their air conditioners turned on and the other half with their windows opened and the air conditioners off. The big savings here don't come from more efficient air conditioner operation but from no operation whatever.

Even the better-insulated stucco bunkers can't rely on continuous artificial cooling without budget-busting results. The goal here is to create an operating flexibility allowing you to turn the machine completely off, or to raise the thermostat setting, and still have tolerable living conditions indoors for as many hot days as possible.

The best summer cooling investments are those that shade the windows from direct sunlight and those that create more internal breeze. Freezing is a scientific term, but sweltering is a subjective matter that depends on humidity, air flow, and temperature. So with proper air flow and humidity control, a person can accept warmer indoor temperatures and still feel cool.

Your first step is to repel the direct sunlight from hitting your windows. Those millions of invading BTUs so helpful during the winter are now a scourge, as anybody who stands in front of a sunny summertime window knows. The chart on page 79 showing the BTUs entering Branfman's house on an average July day illustrates the problem; all the windows here are heat gainers all day, and none of the heat is beneficial at any time.

Double-paned or storm windows, represented by the solid line, do keep some heat from getting into the house. So you can save money by leaving the storms up for the summer, assuming that inhabitants of the house are addicted to air conditioning and that the windows are never opened for natural ventilation. You can see that about 150,000 errant BTUs wouldn't have reached Branfman's house had she kept the storms closed. Over the course of the entire summer, the storms would repel 4 million BTUs, or half the amount that they trap inside the house during the winter. This represents a $15 saving for Branfman, but would be much more in climates warmer than Golden, Colorado.

Shading is a more complete remedy than double glass or storms. Because it is better to stop solar heat before it gets to the house than after it hits the windows, outside shades and awnings are preferable to indoor drapes and curtains. Most people put outdoor shades or awnings on the south windows, but McGrew's window charts suggest that the east and west sides shouldn't be ignored either.

Conventional canvas awnings cost from $5 to $8 a square foot, and some of the newer roll-down varieties, $8 to $18. Trees are cheaper, if you can wait around for them to grow. You should know that the exact returns from any of the outdoor shades cannot be quantified, and you can only go by intuition and feel. If a room gets a lot of direct sunlight and becomes uncomfortably hot, outdoor awnings are the preferred solution. The investment will definitely pay off if the awnings allow you to use the room without air conditioning; it might pay off if awnings allow you to rely on the air conditioner only intermittently.

The indoor window products—drapes, shutters, curtains, shades —are not as good as outdoor awnings at repelling heat from the house, but if you have them you might as well use them while the air conditioner is running. The strategy for winter savings is merely reversed: you close down the shutters or curtains during the day and open them up at night. Again, the tighter the seal the drapes or curtains make on the window frame, the more effective they are at keeping the cool air inside the house. Some of the multilayered roll-down shades even have special layers of film used only in summer for maximum heat rejection. A light-colored backing on the indoor insulating shutters will also help reflect the sun's heat away from the windows. A space blanket attached to the back of a standard roll-down shade serves the same function.

But I wouldn't buy any special indoor shades or curtains just for the summer energy savings, because the goal is to open your windows as much as possible and to ignore your air conditioner. Outdoor awnings and shades allow such freedom, because they still do their heat-stopping job with the windows open.

What I might buy instead of awnings is the self-adhesive plastic film manufactured under various brand names as sun-control film. This thin, flexible plastic film can be glued to windows for less than it would cost to install outdoor shades or awnings—usually $1 to $3 a square foot, including professional installation. The film rejects about 50 to 60 percent of the heat striking the windows, and even in moderate climates like that of Washington, D.C., it can knock off 25¢ to 30¢ per square foot of window area per year from your air conditioning bill.

Traditional sun-control films have a few drawbacks: some of them reject visible light as well as heat; all of them keep solar heat from getting through the windows in winter, thus creating an energy debt, which wipes out some of the energy savings gained in summer. A precise analysis of sun-control-film performance in Washington, done by Lawrence Berkeley Laboratory, shows that while the film can save $50 in an average house during the summer, it can lose $30 during the winter.

Recent developments in film technology have improved matters. Traditional films were more absorptive—that is, they soaked up the sun's heat and didn't allow it to get into the house. The newer films are more reflective, but only in nonvisible parts of the light spectrum, which means that the visible light is allowed to pass through the windows, while most of the heat is reflected out. Moreover, the new films don't make rooms seem dark, while the old films did. The technology also created superior insulating properties, helping keep heat in the house during winter by improving the R-value of the window by about 10 percent. Some of the heat loss caused by the reflective aspects of the film is thereby counteracted.

Stephen Selkowitz, window expert at Lawrence Berkeley, tells me that the best films to buy if you live in a warm climate are the ones that are highly reflective. Look for a product that reflects at least 60 to 70 percent of the sunlight. Such information should be provided on the package or by the dealer.

Selkowitz has also found a good homemade solution to the summer-winter trade-off, although it takes some work. Instead of gluing the film to the windows and making it permanent, you can buy reflective window film attached to simple rollers and use it as a shade. The unit can be rolled down on hot summer days, and rolled up at night and during the winter. Roll-down shades with reflective film are available in some building supply stores, or you can order them from Plastic View Transparent Shades, Incorporated, 15468 Cabrito Road, Van Nuys, California, 91408.

The manufacturers of the higher-performance films are listed on pages 90–91.

Once you have chosen a way to repel the sunlight from the windows, the next step is to consider ventilation, which requires a certain personal and idiosyncratic sensitivity to outdoor temperature levels. A steady diet of air conditioning dulls that sensitivity, like a hot sauce that stultifies the taste buds. I will assert that people who open their windows and begin to use awnings and fans are often surprised at how little air conditioning they really need.

Any fan that moves air around a room helps to make things seem cooler, but the most effective fan is the whole-house unit installed in the attic or top floor. Such a fan sucks air from all parts of the house, creating powerful and cooling breezes. It costs more than $400 installed, but a combination whole-house fan and awnings investment can all but eliminate the need for air conditioning in many parts of the country.

On the negative side, a large fan installed pancake style in the attic can also make for a new winter heat leak. If you get one of these fans, make sure it comes with tightly sealed shutters that close down when the machine is not operating. In rooms that may still require air conditioning, the fan-and-awning approach can cut the time that air conditioning has to be operated by at least 50 percent; this produces big money savings.

LOW-COST WINDOW TREATMENTS

Several people I know have insulated their windows from the inside with rigid sheets of transparent plastic available at building supply stores. They cut the material so it fits snugly inside the window casings, and then seal the edges with silicone or some other neutral-colored caulk. If they want to get fancy, they trim the edges of the plastic with some sort of attractive molding. Holes are then drilled through the molding and the plastic beneath it at various intervals so the whole thing can be screwed into the window casing.

These interior storm windows have an insulating value equal to the exterior storms, and they are ten times cheaper, making the return on your money ten times as great. Because it's the dead air space between the storm and the window which creates most of the insulating effect, it doesn't really make any difference whether the storm window is placed outside or inside, or whether it's made of glass or plastic.

Plastic storm window kits can also be purchased from hardware stores, but the ones I have seen are not as attractive as some of the homemade units. But either way, plastic storms present an alternative for people who don't want to buy exterior storms or who want to add a third layer of insulating protection and don't like the idea of solid insulating panels that have to be opened and closed all the time. If you are not yourself an adept carpenter, you can discuss the plastic storm project with a local handyman to see what the cost would be per square foot. It is not, in any case, a big job to cut the pieces and affix them to the windows.

The more popular low-cost energy choice here is the insulated drape. Regular drapes can be closed on winter nights for some savings in energy, but if they are insulated and tight-fitting, their performance shoots up to equal a second or even a third pane of glass. If you are going to have drapes anyway, they might as well have insulating liners. Large retail outlets like Sears now offer them to go along with their standard lines. A company called windowBlanket (see page 89) sells a quilted polished cotton drape filled with polyester advertised to have an R-value of 2. That's as good as a storm window right there.

Homeowners have found many and ingenious ways to seal the drapes to the sides of the window casing. One of the most effective is to run one Velcro strip around the perimeter of the casing and another strip around the back of the drape or curtain so the two can be joined with a continuous seal. A more expensive approach is to install tracks on the sides of the window casing and insert the drapes the way a sail is inserted into a mast. Russell and Associates, 110 Riverside Avenue, Jacksonville, Florida 32202, makes a product called fluff gasket, which sticks to the backs of drapes and makes a good seal against the adjoining wall.

For people with more advanced carpentry skills, making the insulating indoor shutters described earlier is sure to be rewarding. The place to start is on north-facing windows. If the north rooms are infrequently occupied, an insulating panel doesn't even have to be hinged for easy operation. It can simply be set into the window casing and left there until spring. One way to seal the panel on the edges is to run a length of foam weatherstripping around the perimeter of the panel.

The plans for an insulating panel made of rigid insulation board, black on one side and white on the other, are available from Solpub, P.O. Box 2351, Gaithersburg, Maryland 20760.

Summer and Shading. It seems trivial, but people who get accustomed to living in air-cooled isolation from the elements often don't know when to turn the machine off. The Princeton researchers found that it is common practice among residents in Twin Rivers, New Jersey, to run the air conditioner even when outdoor temperatures have dropped to below indoor thermostat settings. At that point, windows should be opened. Princeton even installed a blue light inside a group of houses and then wired the light so it would flash whenever outdoor temperatures reached the window-opening levels. When the homeowners got the signal device, they did begin to turn off the machines and saved money.

One common misconception about air conditioners is that letting them run all the time is cheaper than allowing the house to cool down, heat up, and cool down again. But continual use is becoming less and less intelligent as electric rates increase. In many parts of the country, it now costs more than 25¢ an hour to operate a room air conditioner, and several dollars an hour to operate big, central units.

Most houses have some thermal storage capacity, or the ability to keep the cool air produced inside the house, and many people have learned to use the thermal storage to reduce the need for air conditioning. One such person is my friend Frank Tenney, who lives in Naples, Florida, and is an expert at thermal technique. He opens up his house completely at night so that the cooler air can reduce temperatures to the maximum natural levels. Then in the early morning he shuts all the windows and closes all the drapes so the cool air now stored in walls and floors cannot escape. At noon, during the hottest part of the day, he turns on the air conditioner to dump the humidity out of the house and to cool it down intermittently. When the air conditioner reduces indoor temperatures to a comfortable level, Tenney turns off the machine. He uses fans to circulate air around the living areas, and uses light- and heat-producing appliances as little as possible.

The result is that Tenney's house remains tolerably pleasant on about one-fifth the electric bill of his neighbors, who air condition full blast from May to October.

Part Four

AUDITING THE AUDITORS

U tilities are beginning to perform home energy audits at the owner's request. An energy audit is the only inexpensive way to get an expert into the house to examine the energy situation, analyze conflicting investments, and advise you where to put your money. A service like this costs between $150 and $200 when it's done by private auditing companies, but utilities that offer it will either do it for free or charge a nominal fee of $15 to $25, with the companies recovering the difference in their rate structures.

That's another reason to ask for an audit. You are paying for it with higher utility bills, anyway, so you might as well spend the few extra dollars and take advantage of the information. Some utilities have launched elaborate advertising campaigns to let their customers know that audits are available. Others keep their programs relatively quiet, which is a bad sign, but you should call them anyway and ask if audits are being done and when you can be scheduled. If your electric utility doesn't perform audits, try the gas company or even an oil dealer (depending, of course, on whether you use one of these fuels).

The drawback is that the quality of the audits is uneven. I don't mean from house to house, but from utility to utility. The companies eager to promote conservation will make their audits as comprehensive and accurate as possible, but utilities upset that the audit program began as a government mandate may take a less than enthusiastic approach. Before you decide to listen to any advice given, do a little auditing of the auditor while he or she is auditing the house. A few pointed questions will help you get the most out of a good audit or identify a bad one.

The auditor will arrive at your door with a questionnaire, a tape measure, and possibly some other diagnostic equipment. Some utilities train auditors to turn down water-heater thermostats or make other low-cost adjustments, if the customer agrees. Take advantage of the offer, if it arises. Low-cost efforts, as we have seen, always pay.

Other utilities run a hands-off program, in which the auditor collects information and asks questions. He is supposed to inspire you to take the low-cost steps yourself, but his main job is to give you a cost-benefit analysis of the big investments. He counts windows, measures floor spaces, checks the caulking and weatherstripping, determines the thickness of the insulation, and figures out what kind of furnace you have. Then he asks some questions about how much it costs to heat and cool the house and so forth.

The answers are put on an audit form, and the whole thing is sent to a central computer, the key to the procedure. The relationship between the auditors and the central data bank is similar to the one between roving paramedics and the doctor back at the hospital. The auditors describe the condition of the house, and the computer makes the decisions. The idea here is to standardize the advice so that two or more auditors don't make wildly divergent recommendations. The computer is programmed with local information about energy prices, average outdoor temperatures, heat-loss calculations, and other factors. After the description of your house is fed into the machine, it spews out a list of possible energy-saving investments, with an estimate of what they will cost (contractor and do-it-yourself prices are given) and what they will save you in the first year.

In some audits, a list of recommendations arrives in the mail a few days after the auditor has visited your house. But in programs with more technical pizzazz, the auditor brings a telephone hookup to the computer, attaches it to your own phone, sends in the numbers, and gets an instant printout of the recommendations. Showmanship doesn't make the advice any better, but the quick feedback at least gives you a chance to discuss the list with the auditor.

On page 103 is a simple result from a California house audited under a pilot program run by Pacific Gas and Electric. The house is owned by John Hailey, a PG and E executive whose total energy bill was $454 for the twelve months preceding the audit in July 1979. Other utilities' audits will differ in form, but the essential categories will be the same. (The newer audits also make recommendations

PG and E
HOME ENERGY USE SURVEY REPORT

NATIONAL ENERGY WATCH

Prepared Especially for __John Hailey__ Phone __595-0513__

Address __273 Arundel Road__ City __San Carlos__ State __CA__ Zip __94070__

Product Description:	CONTRACTOR INSTALLATION			DO-IT-YOURSELF INSTALLATION			EST. FIRST YEAR ENERGY SAVINGS d
Survey Number ___	Priority for Installation a	Estimated Costs b	Payback Years c	Priority for Installation a	Estimated Costs b	Payback Years c	
1) CEILING INSULATION ADD		$ Skip			$		$
2) WALL INSULATION ADD e		$ Skip			$		$
3) FLOOR INSULATION ADD R-11 f	yes	$ 800	7.9	yes	$ 218	2.4	$ 87
4) STORM/INSULATED WINDOWS AND DOORS	yes	$ 345	9.3	yes	$ 253	7.2	$ 31
5) CAULKING OF WINDOWS AND DOORS		$ Skip			$		$
6) WEATHER STRIPPING OF WINDOWS & DOORS	no	$ 300	25.0	yes	$ 24	9.9	$2
7) WATER HEATER INSULATION WRAP		$ Skip			$		$
8) CLOCK THERMOSTAT	yes	$ 80	2.7	yes	$ 45	1.6	$ 28
9) INSULATION OF DUCTS g		$ Skip			$		$
10) LIGHTING CONVERSION	no	$ 607	20.6	yes	$ 229	9.9	$ 19
11) LOW – FLOW SHOWER HEAD (S)	no	$ Skip			$		$
12)		$			$		$
PACKAGE RECOMMENDATION h	no	$ 2132	13.0	yes	$ 769	5.5	$ 126

Notes a through h are listed on the back of this form

REMINDER CHECKLIST

√	Item Description:	√	Item Description:
	1. Check furnace/air conditioner filter monthly. Replace or clean quarterly if necessary.		8. Keep the fireplace damper closed when the fireplace is not in use.
	2. Move furniture and other obstructions away from heater/air conditioner registers.		9. Set water heater at "normal" or "medium" (130°–140°) temperature.
	3. Clean and oil furnace/air conditioner motor annually.		10. Clean refrigerator coils every three months.
	4. Check furnace/air conditioner fan drive belt annually and replace if worn.		11. Defrost freezer before frost buildup is 1/4"
	5. Install reduced-flow heads or flow restrictors on showers.		12. In the winter, set your thermostat at 65°–68° in the day time, 55° at night. In the summer, if you have air conditioning, set your thermostat at 78° or higher.
	6. Install low-volume aerators on sinks.		13. During summer days, avoid use of heavy appliances (air conditioning) between 12:30 and 6:30 p.m.
	7. Repair leaking faucets.		

√ indicates that item needs attention. For more assistance, call PG and E toll-free: (800) 792-8000. In area code 805, call collect to (415) 543-2073 Monday through Saturday, 8 a.m. to 5 p.m.

Enercom® – A service of **PG and E**

© 1979 ENERCOM, TEMPE, AZ

Weatherization Specialist __D. Southwork__

Date __7-6-79__ Specialist ID # __08-806__

White - Homeowner's Copy; Yellow & Pink - PG and E's Copies

on "renewable resources," including solar water heaters.)

Where Hailey had enough insulation or where the audit category did not apply, the auditor marked "skip." The computer gave cost-benefit numbers for the rest of the items and recommended three of them—a clock thermostat, storm windows, and floor insulation. Hailey was told that in the first year he could save $87 from the floor insulation, $31 from the storm windows and doors, and $28 from the clock thermostat.

Should Hailey believe the numbers? Not without knowing something about the computer program used by his utility. Most of them buy audit programs from small companies that specialize in such things, and the programs range from superb to simple-minded. The Lawrence Berkeley Laboratory, for instance, has a computer model that accounts for air leaks, attic bypasses, and other subtleties before determining each homeowner's best investment possibilities. Less elaborate models merely resurrect and rely upon the heat-loss formulas from an old physics textbook, formulas that have proven deficient in predicting energy consumption.

Pacific Gas and Electric, Hailey's utility, has already found places where the audit numbers didn't make sense, and their computer apparently thought weatherstripping always saved the customer $1 a year. But since PG and E cares about the quality of the audits, it has revised the program, gradually refining the recommendations, and it has taught the auditors to apply certain fudge factors and ignore the computer when it seems to miss the point.

PG and E is exemplary in this regard, but you can probe the reliability of your own audit by quizzing the auditor in the following ways:

General Recommendations. Auditors don't measure the furnace's efficiency, which is a major failing. Not only can big savings be achieved through furnace improvements, but such improvements affect the savings from the other items on the audit list. If you are planning to replace or modify the furnace, you should ask the auditor how that will affect his recommendations. What fuel prices are assumed in the audit savings? What happens if you switch from oil to gas? What level of efficiency is assumed for the furnace? The answers to these questions will help determine whether insulation or storm windows make the better investment choice. If you make the furnace more economical and pay less for fuel, you will have less to gain from insulation. The auditor should adjust for that.

Insulation Recommendations. Air leaks, bypasses, gaps in foam insulation, and other imperfections inhibit your return on money spent. Does the utility's computer program take these spoilers into account? Or does it rely on simple heat-loss calculations—so much insulation, so much savings? Does the program figure diminishing returns for higher levels of attic insulation?

Storm Window Recommendations. Does the audit treat windows only as heat losers, or does it assume that some windows may be heat gainers? The economics of storm windows or triple glazing are tied to the choice. If the computer predicts storm window savings greater than 15 percent of the annual heating bill, distrust it.

Solar Water Heater Recommendations. The auditor will suggest that you turn down your water heater thermostat, install flow restrictors in the shower, and wrap the water tank with insulation. The auditor will also make a recommendation about a solar water heater. Does that recommendation account for hot-water use now having been reduced?

If the computer claims you will get more than 70 percent of your hot water from a solar heater, doubt the claim.

Cumulative Savings. The PG and E audit advised Hailey to buy a clock thermostat, which is supposed to save money by lowering the indoor temperatures at night during the winter. The potential savings from insulation are therefore reduced by some amount every time the thermostat is lowered. None of the computer programs deal with these interactions of savings; each item on the recommended list is treated as a separate entity. A good auditor will be able to tell you how one item may affect another.

Contractor Costs. The audit also estimates the cost of carrying out each recommendation, either by doing it yourself or by hiring a contractor. Some auditors even provide a list of approved contractors and sources of financing. You might want to check with one or two of these contractors to see if the computer's cost estimates are realistic.

I'm not suggesting that any one auditor can provide definitive answers to all the questions and challenges described above. But his responses will give you an important feel for the audit and the thinking behind it. If he is unaware of any of the reliability issues or if the program does not involve any fine tuning possible from one house to another, you can politely ignore the whole effort. In some areas of the country, you may be able to get a second audit from an overlapping utility, although this is not supposed to happen.

The purpose of your questioning is also to test the auditor. Even though the computers have become the focus of the program, the value of a good auditor goes beyond collecting data and giving estimates. A good computer model may be a hedge against a bad auditor. But a good auditor can be useful to you even if he's backed by a bad computer analysis.

Most of the auditors hired by utilities will be young, perhaps college-educated types looking to get into a new career line. Even if quickly trained, some of them will have learned a great deal from in-house experience. If your auditor has convinced you that he knows what he is talking about, listen to him.

A utility only has to audit an individual house one time, so you want to schedule one for maximum benefit. The program was supposed to begin in earnest in March 1981, although each utility has its own timetable. Find out when your utility actually started doing the audits, and then wait a few months after that date while the auditors gain experience before requesting an audit. The Princeton house doctors have discovered certain patterns to the energy problems of houses in their area, and their current investigations are much more sophisticated than the ones they performed two years ago.

Another good time to ask for the audit is whenever you are about to buy or sell a house. When selling, try to get the audit several months before the house goes on the market. That way you can leisurely upgrade the insulation or carry out other auditor recommendations you think will add to the selling price. When buying a house, you should demand a copy of the audit from the old owner before you commit to the deal. The auditor recommendations can be used as a bargaining chip in the negotiations.

Part Five

THE
APPLIANCE
DIVIDEND

G ene Jordan lives in suburban New York, one of those areas that already have the kind of punishing electric bills that the rest of us will be paying by the middle of this decade. With no national uniformity on electric rates, Jordan spends 11¢ for the same kilowatt-hour that Greenspan gets for 5¢, and that the people in the Tennessee Valley get for 4¢. Jordan has reached the conversion point early. The conversion point is when it makes sense to scrap an old appliance and buy a new one simply because the new appliance uses so much less electricity or gas.

This is an instance where people who hanker for a fancier new refrigerator or a quieter air conditioner may be able to make the new purchase and actually come out money ahead. The rise in electric rates, combined with notable recent improvements in the energy economy of major appliances, creates money-making opportunities at the appliance store, opportunities that are curiously underplayed. Many people have spent hundreds of dollars on improvements to the shells of their houses, hoping to achieve savings of similar magnitude, only to raise their energy bills capriciously by purchasing energy-guzzling refrigerators or air conditioners. So a five-minute decision at the appliance store can make a $1,000 difference in energy costs over the lifetime of the appliance involved—if it happens to be an air conditioner or a refrigerator.

In a typical home, appliances (and I'm including water heaters and air conditioners but not furnaces) account for one-third to one-half of the total household energy bill, and half of that half can be saved over time by careful buying. Careful buying does not mean calling in experts and often doesn't even require extra money: some energy-saving appliances have purchase prices equal to or less than those of non-energy-saving models. Even when an energy-saving appliance has a slightly higher initial cost, the relative saving in utility bills is displayed right on the new label. The predictability of the returns from appliance conversion is one reason that I give it a general high rating. There are few climatic variables involved, so an efficient refrigerator will provide the consumer in Maine or in Texas with clear energy savings.

Two ways exist to profit from this component of your energy bill. The first is to trade up in efficiency every time you have to buy a new appliance. In a few years you will have naturally replaced the appliance stock, and your household energy consumption will have been naturally reduced by one-quarter to one-third. (In certain cases, as we will see, it makes sense for people like Jordan to buy new appliances even before the old ones break down completely.)

The second is to fix existing appliances so they do the same job on less energy. The modification efforts can be viewed as a kind of holding action, keeping energy costs down until the time arrives to switch to the really efficient models. But with some appliances, the at-home modifications generate large savings, equal to the savings from total replacement and at a fraction of the cost. There are especially good opportunities with hot water, which after heating or air conditioning is usually a household's biggest energy expense. Potential hot-water savings can amount to about $100 to $300 a year.

This section is divided into two parts to reflect the two appliance strategies. The first is about how people like Jordan can maximize the use of their money at the appliance store; the second, about how existing appliances can be more economically managed.

A Strategy for Conversion

Jordan, a newspaper editor, lives in a townhouse condominium, eats most of his meals in restaurants, and uses his home as a bedroom. Although hooked into a communal heating system over which he has no control, Jordan does pay an electric bill for his own water heater, lights, a small room air conditioner, and kitchen appliances. Like many Americans who are cooking less and living alone or in twos, Jordan spends most of his appliance energy money on that continuously running refrigerator. From a booklet I got from the Association of Home Appliance Manufacturers (AHAM), I identified it as a guzzler.

"It's only six years old," Jordan said.

"Doesn't matter," I countered. "It might pay you to scrap this model even if you had bought it last week."

Jordan resisted my argument. In all the magazine and newspaper stories he had read about how to save energy, he had never seen a word about throwing out the refrigerator. But no theoretical calculations or idle speculation was necessary here. I had the figures from the AHAM booklet. Jordan owned a 17-cubic-foot side-by-side refrigerator with automatic defrost, manufactured by Coldspot. The AHAM booklet listed his model as having an energy appetite of 205 kilowatt-hours a month.

"That's where $22.55 of your $50-a-month electric bill goes," I said. "Keeping your beer cold."

"How do you get that?"

"Multiply 205 kilowatt-hours by 11¢. That's what you pay."

My analysis was not entirely lost on Jordan. I told him about the refrigerators of the same size and capacity sold at local appliance stores that only used 90 kilowatt-hours a month. At his electric rates, Jordan would save $12.65 per month by dumping the 205-kilowatt model in favor of the 90-kilowatt replacement, for a saving of $151.00 a year. Over the next ten years, he would keep $1,511 that otherwise would have gone to the electric company, and that's assuming no increase in rates. Given a realistic 10 percent annual hike in rates, Jordan would "make" $2,406 over ten years on an investment of $600, a 40 percent annualized tax-free yield. (Even if one argues that Jordan can never recover the original $600, which could itself have been invested elsewhere for a 10 percent return, Jordan still makes an extra $900 on the refrigerator purchase, a 16 percent tax-free yield. Either way, it's a great deal. Life-cycle costing, which is what this ten- or fifteen-year energy accounting is called, often leads to savings of this magnitude.)

Jordan's case is extreme, since he has an especially inefficient refrigerator and also pays especially high electric rates. I'm not saying that all homeowners would save as much money from refrigerator conversion, and I'm not even sure you can get the kind of information that I found on Jordan's refrigerator, since AHAM no longer includes energy costs in its updated booklet. (Maybe your appliance dealer can look up the energy consumption figures on your existing refrigerator, if he thinks it will lead to a sale.) What I am saying is that appliances deserve much more attention than they usually get in homeowners' plans to save energy.

I went with Jordan to look for a cheaper-running refrigerator in a White Plains appliance store. Energy had already been introduced to the aisles in a big way, with every other machine having a tag or sticker trumpeting money-saving virtue. There were room air conditioners touted as "energy conserving" because they had separate switches to operate the fan. There were "energy miser" refrigerators with switches to regulate humidity control. There were "energy-saving" water heaters with small timers. The advertising claims were confusing and somewhat misdirected. Appliances are not energy bargains because of some auxiliary feature of the kind emblazoned in the advertisements, any more than a car is an energy bargain for having a solar-powered CB radio. The car itself could still be getting 10 miles to the gallon, which of course is the only point of comparison that makes any sense. A heavily advertised room air conditioner, one with the energy-conserving fan switch, has an energy efficiency ratio (EER) of 6.5. The EER is the true measure of an air conditioner's mileage, and 6.5 is *terrible*.

EER is the ratio between the amount of cooling power that comes out of the machine (in BTUs per hour) and the amount of electricity that goes in (in watts). (A 10,000-BTUs-per-hour machine that takes 1,000 watts has an EER of 10.) In any appliance store, one can find a range of EER ratings for room air conditioning units that begin at about 5 and go up to 10 or 11. The higher the EER, the more economical the air conditioner; so a 10 is twice as economical as a 5. I wouldn't buy an air conditioner with an EER lower than 8 for a room unit, or 10 for a central unit.

The Department of Energy now requires manufacturers to put energy labels on their appliances, labels that tell you exactly how much energy each model uses, and how its energy economy stacks up against the competition. I can't think of a more useful thing the

Department of Energy has done. The labels give the consumer his first real chance to make the right decisions, because they pin down the actual operating numbers in black and white. You should understand that it costs much more to run an appliance, over its lifetime, than it does to buy it in the first place. If I had a make a choice, I would rather see the energy label than the sticker price.

Jordan and I had to look hard to find some of the yellow cards with the bottom line printed on it. But we always found them.

We went to the refrigerator section, where each make and model had the energy card prominently displayed on the door. Each card gives you not only the energy cost of running the refrigerator in question but also the cost of the most efficient model of a similar size manufactured in America. Jordan wanted something in the 16.5-to-18.4-cubic-foot size range. The yellow cards showed that there was a refrigerator of this size available somewhere with an annual energy cost of $45. But here the best we could find was a Kelvinator with an annual energy cost of $65.

One of the failings of the labeling is that they say the most economical model exists but don't name it. When we asked the salesman where we might find this $45-a-year refrigerator and who manufactured it, he said he didn't know. The manufacturers were not about to give the competition free advertising via government labeling regulations.

But I had done some of my own research into the refrigerator business, compiling a list of some of the best refrigerators so consumers would know what they are. The list is reproduced on page 115. My compilation is not comprehensive, because new and better models are coming on the market every year. But it will at least give you some of the stand-out brand-name performers, by name and brand number, so you will know whom to call if your local store carries only guzzlers.

Another drawback to the labels is that they lump together the fully automatic refrigerators and the partial automatics, and the side-by-sides with the top freezers. As a result, there is no way to tell which characteristics the most economical model actually has. Interestingly enough, no absolute correlation exists between size, features, and energy costs of new refrigerators. Some 13-cubic-footers require more power than some 18-cubic-footers. There are models with fully automatic defrost that use less electricity than models with partial automatic defrost. So energy cost has more to do with technical features like compressor design than it does with obvious features like size and capacity.

But as a general matter, the best partial automatic defrosts are more economical than the best fully automatic defrosts. Art Rosenfeld of the Lawrence Berkeley Laboratory produced the chart on this page showing the range of efficiencies for refrigerator/freezers with various features. One of the surprises here is that side-by-sides use more energy than the top-freezer refrigerators.

The label on the Kelvinator, as I say, didn't lead us to the competing model with the best energy rating. But Jordan could guess that it was a partial defrost, requiring a sponge bath a couple of times a year. The best top-freezer automatic defrost costs about $60 a year, and the best side-by-side starts at about $70. Jordan could figure that this $65-a-year Kelvinator ($130 for him, since all estimates are based on a 5¢ electric rate and he pays 11¢) was close to the top of the efficiency line for automatic defrosts. He could have saved another $40 a year with partial defrost, but he didn't think the inconvenience was worth it. So he decided to buy the Kelvinator, which was on sale for $550.

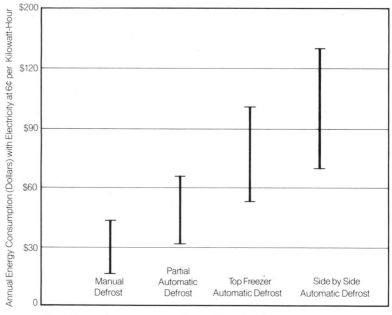

Refrigerator Energy Use by Type of Refrigerator

If you have to replace a refrigerator, the strategy is simple: go for a unit on the low end of the energy consumption scale. You may not be able to get the lowest, as I discovered recently in Miami. I called up the Amana dealer and asked for the model with the smallest energy appetite, was told that it was a special-order item for which I would have to wait six weeks. So much for the nation's, or the dealer's, zeal to save energy. But like Jordan, I was able to find a unit that was close to the most efficient, and I settled for it.

Compared to the old guzzlers, most of the new units represent some improvement in energy consumption, and federal standards now keep the really bad units off the market. But there is still difference enough between the best and the worst that you should do a little shopping around, and the shopping in itself becomes very profitable. Jordan might have bought a new refrigerator with an annual energy cost of $88 a year, or $176 in his case, since we have to double the estimates for his electric rates. That still would have represented an improvement over his existing refrigerator, which costs $270. But by picking a model that will cost him $130 a year, he saves an additional $46 a year compared to the less economical choice, and that $46 may turn into a $1,000 relative gain over the lifetime of the appliance.

This is not, I repeat, an argument to rush out and convert, unless your situation is, like Jordan's, extreme. I do strongly suggest,

HIGH-EFFICIENCY REFRIGERATOR/FREEZERS
WITH AUTOMATIC DEFROST

Capacity (cubic feet)	Make and Model	Estimated Annual Energy Cost
14–15	Amana ESRF-14C	$52
	Admiral NT1595	$54
	Montgomery Ward HMG-1459-0	$56
	Magic Chef RB14A-1	$59
	Coldspot Kenmore 76946-1	$59
15–16	Magic Chef FB165-1	$57
	FB166-1	$56
	Philco RD16G6	$57
	RD16G7	$56

Capacity (cubic feet)	Make and Model	Estimated Annual Energy Cost
15–16	Coldspot Kenmore 76955-1	$60
16–17	Amana ESRF-16W	$53
	Admiral KNT16A7	$59
	KNT1697	$58
	KNT1694	$58
	Crosley CNT16H6	$59
	CNT16H3	$59
	Magic Chef RB16A-2A	$59
17–18	General Electric TBF17BA	$55
	Philco RD17G7	$61
	Magic Chef FB176-1	$61
	Hotpoint CTF17CA	$55
	J. C. Penney 867-0170-0	$55
	Coldspot Kenmore 76977-0	$51
	86077-0	$45
	Whirlpool EHT171HK0	$45
	EET172HKO	$51
18–19	Amana TC18B	$68
	Admiral KNT18A7	$60
	Tappan 95-1870	$60
	Montgomery Ward HMG-1809-0	$60
	Crosley CNT-18H4	$60
	Magic Chef FB196-3	$61
	White Westinghouse RT188A-3	$64
19–20	Coldspot Kenmore 76992-0	$60
	86092-0	$58
	Whirlpool EDT193NK1	$59
	EET203EK0	$59
20–21	Amana TR-20B	$72
	Admiral TR-20B	$64
	Frigidaire FPI-21TB	$70
	Magic Chef RB21A-3A	$64
	Norge NE218B	$64
	Crosley CNT-21H8	$64

Capacity (cubic feet)	Make and Model	Estimated Annual Energy Cost
21–22	Admiral KNT2197	$64
	Crosley CNT-21H6	$64
	Montgomery Ward HMG-2189-4	$64
	Tappan 95-2169	$64

SOURCE: California Energy Commission, Department of Energy

HIGH-EFFICIENCY REFRIGERATOR/FREEZERS WITH PARTIAL AUTOMATIC DEFROST

Capacity (cubic feet)	Make and Model	Estimated Annual Energy Cost
13–14	Amana ESU 13-C	$36
	Whirlpool EEL14CT	$36
	Otasco AMU-1310	$36
14–15	Amana ESR-14C	$31
	Kelvinator TSX140MMO	$48
	White Westinghouse RT142A-0	$48
	Gibson RD14C1-EGD	$48
	Coronado REI-29-GA	$48
	Coldspot Kenmore 7642 series	$48
	Whirlpool EET151DT0	$53
15–16	Magic Chef FB162-1	$30
	Philco RD16G2	$30
	Amana ESU-15-C	$42
	Otasco AMC1510	$42
	Frigidaire ESRC3-16B	$32
16–17	Amana ESR-16D (stand-out model)	$33
17–18	Amana ESU-17C	$46
	Otasco AMU-1710	$46
	Whirlpool-Sears 60771	$45
	Whirlpool EHT171HK	$45
	Frigidaire FCD-170T	$48
18–19	Amana C-19B-1	$51
	Otasco AMC-1910-A	$51

however, that you take advantage of energy-saving opportunities when you need a new appliance. There is no hurry, because the new refrigerators and freezers will probably continue to get more and more efficient. At least it seemed like they would until the new administration put the brakes on the federally mandated appliance efficiency standards. The technology is certainly there for better numbers. A. D. Little, a consulting firm, recently did a study for Amana, the company that already makes many of the most economical refrigerators. ADL says that an automatic defrost model could be built with current techniques to stay within a $33-a-year energy budget, about what the best partial defrosts get today. Art Rosenfeld believes that a $23-a-year refrigerator could be produced right now. (These estimates are based on a 5¢ per kilowatt-hour electric rate.)

Whether manufacturers will be inclined to make superefficient units depends on consumer response to the existing high-efficiency models. It's a little like the automobile business. The government has pushed for improved energy efficiency of all appliances, so even the run-of-the-mill models will have improved energy economy over their predecessors. But because federal standards do not yet exist, manufacturers will certainly not be forced to take existing technology to its limits. Amana has been especially aggressive with refrigerators, with some of its models far outclassing the competition, but its refrigerators are also more expensive. If other manufacturers see that the Amana refrigerators sell, everyone will know that energy efficiency has begun to affect the market.

Art Rosenfeld of Lawrence Berkeley Laboratory hopes this will happen for reasons that go beyond the individual consumer's pocketbook. Rosenfeld says that if manufacturers were encouraged to make only high-efficiency refrigerators, the country could do without fifteen new power plants. Rosenfeld and his colleague, David Goldstein, have made their strongest case for the refrigerator alternative to nuclear power in California, and calculate that by converting the entire state to high-efficiency refrigerators and freezers, the state would save 1,700 megawatts of power, or 5 percent of current California electricity consumption. The 1,700 megawatts equals the output of two proposed nuclear power plants, which together will cost $3 billion to build. The price tag on 16 million improved refrigerators is $750 million, which many people would be spending anyway in routine replacement.

Rosenfeld says the utilities or the government should buy all the new refrigerators and give them away—an approach economically preferable to paying for the energy needed to power the less efficient models. It would also be safer, because efficient refrigerators don't produce radioactive waste. In any case, all of us pay for the peculiarities of the energy marketplace—it is easier to raise $30 billion to pay for fifteen new nuclear power plants than to build and sell efficient refrigerators.

Jordan bought his new refrigerator, and we moved on to the other departments at the appliance center.

Freezers. Because freezers have labels like refrigerators, you can also shop for energy savings here. Your potential savings may not be as great, because the energy costs for freezers don't vary as much from one model to another. But given just small differences in the purchase prices, one might as well buy a unit with the lowest energy appetite. The labels tell the story.

Televisions. There were no energy advertisements in the television section, probably because the new ones are *all* very efficient. For a number of years, solid-state or transistorized television sets have been designed and manufactured to use just under 200 watts of electricity, or about the same as two standard light bulbs. They run on less than half the power it took to operate the old tube-type color sets. Manufacturers achieved the high efficiencies voluntarily, both because the technology allowed it and because the components in low-energy TV sets last longer. Energy makes heat, and too much heat has an unkind effect on the innards of the circuitry.

Because of the general high level of TV efficiency, little is to be gained searching out the stingiest model. Certain companies advertise energy-saving sets that use 100 watts, but the difference here is between one light bulb and two. So it costs you between 1¢ and 3¢ an hour to watch color television. A real bargain (depending on the program).

Clothes Dryers. There are no appliance energy labels for clothes dryers. I suppose that's because not much can be done to make the appliance more efficient. Heat is required for a short period of time, so losses through the walls of the dryer aren't that significant. Unless heat pump dryers are developed, the new electric dryers on the market will continue to use about the same amount of energy as the old ones. At present, it costs 20¢ to 40¢ to dry a full load of clothes.

If you have to buy a new dryer, you might as well find one that has thermostat control and stops the action as soon as the load is dry. That way the machine won't run on another ten to fifteen minutes after the job is finished.

New gas dryers offer the same energy benefits as new gas furnaces —no pilot lights, and vent dampers to recover heat from the flue. Dryers are too expensive to replace just for the energy savings that these improvements bring. But when the old one falls apart, choose a replacement with the energy-saving features.

Air Conditioners. The aisle-long row of new air conditioners was bedecked with tags designed to appeal to an energy saver's instinct —labels touting a machine's "special energy-saving switch" or "power squelcher thermostat." Buyers should ignore such effusions and look for the true measure of economy—the energy efficiency ratio, or EER (see the discussion of this ratio on page 112). Air conditioners have been given EERs for about four years now, and I am surprised that the ratings have not caused a stampede to the high-efficiency models. The potential savings here are as good as they are for refrigerators.

The energy labels on air conditioners provide the same kind of information one finds on refrigerator tags, and each lists the EER for the machine in question, as well as the EER for the most efficient model in the size class. The air conditioner label similarly doesn't name names, so I have included a list of high-efficiency room and central units by brand number and model. The list is not all-inclusive, but it does identify many of the most economical models available in 1981. My work might be especially useful when you are buying a central air conditioner, which, although given an EER, isn't yet required to carry the complete label. So it will be hard for you to compare energy costs for central units in a store.

Some central air conditioner units have a slightly refined EER rating, called SEER, short for seasonal energy efficiency rating. The energy economy of the machines is slightly diminished when the machines cycle on and off, and the SEER rating takes the cycling losses into account.

How do you know if it is profitable to replace an existing air conditioner with a more efficient model? And when do you know if the higher efficiency of two competing models in the store justifies the higher purchase price? The appliance labels for room air conditioners include a chart that enables you to pin a dollar value on the various EER ratings. If you know your local electric rate, and you can estimate how many hours a year you require air conditioning, the chart can tell you how much money you would spend on electricity for any given unit. A glance at two or more labels, and you can immediately identify the best buy.

Comparing air conditioners that don't have labels (say, the one in your house against one in the store) is slightly more difficult, but not impossible. To determine whether replacement makes sense, you need to know these things:

(a) The EER of your existing air conditioner. There won't be a label, but you can compute the number yourself. Somewhere in the owner's manual or on a small plate attached to the machine, you will find the BTU capacity and also the wattage. Divide the watts into the BTUs and you get the EER.

(b) The amount of money you spent last year on air conditioning. You will have to guess at this one by comparing summer utility bills to utility bills from months when no air conditioning or heating is required. Or you can take the wattage of the unit, multiply by 1,000, multiply again by the number of hours you use the unit each year, and again by the amount you pay locally for a kilowatt-hour of electricity. Watts $\times$ 1,000 $\times$ hours $\times$ price will give you an annual cost of operation.

(c) The EER of the potential replacement machine. You can get it from the appliance label or from the salespeople.

With this information in hand, you can set up a simple equation. If the EER of your existing air conditioner is 5, and the new machine has an EER of 8, and your air conditioning bill is $500 a year, then your bill with the new machine will be five-eighths of $500, or $312. One-year savings from purchase would be $188. You can add 10 percent a year for electricity price increases to figure a ten- or fifteen-year return on your investment.

Air conditioning salesmen may try to get you to buy a bigger unit than you have now on the grounds that more power will somehow

SOME HIGH-EFFICIENCY ROOM AIR CONDITIONERS

BTUs	Manufacturer	Brand Name	Model Number	BTUs per Hour	EER
5,200–5,799	Friedrich	Friedrich	SP05D10	5,200	8.8
	Edison Products	Frigidaire	A5-LECD-H	5,300	8.7
	Edison Products	Montgomery Ward	VWE-5120	5,300	8.7
5,800–6,299	General Electric	General Electric	AJC06LA	5,800	8.7
	General Electric	General Electric	AJ106LM	5,800	8.7
	General Electric	General Electric	AJ906LM	5,800	8.7
6,300–6,799	Friedrich	Friedrich	YP06E10	6,300	8.5
	Friedrich	Friedrich	SP06D10	6,500	8.7
	McGraw Edison	McGraw Edison	061F-A	6,600	8.8
	General Electric	General Electric	A2B388E	6,700	8.3
6,800–7,799	General Electric	General Electric	A2B3868D	6,800	9.3
	Friedrich	Friedrich	SS07D10	7,000	10.2
	Amana	Amana	ES7-2MT	7,200	9.8
	Fedders	Airtemp	R08-1WJNN	7,600	8.9
	Fedders	Airtemp	R081WKRK41	7,700	8.7
7,800–8,299	Belding Products	J. C. Penney	865-1978-00-00	7,800	8.7
	Belding Products	Kelvinator	MH 308 RI QA	7,800	8.7
	Fedders	Fedders	AST08F2HEA	7,900	9.4
	Fedders	Airtemp	R081W6RH	8,000	9.3

Amana	Amana	ES108	8,200	8.8
Friedrich	Friedrich	SS08D10	8,000	9.0
Friedrich	Whirlpool	AFF-P80-2	8,000	9.0
General Electric	GE	AF108FM	8,100	8.8
Whirlpool	Whirlpool	ADF-P80-2	8,000	8.8
Carrier	Carrier	51EA0081B	8,000	8.8
Montgomery Ward		UFO-5168	8,050	8.7
8,300–9,299				
General Electric	GE	AGFE908FA	8,300	9.0
York	York	R2WC009A02	8,500	9.2
Fedders	Airtemp	R09-1WJNN	8,600	10.0
Amana	Amana	ES9-2MR	8,500	9.3
Fedders	Fedders	ASL09E2HBB	9,000	10.5
Friedrich	Friedrich	EW09A33	9,100	9.1
Friedrich	Friedrich	51FE0091	9,200	10.5
9,300–10,299				
Carrier	Carrier	51FE0101	9,300	10.2
General Electric	GE	AD910FD	9,700	10.6
General Electric	GE	AD910FM	9,800	10.7
Friedrich	Friedrich	SM10D10	9,900	10.7
Fedders	Fedders	ASL10E2HB	10,000	11.6
10,299–11,799				
Friedrich	Friedrich	ES11E33	10,600	8.7
Fedders	Airtemp	M124RKRK21	11,000	9.1
Fedders	Fedders	ARL12E7HD	11,000	9.1
Fedders	Airtemp	R122WRK41	11,500	8.7

SOME HIGH-EFFICIENCY ROOM AIR CONDITIONERS—continued

BTUs	Manufacturer	Brand Name	Model Number	BTUs per Hour	EER
10,299–11,799	Fedders	Fedders	AST12F2HD	11,500	8.7
	York	York	WCH121-6A	11,500	8.2
11,800–12,799	Fedders	Airtemp	R12-2WJNP	12,000	8.8
	Frigidaire	Montgomery Ward	UFO-5195	12,350	8.7
	Addison	York	R2WC013A02	12,600	9.1
	Addison	Comfort Aire	WQ141HF	12,600	9.1
12,800–13,799	Amana	Amana	ES213-2MK	12,800	8.9
	General Electric	General Electric	AD913AM	12,900	8.9
	Belding Products	Kelvinator	MHX4-13N10A	13,000	8.8
	Edison Products	Montgomery Ward	VWE-5190	13,100	9.0
	Edison Products	White Westinghouse	AS138B1K	13,300	9.0
	Fedders	Airtemp	M142WJRH	13,500	9.6
	Fedders	Fedders	ASL14E2HEA	13,500	9.6
	Whirlpool	Whirlpool	AGF-135-2	13,500	9.4
	Emerson	Quiet Kool	14FD1E	13,500	9.4
	Emerson	Quiet Kool	14DE1E	13,600	9.4
13,800–14,799	Amana	Amana	ES614-2R	13,900	9.3
	Whirlpool	Kenmore	779149	14,000	9.8
	Fedders	Fedders	ASL14E2HB	14,000	10.2

Price range	Brand	Brand	Model	Capacity	EER
	Whirlpool	Kenmore	870149	14,000	9.6
	Carrier	Carrier	51FE1153	14,700	8.4
	Whirlpool	Whirlpool	106.8701490	14,000	9.6
14,800–16,499	Addison	York	R2WC015A06	15,000	9.0
	Friedrich	Friedrich	SM16E30	15,200	8.3
	Addison	York	R2WC015A06	15,200	9.1
	Addison	Comfort Aire	WQ163HE	15,500	8.8
	Heat Controller	Comfort Aire	WQ163HE	16,000	8.8
	York	York	R1AC015A06A	15,050	9.0
	Addison	York	WC 155-6A	16,000	8.8
16,500–19,499	Emerson Quiet Kool	Emerson Quiet Kool	18ED48	17,000	8.7
	Emerson Quiet Kool	Emerson Quiet Kool	18FD4E	17,500	8.6
	Fedders	Airtemp	M18-4WHNL	17,600	8.5
	Amana	Amana	ES619-3R	17,800	8.5
			ES619-3S	17,800	8.5
	Fedders	Fedders	ASD19E7HB	18,500	8.8
	Friedrich	Friedrich	SL19D30	19,000	8.5
	Fedders	Fedders	ASD19E7HB	19,000	8.5

SOURCE: California Energy Commission Directory of Room Air Conditioners, June 1980

SOME HIGH-EFFICIENCY CENTRAL AIR CONDITIONERS

Manufacturer	Condensor Number	Coil Number	BTUs per Hour	Seasonal Efficiency Rating
Bryant	570AJ024	522A001	24,000	13.20
	570AJ030	507D060	29,000	11.00
	570AJ030	522A001	29,200	12.10
	570AJ036	522A001	36,000	12.10
	568CJ042	505C060	43,500	10.40
Carrier	38VH00231	28Vh002	23,800	12.30
	38VH00231	28Vh002	24,000	12.70
	50BB08	9AB12	93,000	10.30
Coleman Presidential II D.E.S.	9430C901	9435C830	29,600	12.80
	9435C901	9435C830	35,000	12.00
Day and Night	570AJ024	507D060	23,400	11.40
	570AJ024	522A001	24,000	13.20
	570AJ030	522A001	29,200	12.10
	570AJ036	522A001	36,000	12.10
	568CJ042	505C060	43,500	10.40
	568CJ048	505C060	46,500	10.15
Friedrich	RCE042GCB	CCF036CA	42,000	10.70

General Electric Executive II	BTN936B	BXF060A	35,600	11.45
	BTN736B	BWV760S	36,800	11.60
	BTN948B	BWE960C	45,500	10.40
	BTN748B	BWV760S	47,000	10.70
	BTN948B	BGXA072A	47,500	10.75
Lennox	HS13-261V-2P	CB 15-900	22,800	13.00
	HS14-411V-1A	CB10-51-1P	37,000	11.70
	HS14-411V-1A	CB 15-900/41-1P	39,000	14.00
	HS14-511V-1A	CB 15-1200/65-1P	51,500	12.65
Landmark II	HS11-311/511V	CB 15-1200/65 1P	50,000	11.00
Landmark III	HS13-311V-2P	CB 15-900/41-1P	27,000	12.20
	HS13-41V-2P	CB 15-900/41-1P	34,400	11.30
	HS13-461V-2P	CB 15-900/46-1P	42,000	11.40
Montgomery Ward 900 "Super High Efficiency Series"	SRM-51350A	SRM-51463A	23,600	12.30
	SRM-51351A	SRM-51464A	29,400	11.70
	SRM-51352A	SRM-51465A	36,000	12.10
Payne	570AJ024	522A001	24,000	13.20
	570AJ030	522A001	29,200	12.10
	570AJ036	522A001	36,000	12.10

SOME HIGH-EFFICIENCY CENTRAL AIR CONDITIONERS—continued

Manufacturer	Condensor Number	Coil Number	BTUs per Hour	Seasonal Efficiency Rating
Rheem Super High Efficiency	RAGC-024JA	RCTB-A025	23,600	12.30
	RAGC-030JA	RCTB-A036	29,400	11.70
	RAGC-036JA	RCTB-A037	36,000	12.10
	RAGB-042JA	RCTB-A048	41,500	11.05
Ruud Super High Efficiency	UAGC-024JA	RCTB-A025	23,600	12.30
	UAGB-024JA	RCTB-A024	24,200	11.05
	UAGC-030JA	RCTB-A036	29,400	11.70
	UAGC-036JA	RCTB-A037	36,000	12.10
	UAGB-042JA	RCTB-A048	41,500	11.05
Sears Best	867.819620	867.815321	27,400	10.00
	867.819640	867.815360	42,500	10.35
York	CDHE42-6A	44CF22	40,000	10.10
	CDHE42-6A	60A22	45,000	10.20
	CDHE48-6A	60A26	49,000	10.00
York Embassy	C1EW 105	A25A145A	100,000	11.00

SOURCE: Air Conditioning and Refrigeration Institute, 1981 Directory. Copyright © 1981 by Air Conditioning and Refrigeration Institute. All rights reserved.

save energy and money. Don't believe it. There is a misguided notion that an overpowered unit is more efficient, since it can coast on the off cycle more than a smaller unit. The reverse is true. Like a furnace, an air conditioner is more efficient if it stays on for longer periods of time. Since part of the function of an air conditioner is to remove moisture and dehumidify the living space, an air conditioner that operates intermittently is failing at this job. When a house is too humid, people feel discomfort and may turn the thermostat down, thus resulting in more work for the machine and higher energy bills. If you have shaded or insulated your house since you bought the last air conditioner, you ought to be able to get by with a smaller unit than before, saving both on first costs and on energy costs. There are local sizing formulas; find a contractor who will review them with you so you aren't stuck with muscle-bound equipment.

Stoves. With turbo ovens, small electric-toaster-broilers, and a general retreat from home baking and heavy meat, the stove/oven is losing its importance as an appliance. The average American family now spends only $40 a year to bake, broil, sauté, braise, and make coffee on the burners. Although there are ovens on the market with more insulation, it would take a long time for the energy savings to make conversion profitable. There may be some inducement to switch from electric to gas stoves, especially since the new gas stoves don't have wasteful pilot lights, but even at 1985 energy prices, the incentive to do so is not very compelling. Stoves aren't used enough for the difference in energy costs to add up to important money.

If you have to buy a new electric stove, the only energy feature to look for is extra insulation in the oven cavity, and as I say, even that doesn't make much of a difference. If you have to buy a new gas stove, it makes sense to choose one with pilotless ignition, which may cost you an extra $50 or so. But a gas stove with three pilots can burn 400 cubic feet a month, at a cost of $2, or $24 a year. And the expense will increase rapidly as gas is deregulated, making pilotless ignition more attractive. Kits are available to convert existing stoves and other gas appliances. You are probably burning 50 percent of the gas in the stove on pilots alone. The gas company can help you estimate the costs of burning the existing pilots, and then you can decide whether converting to pilotless ignition is going to pay off.

Water Heaters. The energy-saving prospects for electric and gas water heaters are quite different, so I will treat them separately.

It is not possible to list all the energy-saving electric water heaters by model and brand name, since there are dozens of manufacturers and since the appliance stores often attach their own names and labels to the heaters. With standard electric water heaters, not much can be done to make them more or less energy efficient. If you have to buy a new one, you will save some small amount of electricity and money by picking a model with better insulation—in other words, one that shows up on the appliance labels at the low end of the energy cost scales.

But if you don't have to replace for a year or two, you might find big savings in switching to a heat-pump electric water heater. A tremendous excitement exists around the research labs where the innovation has been tested. Enthusiasts believe that the device can put the solar water heater out of business: the heat pump saves as much energy on an investment of $650 to $800 as a solar heater can for $1,500 to $3,000, and the less expensive item doesn't require collectors on the roof. The machine, no bigger than a toolbox, can be installed on an existing water heater, or sold as part of a complete water heater unit.

The heat-pump water heater works just like a heat-pump space heater. It extracts, or pumps, heat from the surrounding air and uses that to warm up the water—a process cheaper than generating the heat with standard elements, which is what regular water heaters do.

The real savings from a heat pump depend on the climate in which it operates, and also on the location of the water heater in the house. When the heat pump is working, the air surrounding gets colder. In warm climates, therefore, the device is doubly attractive because it also serves as a small air conditioner, and the residual cooling costs nothing. To benefit doubly, of course, the heat-pump water heater has to be located in the living area of the house.

In cold climates, the heat pump loses some of its efficiency, because the unit has to extract heat from air that has already been warmed by the furnace. Indirectly, you are using your furnace to help produce hot water, if the water heater is located in a heated part of your house. If the water heater is located in an unheated basement, the heat pump can function as long as the basement temperature stays above 20 degrees or so.

But even in the North, the heat-pump water heater will outperform the regular electric water heater, and in the South, it can cut water heating bills by as much as 70 percent. The new device is another investment that can give a better than 25 percent return. At 5¢-per-kilowatt-hour electric rates, the heat pump can save you $150 a year in warm climates and $90 a year in cold ones. In Jordan's area, where people pay 11¢ for electricity, the heat pump will pay for itself in less than two years. Over its lifetime, it is likely to generate $1,000 in tax-free returns.

There are three companies that manufacture the units. Fedders has begun to promote an add-on heat pump that connects to the existing water heater. It costs about $800 and is available through Fedders dealers. E-Tech, Inc., 3570 American Drive, Atlanta, Georgia 30341, also makes an add-on device; and Temcor, 365 Plum Industrial Court, Pittsburgh, Pennsylvania 15329, manufactures a complete water heater with a heat pump integrated into the design.

If you now have an electric water heater, I suggest you insulate it with an extra layer of fiberglass to cut hot water costs as much as possible, and then replace it with a heat-pump unit when the old unit breaks down. If the federal energy tax credit is ever extended to the heat pump, it will become one of the consumer's great energy buys. Meantime, it is hard to understand why solar gets the tax advantage, and this doesn't.

Gas Water Heaters. The run-of-the-mill gas water heater wastes 40 percent of its gas on pilot lights and on heat that escapes up the flue. Manufacturers may respond with new models that have no pilot lights and flue dampers to recover some of the loss, but these are not readily available. Until they are, there will be no particular advantage in converting to a new gas water heater for the energy savings alone; some new models have thicker insulation to reduce the standby losses, but those losses are small in comparison with pilot and flue losses.

Lights. You probably spend about $50 a year to burn lights. That's not a large chunk of the utility bill, but the rising electric rates and the rising costs of bulbs themselves create some opportunities to save money at the light-bulb counter. Incandescent bulbs, the kind everybody uses and the kind Edison invented, are the most inefficient of light sources. Ninety percent of the energy that goes into some incandescents is converted into heat, not light. Such heat helps in the winter, but electricity, as we have seen, is not the cheapest way to keep warm. The EPA mileage equivalent for light bulbs is lumens per watt, or the amount of light that comes out for the amount of electricity that goes in. As the chart on page 133 shows, the energy economy of the different light sources varies from less than 10 lumens per watt to over 130, and incandescents, as a group, are down at the bottom.

But there are ways to get slightly more light for your money, even from among the incandescents. The first thing to recognize is that a single high-wattage bulb throws off more lumens per watt than two or three medium-wattage bulbs. A 100-watt incandescent produces 18 lumens per watt, while a 60-watt incandescent produces only 14. The single, more powerful bulb not only saves electricity but costs less than two or three smaller bulbs. So in fixtures with three sockets, you are better off with one high-wattage bulb.

A trade-off also exists between a bulb's life and its energy efficiency. Those advertised as long-life are energy losers, and the reason they last longer is because they give off less light per watt consumed. The only advantage to long-life versus standard bulbs is that they don't have to be changed as often, so if you like convenience, they may be appropriate for hard-to-reach fixtures. Otherwise, they should be avoided.

The best way to shop for incandescents is to compare all the features—lumens, watts, and bulb life—described on the side of the package. You want the most lumens for the least watts.

As the chart indicates, other kinds of bulbs offer better energy performance. Fluorescents, for instance, give three times the light for the same amount of electricity. Some energy-saving manuals advise scrapping incandescent fixtures and replacing them with fluorescent units. I don't like this idea, because installing a fluorescent fixture is expensive and often requires a carpenter and/or an electrician to do the work. You can now buy screw-in fluorescent bulbs at hardware stores, and these give you the same energy savings as fluorescent fixtures without the high cost of installation.

Super-efficient non-fluorescent residential bulbs are beginning to reach the market now. Norelco makes such bulbs; other manufacturers are expected to follow suit. I can only suggest that you try them.

What you should remember is that the savings from any kind of bulb can be computed from the lumens-per-watt information as long as you know how much your utility is charging for 1,000 watts (a kilowatt-hour) of electricity.

Heating Water with Oil. Like thousands of other people who heat their houses with oil, my friend Greenspan gets his hot water from a coil inside the oil boiler itself. In warm months he has to keep the furnace fired up just to provide the hot water. And using that for a single family's hot-water needs is about as economical as

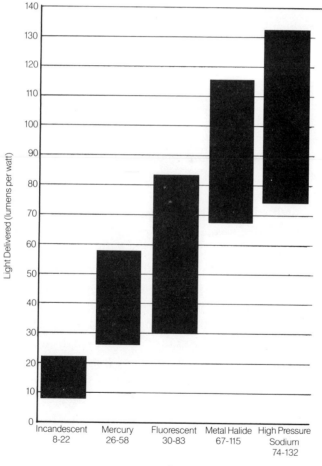

Efficiency of Various Light Sources

getting into a moving van for a quick trip to the grocery store.

There is a no-cost remedy Greenspan can pursue before he considers an expensive one—and that is turning down the boiler temperature during the period when the boiler is used only to make hot water. Some backyard energy technicians swear by this technique, which they say can cut their hot-water cost to $10 a month. It can't hurt to try. Ask your oil dealer how to do it.

If that doesn't work, you might benefit from one of three strategies: (1) installing an electric heat-pump water heater; (2) installing a gas water heater; or (3) installing a smaller reservoir that will reduce the volume of water heated with the oil. To make the proper energy-saving calculation, you're going to have to get local estimates on the initial cost of the three approaches. You already know what your oil bill is during the nonwinter months, so that gives you a basis from which to compare. The hard part is figuring out the fuel benefits of either gas or electricity. A heat-pump electric water heater will cost twice as much as the gas equipment, but it may be the best long-term choice in warm climates where heat pumps perform the most economically. Gas-heated water is the likely choice in northern areas where heat pumps work at a disadvantage.

Notice I didn't say anything about a standard electric water heater. I can't imagine a situation when you should convert to regular electric-resistance heating, since electricity is the most expensive form of household energy in most areas.

Dishwashers. The dishwasher that saves the most energy is the one that uses the least hot water. It doesn't take much electricity to run a dishwasher motor or even to dry the dishes after they are washed. Eighty percent of the energy cost of operating this appliance comes in the hot water it requires. I doubt if there is enough savings from one model to another to justify trading in a dishwasher the way Jordan traded his refrigerator. But there is some small advantage to be gained by careful buying when you need a new machine.

Here again, what is advertised as the energy-saving feature may not be the most important factor. I refer to the "air dry" switch, which allows you to conserve some electricity by stopping the machine's cycle before the dryer heater comes on. You can do the same thing manually on any unit. Two other features are worth more attention. One is an internal booster to raise the water temperature inside the machine. When a dishwasher has its own water heater, you can turn down the thermostat on your home's central water heater to 120 degrees or even lower without affecting the dishwashing results. This will save you money.

Second is the water level inside the dishwasher. A machine that does the job with the smallest amount of hot water is the most economical from an energy standpoint. Standard machines require sixteen gallons or more for each load of dishes. Appliance labels are very useful here.

Clothes Washers. Look for the same thing here—a machine requiring the least amount of hot water, or one with variable water volume settings for large and small loads. It takes 35 gallons to wash and rinse a load of clothes in a standard machine. A machine that gets by on less will cut your hot-water bill. Again, the labels reveal which machines are stingiest with the commodity.

The Low-Cost Approach

I had one of my 10¢ solutions, a small plastic flow controller, in my pocket when I visited my neighbor Ben Stanfill. (I carry these items around like a Johnny Appleseed of the showerheads.) Stanfill was impressed with my solar water heater, even after I told him that a 10¢ gadget plus a little insulation might save his household as much electricity as my $1,500 investment in sunshine. He didn't believe me, so I wanted to prove it to him on his own shower.

Aside from the thermostat setback with the furnace, hot water is the place a homeowner can conserve his way into the biggest returns. Hot water is getting to be ridiculously expensive, and the costs increase dramatically when the ground temperature drops. The chart on page 136 shows you what we pay for hot water, at the going national rates. An average family uses 100 gallons of hot water a day, which can result in a $2-a-day habit. My four-part plan for hot-water savings, including the flow controller, could cut these costs in half, which equals the 50 percent contribution from rooftop solar collectors.

The plan begins in Stanfill's shower, which I found out was spurting hot water at a rate of six gallons per minute. Stanfill wondered why that mattered.

"You and Cybele and the two kids shower every day, right?" I said. "The combined shower time is at least 20 minutes. Your shower puts out 6 gallons per minute, so that's 120 gallons down the drain just for daily human cleanliness. Half of that water is hot. At local Florida prices, you are paying 50¢ a day, or $185 a year, for hot showers. The 10¢ flow controller will save you $90 of that."

The Department of Energy thought enough of the flow controllers that they sent them out, free, to every mailbox holder in the Northeast. This was a very successful program, and nobody knows why DOE didn't make a present of the gadgets to the rest of the country. I have tried to find them in hardware stores and have gotten only blank looks, so you may have to write the manufacturer—WF Products, 3625 Dividend Drive, Garland, Texas 75042. Or you can

COST OF HEATING WATER IN AN ELECTRIC WATER HEATER (ELECTRICITY AT 6¢ PER KILOWATT-HOUR)

Temperature to Which Water Is Raised (degrees F.)	Amount Heated (gallons)		
	50	100	150
50	43¢	85¢	$1.28
70	60¢	$1.20	$1.80
90	77¢	$1.55	$2.31
110	94¢	$1.87	$2.84

COST OF HEATING WATER IN A GAS WATER HEATER (GAS AT 40¢ A THERM)

Temperature to Which Water Is Raised (degrees F.)	Amount Heated (gallons)		
	50	100	150
50	16¢	32¢	48¢
70	22¢	45¢	67¢
90	29¢	58¢	87¢
110	35¢	70¢	$1.06

spend a few more dollars and buy a flow-controller showerhead, available in hardware stores.

The flow controller is inserted in the shower arm to restrict the output. Older varieties, which look like dimes with holes in them, were accused of producing limp showers. But the newer plastic types, which resemble funnels, have gotten more favorable response. They allow enough air to pass through the showerhead so that the pressure stays high, even though the amount of water issued is reduced.

At least that is the theory. Stanfill wanted to see the controller in action. I unscrewed his showerhead with a wrench, something an amateur can do, provided that the showerhead isn't stuck on the shower arm too tightly. If it is, too much twisting might damage the arm, and an plumber's help might be required.

I inserted the flow controller into the pipe of the shower arm, large end first, and then replaced the showerhead. I turned on the shower and measured the flow rate again with a calibrated bucket I use for the purpose. The flow was down to 2.5 gallons per minute, less than half of what was coming out before. The little plastic insert would cut Stanfill's total water consumption by 60 gallons per day, and the hot-water consumption by 30 gallons per day.

Stanfill was pleased by the savings and equally pleased by the strength of the spray. Had he been unhappy with the oomph in the shower, I would have brought him a flow-controller showerhead. These are more expensive than the insert devices, but some of them offer variable sprays and may work in places that the controllers don't. A replacement showerhead costs from $10 to $20, and the energy savings will pay for that in less than four months. The important thing is to get a showerhead with a 3-gallon-per-minute flow or less.

Carrying out the first part of my plan took about five minutes. For the second part, we moved from the bathroom to the basement, which is where Stanfill keeps his water heater. I told him I wanted to reduce his water heater thermostat settings. He had heard about the modification, but never understood the rationale. Stanfill thought that a lower hot-water temperature would force him to put more hot water in with the cold to get the right temperature mix at the shower-head or at the faucets. He couldn't see how that would save any energy, and he was right.

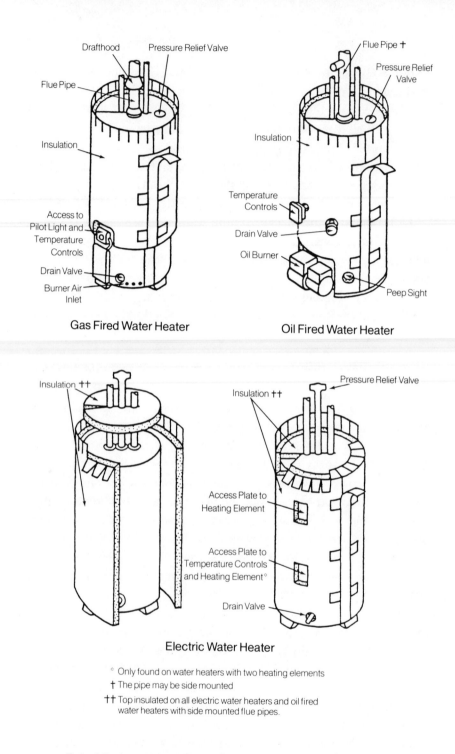

Gas Fired Water Heater

Drafthood

Pressure Relief Valve

Flue Pipe

Insulation

Access to Pilot Light and Temperature Controls

Drain Valve

Burner Air Inlet

Oil Fired Water Heater

Flue Pipe †

Pressure Relief Valve

Insulation

Temperature Controls

Drain Valve

Oil Burner

Peep Sight

Electric Water Heater

Insulation ††

Insulation ††

Pressure Relief Valve

Access Plate to Heating Element

Access Plate to Temperature Controls and Heating Element ⁎

Drain Valve

⁎ Only found on water heaters with two heating elements

† The pipe may be side mounted

†† Top insulated on all electric water heaters and oil fired water heaters with side mounted flue pipes.

SOURCE: Federal Register, Vol. 44, No. 54–Monday, March 19, 1979

But Stanfill didn't know about standby losses. Some of the heat that sits in the water tank all day dissipates through the walls of the tank. We pay for the losses in return for the privilege of having hot water available immediately, day or night. A miniature "thermal dam" effect is also at work here. The higher the water temperature inside the tank, the more heat is lost. Lowering the temperature here has the same effect, on a smaller scale, as turning down the furnace thermostat at night.

I found a screwdriver while Stanfill turned off the circuit breaker to the water heater, something you *must* do. I unscrewed the two metal plates on the front of the water heater and removed them. By pushing back the insulation, I could see the two thermostats.

Some water heater thermostats have a series of degree markings —120, 140, and 160—and some have high, medium, and low settings. Stanfill's thermostats were showing high, which corresponds to a 160-degree level. I moved them back to 140, or medium. That small adjustment is worth $10 to $15 a year with electric water heaters, and $5 to $10 with gas.

I could have gone to low and saved Stanfill a little more money, and many people are doing just that. The problem with low is that 120 degrees may not provide water hot enough for the automatic dishwasher. The dishwasher is the critical factor here, the only appliance that requires truly hot water. If Stanfill had one of those machines with its own booster to heat water, then low would have been the correct water-heater setting. But with a standard machine, the low setting on the water heater is sometimes blamed for putting spots and stains on the glasses and dishes. This is not an issue of health, since even the highest water-heater settings don't actually sterilize your dishes. It's a personal aesthetic matter.

Some homeowners are willing to accept a few extra spots in return for the extra savings. I doubted if Stanfill would. I also sensed that he would never look at the water heater again, which eliminated the possibility of turning the setting to low and then upping it to medium if the results didn't please him. So I told him that medium was the most reasonable choice.

That brought us to part three of my plan, wrapping the water heater with another layer of insulation. What you can save here is somewhat diminished when the thermostats are turned lower, but the insulation is cheap enough that the effort still pays off. Three-and-a-half-inch fiberglass with the foil backing will do the job. You can buy water-heater kits for about $20, but you can get the same insulation from a leftover roll or from an insulation contractor willing to give or sell you a small piece. The only other thing you need is duct tape.

I encircled Stanfill's tank with the insulation, keeping the foil to the outside, and closed the vertical seam with duct tape. I wrapped duct tape around the tank like a belt, to hold the insulation in place.

I had to cut a separate piece of insulation for the top of the tank, and tape it to the insulation on the sides, as shown in the illustration on page 138. (Do *not* cover the top of gas water heaters, because that's where the air intakes are often located. If these are smothered or clogged, fires and even explosions can result.) Even on electric water heaters, one should cut holes for all the valves, temperature controls, and drains, as shown in the illustration on page 138. Anyone who is confused about where the critical places are on gas or electric water heaters should not undertake the project.

By the time we left the basement, I had saved Stanfill perhaps another $20 a year, in addition to the $90 for the flow controller. The money pocketed on a cash outlay of about $5 could be extended with the final part of the plan, which has more to do with a conserving personal attitude than any single mechanical adjustment. The Stanfills could save another $25 to $35 a year—apart from the shower—and the place to save most of that is the laundry room.

It takes 35 gallons of water to do a load of clothes in a standard clothes washer. Because the Stanfills do three loads a week, they require 5,000 gallons of water a year for laundry. Obviously, if they used 5,000 gallons of cold water, there is no energy cost. If all of the 5,000 gallons were hot, the cost would amount to $80 a year. On hot wash/warm rinse, the highest setting on Stanfill's machine, the cost is about $60, which is to say that every time the settings are made one notch colder on either the wash or the rinse cycle, the energy costs are reduced by about 25 percent. On warm wash/cold rinse, the money comes down to about $25 a year.

By itself, the $25 saving may not seem like much, but when it is added to other savings from the low-cost hot-water plan, the first-year profit for the Stanfills comes to $160, just under half of their annual hot-water bill. (The potential benefits of the low-cost plan to

STANDARD WATER HEATER WITHOUT EXTRA
INSULATION IN HOUSE OF LARGE FAMILY

Losses through tank	$35
Hot water for showers, baths, sink	$45
Hot water for washing clothes	$15
Hot water for dishes	$ 5
Annual Gas Bill for Hot Water	$100

Losses through tank	$ 55
Hot water for showers, bath, sink	$185
Hot water for washing clothes	$ 60
Hot water for dishes	$ 35
Annual Electric Bill for Hot Water	$335

IMPROVED WATER HEATER WITH EXTRA INSULATION,
THERMOSTAT SETBACK, FLOW CONTROLLERS IN SHOWERS,
FAMILY TAKES CONSERVING APPROACH

Losses through tank	$20
Hot water for showers, baths, sink	$16
Hot water for washing clothes	$ 9
Hot water for dishes	$ 5
Annual Gas Bill for Hot Water	$50

Losses through tank	$35
Hot water for showers, bath, sink	$90
Hot water for washing clothes	$15
Hot water for dishes	$35
Annual Electric Bill for Hot Water	$175

families with electric and gas water heaters are itemized above.) So, with an investment of $5, Stanfill's savings represent a 3200 percent return. People with gas water heaters won't do quite that well, since gas is still relatively cheap; for low-cost efforts here, the return is 1600 percent on a $5 investment.

Or let's say that Stanfill's results are disappointing, as disappointing as my results with solar, and the savings come to half of what we are predicting here, or $85 a year. That's still a 1600 percent profit on an investment of $5, and that is precisely the beauty of doing the low-cost things first. Even with the usual variability in returns from energy-saving investments, the up side on this one is still terrific.

This still may not be Stanfill's last move. Someday, he may want to buy a heat-pump water heater and cut hot-water costs in half again. Meanwhile, he will be getting the benefit of that $1,500 he didn't spend on his solar water heater, plus the same direct return had he spent the money on the piece of complicated technology.

The low-cost opportunities don't end with water. Stanfill could further his advantage with cut-rate remedies in the following areas:

Air Conditioners. There are a couple of operational secrets that go beyond the obvious advice, which is to keep the machines free of dust and clean the filters regularly. It doesn't cost you much more money to run a room air conditioner on high/cool rather than low/cool. The different settings affect only the fan speed, and fans burn small change compared to the compressor. The thermostat is what needs to be set high. Sometimes it is possible to circulate more air on the high fan speed and get by with a higher thermostat setting, which may mean less work for the compressor.

Many central air conditioners have a sump or crankcase heater that keeps the innards of the machine warm, and therefore dry and undamaged. On many units, the heater operates full-time all year long, adding up to $25 to your annual electric bill. You can save most of this money by switching off the sump heater after the summer air conditioning season. You do this by turning off the circuit breaker in the main switch box, the one marked "air conditioner."

But the circuit-breaker switch must be turned on at least twenty-four hours before the air conditioner is actually used again. That gives the heater a chance to evaporate the moisture that may have accumulated. If you don't allow for the warm-up, the compressor might be ruined and your $25 savings could be lost in a $500 repair bill.

Dishwashers. It costs you about $10 a year to dry the dishes with the heating element in the dishwasher, and during the summer, it takes another $5 for the air conditioner to cope with that extra heat. (The winter heat from the dishwasher is of course useful.) You can save a few dollars in warm or moderate climates by opening the door to the dishwasher after the rinse cycle is complete, and letting the dishes dry by themselves. Newer machines may have an air-dry switch that takes care of this automatically.

Clothes Dryers. It now costs you between 40¢ and 60¢ an hour to dry clothes in your machine, depending on your electric rates. In some areas, electric rates are so high that drying clothes at home isn't much cheaper than doing it at the coin laundry. And this makes the old clothesline a more attractive investment.

Hardware stores now carry dryer vent kits that allow you to pull the exhaust hose into the house during the winter so the heat that went through the clothes can be used a second time to warm up the room. Experts disagree as to whether this purchase produces any saving.

Refrigerators. Unplugging a second refrigerator, especially if it is used to store marginal items, has an attractive yield—up to $150 a year.

A smaller amount of money can be recovered from the primary refrigerator if it has a power-miser or energy-saver switch. Small heaters are built into the walls or doors of refrigerators to burn off condensation and prevent sweating. The heaters work full time on older units, but the above-mentioned switch allows you to periodically turn them off. When you flip on the energy-saving switch, it simply means that the sweat heaters are disconnected.

In most parts of the country, refrigerators never need the anti-sweat heat, especially if the house is air-cooled and climate-controlled. In warm climates where the houses are not air conditioned, one can use the sweat heaters only when moisture appears on the walls of the refrigerator, and keep the energy-saver switch on the rest of the time. Oak Ridge National Laboratories estimates that the energy-saving switch will save between $9 and $19 a year.

Pilot Lights. Pilots on gas appliances burn up to 400 cubic feet of gas per light per month. It now costs between 30¢ and 60¢ to buy 100 cubic feet of natural gas, so a stove with three pilots adds about $2.00 to the monthly gas bill. Pilots on gas dryers, furnaces, and water heaters cost you about $1.50 to $2.00 a month each.

Since families do less cooking at home these days, it is possible that your stove pilots are consuming more gas than you use for the actual cooking. I turned off the burner pilots on my stove a couple of years ago, and I now light the burners with a match. And whenever I need to use the oven, I reset the pilot and light it manually.

Some gas companies say what I do is unsafe. Others send out little booklets that show their customers how to turn off pilot lights. If you want the local expert opinion, call the gas company and ask how difficult or dangerous it would be for you to douse pilots on the oven or stove, or on the furnace during the summer. They may suggest an electronic ignition kit, which is undisputedly safe because it eliminates the match. The gas company can tell you exactly how much it costs to maintain your pilots; that cost can be measured against the cost of electronic ignition.

Off-Peak Pricing Strategies. All electric utilities worry about meeting peak demand at those times of day when electricity usage is very high. Like the highway builders, the power producers must provide enough generating capacity to handle the rush-hour traffic, even if the extra equipment is idle the rest of the time. Since many utilities don't want to build new power plants, they are searching for ways to cut peak demand. You can benefit from their anxiety.

The plan is to lure customers off the peaks with lower electric rates for the nonhectic hours. You might pay a dime per kilowatt-hour during an 8:00 A.M. to 10:00 A.M. rush, but only a nickel during the 10:00 A.M. to 12:00 P.M. slack period. To my knowledge, no utility yet offers the special off-peak rates to all the customers, but they are beginning to take volunteers for off-peak experiments. If you don't mind adjusting your appliance schedule a bit, you might profit by joining. You will also be preparing yourself for the day when off-peak is an integral part of the rate structure, as it already is for phone calls.

Rate formulas vary from utility to utility. Some merely reward the off-peak use with lower rates (the carrot approach you want), while others penalize the peak use by adding an extra charge for electricity consumed during that period. I wouldn't join a program where the stick was stronger than the carrot. But if there is enough carrot, you can reduce your utility bill perhaps one-third by running your appliances at odd hours and doing nothing fancy to the structure of the house. Timers on water heaters and other appliances give you a way to get this price break without inconveniencing yourself. Call your local electric utility and ask what off-peak programs they will be offering.

Part Six

THE FASHIONABLE ALTERNATIVES

The most favorable publicity has been given to energy-saving devices that remind one of the nineteenth century or that suggest the twenty-first. Woodstoves are sold on the notion that the best way to fight OPEC is with old-fashioned New England grit, to burn what is above ground to avoid the price-gouging by those who sell what comes from below. People have marketed solar devices by implying that we can sun ourselves to independence by dealing directly with the thermal source and cutting out the middleman. The solar that we can buy today is really part of an old technology, but it has acquired a curious kind of Buck Rogers image.

One would think that the pioneers and visionaries among us have hooked their houses up to forests and the sun. Actually, a fair number of suckers among us have done that. Because of the national scope of the conservation effort, the fashionable alternatives have undergone widespread migration from places where they once made sense to places where they may not. Woodstoves have moved from rural areas into the suburbs and cities of the Northeast, where in recent years winter cocktail parties were dominated by talk of splitting, stacking, and burning ash or oak. Meanwhile, solar water heaters made their initial appearance in Florida and California and can now be found in colder climates where collectors must be filled with antifreeze.

The following investigation into woodstoves, fireplaces, solar water heaters, solar space heaters, solar pool heaters, passive solar additions, and coal-burning is an extended cautionary tale.

Solar Heaters

The solar heater has been awarded the energy saver's medal of honor. President Carter, for example, didn't insulate the White House or put storm windows on the West Wing; he installed a bank of solar panels on the roof. Solar alone, his action implied, was worthy of presidential invitation. The IRS has also sweetened the solar purchase for the rest of us, offering tax credits for solar devices that exceed anything available for furnace improvements, clock thermostats, insulation, and the rest of the conservation list. While the maximum residential energy credit is $300 for any of the above items, the solar credit has been increased to 40 percent of the cost of the equipment, or up to $4,000.

Some local and state governments have bestowed their own special status on solar. With the California state solar tax credit, a homeowner pays only 45 percent for a solar device and the government covers the rest. That kind of break is supposed to help millions of homeowners find solar irresistible. But should you buy this product even under such favorable conditions? Does solar deserve heavy subsidy?

My doubts started with my own rooftop solar water heater, and they intensified as I investigated solar water heater performance across the country. While other solar products, such as photovoltaics, are still under development, I found plenty of problems with this supposedly proven form of technology, so proven that solar water heater dealers are listed in the Yellow Pages.

ONE FAMILY'S SOLAR EXPERIENCE

In 1978 our family decided to bypass Lee County (Florida) Electric and get our hot water directly from the sun. The motivation was partly economic—we were convinced solar water heaters would save us $240 a year. And it was partly a misplaced desire for self-reliance. We took comfort knowing that we could take showers with solar during a utility-company blackout (at least until we discovered that solar water heaters have electric pumps). It was also partly moral.

I was writing about energy conservation and wanted to make a major commitment to it.

Solar enthusiasts were called pioneers even in 1978, but the solar water heater is no space-age product; it is a simple and old-fashioned device attached to homes in Florida and California, Israel and Japan, long before these homes even had electricity. I was surprised to discover that more solar heaters could be found in Miami in 1935 than in the entire state of Florida in 1980; in fact, many of the old systems still sit on Miami rooftops.

How does the solar water heater work? The principle is identical to what makes a car dashboard get hot on a summer's day. The sun's heat is trapped, or collected, inside large, copper-lined boxes covered with glass. Cold water moves slowly through the collectors inside some copper pipes. As the water gets hotter, it rises naturally to the water tank, located above the collectors on the roof—a natural upward flow that is called thermosiphoning. The need for pumps was thereby eliminated, which is why solar heaters could be used before electricity was introduced in a region.

The hot water is stored in the tank until somebody turns on a faucet in the house below. Gravity provides the water pressure.

By the time I went solar shopping, the simple old thermosiphon systems were not the most popular solar units. When the industry revived in the 1970s, the market offered a much more complicated product. The water storage tank was now situated below the collectors, which meant that a pump had to push the water up. In addition, the pump needed temperature sensors to tell it when to turn on and off. Finally, since solar heaters were now being installed in cold climates, the collectors required freeze-up protection. Some of the new models came with drain valves to purge the collectors of water during subfreezing weather, which means another set of temperature sensors. Other models used antifreeze instead of water to absorb the sun's heat. But because hot antifreeze showers are very unpleasant, a heat exchanger was needed to transfer the heat from the antifreeze to the water inside the storage tank.

Adornments helped make the solar heater appear to be something futuristic when it's really just a hot box and a water tank. The gadgetry also made solar more expensive and harder to maintain. Not only did the pumps, valves, and antifreeze loops add several hundred dollars to the cost of a simple thermosiphon system, but they were also all things that could break down.

What the adornments didn't do was improve performance over the old-style solar heaters to any great extent. In its review of eighteen solar water heaters in California, the California Energy Commission found that "the highest solar fraction was attained by a thermosiphon system." The reason, as we will discuss below, had nothing to do with the technology, but with how the family used the equipment.

I was forced to reject thermosiphon because I had no way to put a large water tank above the collectors on my roof. I bought my solar heater from Grumman, but the model uses antifreeze, an unnecessary complication in South Florida. On the other hand, Grumman makes jet aircraft, so I had confidence in their technical and manufacturing abilities. The solar revival in the early 1970s was led by hundreds of small companies that made collectors in garages or backyards. Many of the solar believers who formed a lobby in Washington liked the arrangement; it meant, they thought, that solar could represent clean politics as well as clean energy. Big dirty companies, they felt, should be kept off the soft energy path. But because so many of the moms and pops went out of business, the entire industry got a reputation for unreliability.

The entrance of Exxon and Grumman into the solar market (Exxon has since gotten out of the collector business) meant to some that the industry was finally growing up. Consumers could choose, at least, between buying their sun from a neighborhood expert or from a member of the Fortune 500. I had heard so many stories of small solar outfits that went bankrupt that I ignored my preference for decentralized energy in favor of a company that could honor its warranty. Grumman, for one, offered a five-year guarantee on all the parts that went into the solar package. And because they were selling the package throughout the country, I assumed that they had worked the bugs out of the system.

All I had to do was find somebody to put the collector panels on the roof and connect them, with copper pipes, to the water tank in the basement. This seemed like a simple enough job, especially since the Grumman equipment came with step-by-step instructions.

The dealer was seventy miles away, so he suggested I find a local installer. I contacted our plumber, who said he had handled a number of solar heaters. The fact that he had done good work for us in the past set my mind at ease. It shouldn't have. Our plumber-installer drilled holes in our roof, leaving leaks in three places. He soldered the wrong pipe to the wrong end of the collector, blocking the antifreeze. The electric pump pushed air around until it overheated. I was out of town when all the damage was done, and I returned not to solar heat in the shower but to rainwater in the living room. The installer had left us with crippled collectors, a $500 payment-due notice, and about $800 worth of repairs.

I never paid the $500, but it still took two more installers and about three weeks' worth of effort before we had a functioning unit. (The second installer, who said he was appalled at the work of the first, rerouted the pipes yet again incorrectly.) Grumman didn't guarantee proper installation, and the repair costs exceeded what I budgeted for the project by $300, which changed the economics of the investment. I could have sued the plumber, but it wasn't worth the effort.

At least the thing was finally pumping, though, and we could start to get our money back.

For several months I scrutinized electric bills, with the result as discouraging as the leaky roof. I could see no great difference between pre-solar bills and post-solar bills. The popular belief, as I mentioned, was that solar water heaters in Florida save $200 a year for families of four previously using electric water heaters. We are a family of five. But even when I adjusted for the rate increases that sometimes disguise energy-saving profits, I figured we were saving $5 a month at most—only $60 a year. Our investment, minus tax credits, was $1,500. We were a long way from breaking even, and we live in a part of the country where solar is supposed to be especially profitable.

Two conclusions were possible. One was that our case was unfortunate but atypical. I had hired a bad installer and I bought the wrong solar collector. The other was that the industry has more problems than are generally admitted, that the special tax advantages may be undeserved, that a product of dubious merit has been foisted on the public because of its connection to fashionable political, moral, and mythological imagery. I traveled across the country to find out whether we, or the nation, had been sold on a lemon.

THE FLORIDA SOLAR ENERGY CENTER

The Florida Solar Energy Center sits just outside of the security gate to Cape Canaveral, a good symbolic stop on the soft energy path. It is a state agency established to do solar research, a place where you would expect to find enthusiasm for things solar.

I imagined that the employees of the center would regale me with stories contradicting my experience. They didn't. None of their solar water heaters seemed to be working very well, either. Art Litka, one of the center project directors, had been carefully monitoring his electric bills since he went solar in 1977. "If you look at the numbers," he told me, "you wouldn't even know I had a solar heater.

"I want solar to go," Litka said, "but I also want to be objective. What we are seeing is unfortunately somewhat discouraging."

In 1977, Litka's family used 11,843 kilowatt-hours of electricity without a solar water heater. In 1978, the first solar year, they used 11,727 kilowatt-hours. In 1979, after they had gotten thoroughly familiar with the equipment, they used 11,582 kilowatt-hours. A kilowatt-hour costs about 5¢ in Florida. So the difference between the Litkas' 1977 and 1979 electric bills amounted to just $15.

The same story came out of other offices at the center. The experts who had taken the technology home were saving $40 or $50 or perhaps a maximum of $85 a year with their $1,500 solar water systems. "If you really want to look at hard cash flow," Litka said, "you take the $1,500 and invest in a four-year treasury note."

The news was also bad out in the field, where thousands of solar units have been purchased in the last five years by consumers who know much less than Litka. Under the guidance of Marvin Yarosh, the Florida center made some house calls to find out just how well solar water heaters were working. Their three general conclusions:

1. A disturbing percentage of installations were defective. About 50 percent of them had flaws, and 10 percent have flaws that could damage the house or the solar components over time.

2. Even units that are installed properly do not always pay back what is predicted.

3. In spite of this, people seemed delighted with their solar heaters. Yarosh found several homes where the solar output never reached the water tank. The owners were getting all their hot water from electricity and bragging about their solar investments to neighbors.

Yarosh described the findings as cursory and preliminary. Still, they bothered him, especially the part about the owners' perceptions. Most solar surveys, he said, are questionnaires that merely ask people how they like their purchases. Because solar owners sometimes overlook the problems, the questionnaires may not reflect solar's true performance. "We need more hard data," he said. "More monitoring."

THE NEW ENGLAND EXPERIENCE

One of the most closely monitored solar projects in the country was organized by the New England Electric Company in 1976. The utility put solar heaters of various types and designs on the rooftops of a hundred customers. The early results showed how many things can go wrong with complicated hardware and an inexperienced industry, even in a supervised project. The valves tended to stick on the drain-down systems. Pipes burst and collectors froze up. A panoply of other problems kept the repair trucks busy. In the first year, the worst fifteen systems in the experiment averaged only a 5 percent savings on hot-water costs, while the best systems got 37 percent. The expectation had been that solar could provide 60 percent of the hot water.

In New England, the drain-down systems were scrapped and replaced with solar heaters using antifreeze for cold-weather protection. The performance of the hundred solar heaters improved during the second year of the experiment. Still, the sun was putting only 40 percent of the heat in the water tank of the average home in the project. New England Electric lost interest in solar water heaters and discontinued the experiment in 1977.

I talked to Jack Meeker, who worked on the utility's project and then moved over to the Northeast Solar Energy Center in Boston, one of the DOE-funded regional offices. He said not much field testing of solar heaters was going on since New England Electric got its mixed results. He did mention a small monitoring program of twenty-four solar units where the average installation was saving its owner $140 a year, which is more money than people seemed to be saving in Florida. Meeker's explanation was that it costs more to heat water in the North, where the ground temperature is lower. The solar returns may therefore be paradoxically greater in cold climates, even though one sees the sun less often.

But solar heaters cost twice as much to put in place in the Northeast as they do in Florida. While the installed price hovers between $1,500 and $2,200 in Miami, it reaches $3,000 to $4,000 in New York or Massachusetts because of the antifreeze adornments and because the industry is smaller. Whether solar pays off in the Northeast, even with the federal tax credit, is hard to determine. Meeker said the returns from solar were still highly variable, just as they had been in the New England Electric experiment. The improvements in technique had not standardized the savings.

MORE DOUBTS FROM COLORADO

I found more evidence of the general unreliability of solar heaters after contacting the Solar Energy Research Institute (SERI), the national center for solar research. SERI is located just outside of Denver, Colorado. Marvin Yarosh, from the Florida center, suggested I call Gordon Gross in Colorado.

I had a long conversation with Gross about his investigations into solar water heaters in Grand Forks, Atlanta, and Tucson. He said a formal report could be expected soon, but he would give me a preview.

"We've had an incredible number of installation problems," Gross said. "Installers left out parts, or designs were inadequate, or the size of the systems was wrong. There are so many different models on the market, some of which are unworkable designs.

"It's almost unbelievable the number of faults that we've found. Solar heating is almost where aviation was in 1914. The people who did it then were daredevils.

"Of one hundred systems we've looked at, only one system was well installed, well designed, well operated, and got a clean bill of health. The owner of that system was an engineer. The system was saving him $5 to $6 a month."

I arrived at SERI a few months later, expecting to pick up a copy of the Gross report. I was told it was never released. Gross wasn't around, so I talked to Rebecca Vorhees, another solar specialist disappointed with the record of the water heaters. Vorhees had done some thinking about the reasons for the failures I've described.

In the case of the solar water heater, she said, the installer has to be as talented as the manufacturer. It is just as difficult to connect all the parts, especially on the modern systems with the pumps and sensors, as it is to build the collector boxes. Every house and every piece of solar equipment presents its own special problems, allowing a big margin for error. While the research money has gone into improving the collector panels themselves, installation is where a solar heater succeeds or fails.

A solar installer must possess a variety of skills, from roof repair to plumbing to electrical work, plus an intuitive sensitivity about the habits of the sun. One doesn't often find all these qualities in a single person, especially a career wrench-twister. Training programs have been few and far between, and Vorhees wonders how enough installers can be taught to handle hundreds of thousands of solar jobs, if the industry ever catches on. Even with the small existing market, there is a paucity of good installers.

On top of that, few people are being trained to check the work and provide official quality control. States and localities are now enforcing licensing and building code requirements for solar. But places that do require permits routinely issue them only to licensed plumbers or contractors, who do not have to prove any solar knowledge. In parts of Florida, for instance, an untrained plumber can get a permit to install a solar heater, while a trained solar installer who is not a plumber cannot. Plumbers, as I discovered the hard way, are not always acquainted with the subtleties of solar equipment. And the building inspectors who approve the work often know less than the plumbers.

"There are some good manufacturers and installers," Vorhees said. "But the group is small compared to the potential market, and the amount of experience is small compared to the potential market. How can a consumer be sure he will get a good guy? He can't.

"Neither government nor industry has taken the responsibility to solve these problems," she said. "And government isn't just being neutral about solar products. It is approving them."

THE CALIFORNIA EXPERIENCE

One cannot judge the solar water heater without hearing from California. Florida also has the sunshine, but California has cultural and political support for alternatives in food, consciousness, lifestyles, and energy. Nobody keeps accurate records, but the popular guess is that half the solar units in the country are to be found in California, where an estimated 100,000 homeowners have installed solar water heaters, space heaters, swimming pool heaters, or a combination of the three. (That means there are only 200,000 solar units in the entire country, a figure which, if accurate, suggests the promotion has been much stronger than the reception.)

California is the hope of the solar water heater advocates, who claim that once the industry gets big enough the problems will disappear. The market there is stimulated by a 55 percent tax credit, as I've said before, a licensing program, a consumer affairs office to handle complaints, and an active involvement by the Public Utilities Commission and by some individual utilities. I wondered if solar did any better with heavy institutional support.

As in other parts of the country, the available evidence was scarce. I got some idea of consumer satisfaction from the Energy Unit of the state's Division of Consumer Services at Sacramento. From May 1978 through June 1980 the agency received eighty complaints about defective solar water heaters, or more elaborate solar installations that included water heaters. Most of the complaints involved companies that did damage and then quickly went out of business. Some examples:

Case 011-78. Solar system was installed on four-bedroom home. System is leaking. Client called company and phone had been disconnected. [This one was resolved when the company was finally located at its new address and agreed to do repairs.]

Case 013-78. Solar system installed in January 1976. The pumps malfunctioned and burned out three times. The system was never designed properly for house. Client is using more gas and electricity than before the installation of the system. System disconnected. [An impasse was reached between manufacturer and consumer. Possible civil action by consumer.]

Case 020-78. $12,489 paid out by client to have solar systems installed. Work has never been completed. It has been one year since contract was signed. [Mediation resulted in some action by company.]

Case 037-78. $8,900 to install solar systems for pool, hot water, and insulation. Nothing is working. [Company out of business. Corrections made by another installer sent by manufacturer.]

Case 024-78. $15,000 solar space, hot water and pool heating system. Inadequately and improperly designed system, using inferior materials. Was ineffective and now system is completely inoperative. [Company has promised for eighteen months to redesign system. Civil action anticipated.]

Case 050-78. $5,500 solar space and hot water system. Company paid in full before job completed—then they went out of business. [No action from company. Lawsuit being filed.]

Case 061-79. $7,860 solar space and domestic hot water system. Utility bills three times higher than before solar. [Company could not resolve. Systems removed. Case closed.]

Case 105-79. $1,187 solar system not operating. Contractor's license expires. [No response from contractor.]

A close reading of the complaint list makes for solar caveat emptor. A business that takes several hundred pounds of glass, metal, and wood; attaches it to exposed rooftops; puts an eighty-gallon tankful of water in the basement; and sends antifreeze flowing through pipes between the tank below and the collector above is bound to produce major disasters, even in California. The state licenses its solar contractors and requires a building inspection of all solar installations, but that doesn't help the customer when the solar company wrecks the roof and then goes out of business. And price is no reason for a customer to feel more secure. Many of the biggest complaints were lodged against flawed equipment costing over $10,000.

Still, eighty complaints is a small number, considering the thousands of solar heaters that have been installed in California. Based on the Florida findings, one suspects that many more customers aren't aware that their equipment is defective, or else they don't want to talk about it. But given the magnitude of troubles described in other places, it appears that solar is more reliable in California, a state where solar companies can lose their licenses and where consumers may be better informed about the product.

Do solar water heaters give an improved rate of return in an area with more solar experience? It was hard to get solid information on this point, but the data I did assemble suggests that the returns are just as variable in California as they are in New England. The California Energy Commission monitored eighteen solar water heaters in 1979. Some owners got 30 percent of their hot water from the sun, and some got as much as 80 percent, and the majority got between 40 and 50 percent.

Where one is within the range of returns determines whether solar is a good or a bad investment. Let's assume a family buys a $3,500 solar water heater (a reasonable price in California) and gets the full 55 percent tax credit, reducing the actual expense to $1,575. The family has an electric water heater, which costs them $200 a year to operate. If the solar unit provides 30 percent of that hot water, the family saves $60 a year. Depending on inflation, future energy prices, the family's tax bracket, and a variety of other factors, it may take them a decade or better to recover their investment. If solar provides 70 percent of the hot water, they save $140 a year and the economics are considerably improved.

The problem is predicting whether one will be a 30 percenter or a 70 percenter. There are fancy computer hookups to tell homeowners what their solar fraction will be, but the numbers given are misleading at best, based as they are on how much sunlight falls on the roof and the theoretical efficiency of the collector panels. The news from California is further proof that collector efficiency has little to do with how solar works on any given rooftop. Once the equipment is correctly installed, the important variable turns out to be the people living in the house below it, and human behavior explains why solar may have worked better in 1935 than it does now.

In Miami during the 1930s, nobody thought about solar percentages. People who owned those old thermosiphon systems got *all* their hot water from the sun. On cloudy days they learned to live without a warm bath. They adapted the housekeeping routine to the vicissitudes of weather. They washed clothes in midmorning so the sun could heat another tankful of water by midafternoon. If people were careful, they could stretch their supply of solar water over two or maybe three days. In any case, there was enough sunshine that they ran out only infrequently.

The modern solar heater does away with all inconvenience. Connected to an electric or gas backup heater, hot water is constantly available. In fact the backup often does more work, certainly more reliable work, than the solar unit, but the homeowner doesn't know that. He has no way of telling how much of his hot water can be credited to the sun, and how much to the local utility.

Nobody tells the solar customer that *in addition to* his initial investment he has to be vigilant about how and when he uses hot water to make solar pay. People who put up that kind of money for a technological way out of a problem don't like being told that they have to watch their behavior as well. But they do have to watch it. The California Energy Commission once explained why one solar family got the highest solar fraction in their test group: "the residents were exemplary in working with the solar system so as to use solar energy as much as possible. That is, the residents adjusted their hot water demand depending on the solar energy available."

Consumers like to use the solar heater at their convenience. Why not? The gadgetry is the advertised solution to the problem. When we installed our solar heater, it didn't occur to us to no longer do laundry or wash the dishes or take our baths at night. Yet that routine of nighttime tasks ensured a small solar contribution. Once we used up the eighty gallons of solar water stored in the tank, we took hot water from the backup system. The sun couldn't provide more heat until midmorning, and by that time nobody was inside the house using hot water. By evening, when we needed hot water again, some of the heat collected in the solar unit was lost through pipes and through the walls of the storage tank.

These system losses were the only way the experts at the Florida center could explain why actual solar performance fell so far below what was predicted from solar research. In summer you get more solar heat than you can use, but in winter you often get less than you need. In either season, you achieve high solar percentages (the 70 percent range) by doing the chores on the sun's own time: laundry at 11:00 A.M., when heat has built up in the solar tank; dishes at 3:00 P.M., when the tank has been replenished with solar heat; showers at 6:00 P.M., when the afternoon sun has warmed up more water.

But how many people are willing to adapt to a compulsive schedule of this sort? If you start worrying about how and when you use hot water, you might as well do all the low-cost things and get a potential 30 percent savings on an investment of a few dollars. The low-cost approach doesn't rule out solar, but you may conserve yourself out of the solar market this way, because your hot-water needs are so reduced that the solar purchase becomes overkill.

People who are not compulsive can always put up larger storage tanks to hold more solar water and more collectors to produce more solar heat. That will increase your solar percentage. But the modifications cost money, and tend to make solar much too costly for what you'll get back. The standard eighty-gallon solar tank and the two collector panels are already expensive enough.

The Tennessee Valley Authority is placing 10,000 solar heaters on residences in Tennessee, and early results prove that in a closely monitored situation like this, people can get 60 percent of their hot water from the sun. But even in these favorable conditions, the solar purchase may not be able to stand up against the heat-pump water heater, which costs between $450 and $800. One of the TVA's own conservation directors told me that "the heat-pump water heater will beat the pants off solar."

So why the federal support for the rather cumbersome solar water heater, which is more old-fashioned than futuristic, presents a big chance for foul-up, requires a lot of vigilance for a payback, and is very expensive in the first place? I don't have a real answer.

I'm not saying never buy a solar heater. But don't buy one without first doing the following:

1. Reduce hot-water consumption as much as possible with low-cost measures. No reason for an iron lung when nasal spray will do.

2. Assess hot-water consumption carefully after its use has been cut back with the showerhead flow restrictors and other devices and measures. People tend to think that they use more hot water than they actually do, which makes solar look better. A utility company

energy auditor or perhaps a solar heater salesman can help you figure out how much hot water you require for dishes, showers, and laundry, and what the annual cost of that hot water is. That cost can vary from house to house by as much as 100 percent. You need to know how much you spend before you could in any way estimate how much solar would save.

3. Investigate the solar heater company that wants to sell you its product. I wouldn't deal with a company that has been in business for less than two years, and it should guarantee its product, materials, and installation for at least five years. The installer is very important. Find out whom the company is going to send, and talk to somebody who has had the work done by that particular installer. Ask the solar company for references from other customers. Call the Better Business Bureau or other agencies to check on possible complaints. I know you wouldn't go to such trouble for a new air conditioner or refrigerator, but solar demands it.

4. View the payback predictions with a great deal of skepticism. Some solar companies claim that their product will provide as much as 70 percent of your hot water. You already know better. Find out how they come up with their numbers. If claims are based on collector efficiency or computer simulation, dismiss them. Find out if what they say has been verified with monitoring or field-testing in any homes where this company has installed equipment.

5. If you have an electric water heater, don't buy solar without considering the heat pump. This device can do the same job at one-fourth the cost and without all the installation problems.

6. Less trouble is encountered in closely monitored projects like the TVA solar water heater experiment. Outside of these carefully regulated programs, it's caveat emptor.

SOLAR SPACE HEATING

Most of what I've said about solar water heaters also applies to solar collectors designed to heat the entire house. The principle is the same: that is, water or air is directed through collector boxes on the roof, heated in those boxes, and then circulated through radiators or ducts to the various rooms. The investment is much larger, because you need more collector area, more pumps and sensors, more auxiliary equipment. Solar space heating systems routinely cost more than $10,000 and the collectors cover the entire south side of your roof.

A few hundred Americans have decided that the investment makes a sensible heating system, but I fail to understand why. There are even more maintenance problems with these huge collector systems, plus all the hardware it takes to move the heat into the house, than with the simpler solar water heaters. The large heating systems don't store the collected heat for nighttime use very well, and various leaks and heat losses can rob them of their theoretical efficiency. With so many less costly and less risky alternatives—better furnaces and passive solar greenhouses and more insulation—I can't imagine a sillier heating choice.

SOLAR SWIMMING-POOL HEATERS

Here a solar investment makes more sense. Although most solar swimming-pool collectors are installed on rooftops, it is also possible to install them on the ground, where components are more easily replaced. Solar pool systems do not require antifreeze or water storage tanks. Moreover, the benefits are less esoteric, because most pool owners know how much it costs them to heat their pools, and therefore can predict the savings from solar more exactly. Solar pool heating systems can cost several thousand dollars, but then again, people who own pools can often afford the investment.

The important thing here, as usual, is not the equipment, but the installer. As I said with solar water heaters, find a company that has been in business for a few years and that offers a five-year warranty on parts and installation. Visit a couple of their installations and quiz the owners about performance. Call the Better Business Bureau and the local or state energy office and ask if complaints have been filed against the solar company, and how they were resolved.

Because most pools are heated with natural gas, recent price increases make a warm pool very expensive. If you are planning to put in a swimming pool, by all means heat it with solar and not gas. In the future, you may be forced by the price of fuel to abandon the gas equipment, so there is no percentage in paying for it now.

A low-cost solar pool heating alternative does exist, and that is the plastic pool blanket, which is rolled across the top of the pool. The plastic acts as an insulator to keep heat trapped in the water below. According to Art Rosenfeld of the Lawrence Berkeley Laboratory, pool covers are so effective that they can often do the whole heating job. The trade-off is between cost and convenience. The pool cover costs from $200 to $500 depending on the quality of plastic and the roll-up system, but the cover has to be furled and unfurled in the winter. The solar pool collectors can cost several thousand dollars, and don't require any homeowner effort. Whether it's worth an extra few thousand to avoid rolling plastic is a matter of personal preference. Solar collector systems may last for ten to fifteen years, while the life span of a pool blanket is only two to four, so there is an economic trade-off to consider here, too.

Rosenfeld suggests a hybrid system—the roll-up plastic blanket and a much smaller solar collector. This can produce higher water temperatures than a more expensive pure collector system, because the plastic cover holds the heat in and preheats the water. When less auxiliary heat is needed for the pool, the owner can ignore the plastic cover and get by with the collectors alone. When it's cold, both devices can be used in tandem to get the highest water temperatures for the least cost. Swimming-pool companies and local solar heater companies can explain what the installation might entail. But don't buy a collector system without considering the blanket.

Passive Solar Additions

Passive solar additions, particularly greenhouses, have replaced woodstoves and solar rooftop equipment as the promising new soft-energy response. One can mark the trends by driving around wealthy neighborhoods. In 1979 houses sprouted chimneys for the recently installed woodstoves. In 1980 more were sporting greenhouses, and the front elevations of severe New England saltboxes began to look like Czechoslovakian Easter eggs.

For those who haven't kept up with the terminology, passive solar is a rhetorical refinement on active solar, which used to be called simply "solar." The difference is between getting a tan from a day at the beach and getting a tan from a sunlamp. Active solar requires machinery—valves, pumps, and moving parts. Passive solar is finding the hottest spot on the beach, and a house designed this way is oriented to catch and hold the sun's rays.

A passive solar house is best made from the ground up, a prospect discussed in the next chapter. Here we are concerned with what can be done to an existing house to improve its solar input and take a load off the furnace. Your house is already partially solarized if it has windows, since any hole that lets in sunlight can be considered a passive solar device. In fact, you probably already get 10 percent of your heat from the sun, according to the Princeton research. The challenge is to fiddle with the structure of the house to get more.

Greenhouses are the most convenient retrofit here. You install the greenhouse directly against the south-facing wall of the house, the wall that already gets the most sun. Sunlight is trapped inside this greenhouse, raising the temperature on the south wall. If this extra heat can somehow be sent into the living area, either through a sliding-glass door or through large windows on the south wall, then you have accomplished something clever. You have expanded the square footage of the house while reducing the energy bills. The greenhouse itself can be used as a breakfast room or a place to grow plants in the winter.

A manufactured lean-to greenhouse costs between $1,500 and $2,000, and by the time you pay the carpenters, the architect, and whomever else is involved, the passive solar tab may reach several thousand dollars. Doug Balcomb, perhaps the nation's most prominent passive solar spokesman, tells me that you probably cannot justify the alteration on the energy savings alone. He estimates that passive solar retrofits at best cut one-third off a heating bill, and might not do that well in many circumstances.

Balcomb, however, wants us to consider other factors, as he takes a more expansive economic view. The greenhouse, his favorite passive solar alteration, offers both tangible and intangible benefits; the spirit of the house is enriched by the foliage and the extra sunshine. Balcomb can't put a dollar figure on this, but he says passive solar homes have a higher resale value, and this is where he thinks the investment can be recouped. Already the cost of a passive solar addition has been more than covered by the increase in sales price in the few houses he has tracked.

I have no information to prove or disprove Balcomb's claim, and it is too early to draw general conclusions. The worth of passive solar will ultimately depend on its performance, which brings us to the crucial point. How can you be sure that this project will work?

Just sticking a greenhouse against the outside wall of your house isn't enough; there are already stories of people who tried it and failed. There are several hurdles: the south wall has to get plenty of direct sunlight; the heat has to be properly routed into the house through vents or windows; some method must be found to store the heat; and the windows or sliding doors that open into the greenhouse must be closed at night with insulating panels so that the solar benefits don't escape in the other direction.

Overheating is the technical bugbear of passive solar. The room adjacent to the greenhouse needs some thermal mass to absorb the heat and release it gradually. Flagstone floors or concrete interior walls or even brick walls make good thermal mass. Wood-frame houses don't have the same natural heat storage capacity, and unless some thermal mass is added to the house (one unattractive but effective method is with 55-gallon drums filled with water and painted black), the greenhouse may make the living space intolerably hot during the day, with none of the heat lingering into the night, when it is most useful.

You must find a good passive solar architect to sort all of this out; the designer, again, is more important than the hardware. The field is somewhat treacherous, because passive solar is new and yet there is a faddish bias in favor of it. Some architects understand theories of heat loss and heat gain and can predict the costs and thermal benefits of a passive solar project so you know what kind of deal you are getting. That is half the battle. The other half is making certain that the architect has put the theories into practice. I would never open my checkbook to a passive solar expert who could not show me some of his own retrofit projects that *work*. Get a list of all his or her passive solar credits and then make a few phone calls.

There are two other passive solar retrofits that are less popular than the greenhouse but are still worth a mention. One is a Trombe wall, basically a thermal sandwich created by glass, an air space, and a thermal mass behind it. Brick houses are the likely candidates for the Trombe wall, because brick makes a good thermal mass. Since there is no easy way to insulate a brick wall, you can turn it into a heater by installing a huge piece of glass in front of the brick on the south side of the house. Heat is trapped in the air space between the glass and the brick, and when a few vents are cut into the wall, a natural circulation system will carry the heat into the house.

The other retrofit involves cutting more windows into the south wall, but this gets messy and expensive, and unless the windows are properly insulated at night, they can lose you more heat than they bring in.

Again, you'll have to defer to the architect on which of these choices, if any, to make. I think you'll find very few architects who push passive solar as a substitute for other, more conventional investments. If a house is not well insulated or well sealed, much of the passive solar benefit will be lost, anyway. Passive solar additions are neighborhood attention-getters, but they only perform well if the behind-the-scenes stuff is done first.

The cost-benefit numbers have to come from a local source, but the Solar Energy Research Institute has come up with these ball-park guesses:

Retrofit	Cost per Square Foot	Annual Savings, in Terms of Value of Heat Produced at 1980 Prices
Greenhouse	$4–$30	$27–$360
Trombe wall	$3–$15	$14–$140
More south windows	$5–$25	$28–$190

The Tale of Two Woodstoves

There are already 5 million woodstoves and 18 million fireplaces inside American homes, and they burned 1 quad of energy, or the equivalent of 500,000 barrels of oil, in 1980. That figure is expected to double by 1990. Whether this wood craze makes any sense depends on who is doing the burning. I have two friends, Dan Palmer and Paul Falcone, who represent the limits of woodstove triumph and folly.

First, the triumph.

In 1978, Dan Palmer gave up his New York apartment for an eighteenth-century country house in the Berkshires of western Massachusetts. The house had certain quaint features, such as a sagging floor through which cold air readily seeps. But Palmer wasn't worried about energy costs when he made his purchase. He and his wife, Rebecca, thought they could survive on less money outside of Manhattan—half as much, in fact.

The projected country budget was revised during their first winter, when home heating oil hit 80¢ a gallon. When Palmer wasn't playing computer chess or devising mail-order schemes to pull up his income, he was thinking about ways to bring down his fuel bills. He spent $1,250 on oil in four months.

Dan and Rebecca collect books. An entire downstairs wall was covered with volumes that presumably prepare city people for country living by telling them how to make things. In any case, the books created a kind of inadvertent insulation, since they kept some heat from getting out of the house. Dan talked about filling the walls of the house with fiberglass or caulking the cracks in the floor, but with such a large house and with so many cracks having origins in the eighteenth century, the job seemed hopeless.

Instead, he stuck on an alternative solution—find cheaper heat. Dan's idea had local support, since many of his neighbors already had woodstoves. These weren't people who ran out last year to buy their Jøtuls when they read about them in the *Wall Street Journal.* These local families had been heating with wood for about as long as Dan's house had been standing.

After a number of technical sessions with the neighbors, Dan bought two woodstoves and placed them at strategic points. The first one was a cast-iron radiant stove, which Dan put in the living room. This stove is your standard black hotbox, made by dozens of companies and marketed under such names as Jøtul, Ashley, All-Nighter. When wood is burned, it heats up the sides and top of the metal box to finger-singeing temperatures, the hot surfaces releasing a lot of heat into a limited area.

The second one was a circulating stove that looks like a space heater, which Dan put in a downstairs bedroom near the staircase leading upstairs. This stove is a box within a box. By bringing air into a channel between the outer box and the hot inner box, the stove creates a draft that carries heat beyond the ambit of a radiant stove. Dan hoped it would heat the upstairs bedrooms.

The two installations—with flue pipes and roof attachments and fireproofing around the stoves—cost Dan $2,000. The final bill was an unpleasant surprise, because the woodstoves alone only came to $800. Dan didn't figure on the high price of insulated flue pipe. People often don't.

The Palmers were better prepared for the qualitative difference between a winter with oil and a winter with wood. Neighbors had warned them. A woodstove is not an appliance, they said. It is an obsession.

The arrival of the two woodstoves in the house was like the arrival of a baby. Evenings were interrupted by the four-hour feedings, which meant Dan or Rebecca had to put on a coat, go out to the garage, drag in some wood, shove it into the two stoves, and adjust the dampers. Dan was forever changing dampers. You couldn't have a conversation or a chess game with him during which he didn't leave the room at least once to prod and stoke and shuffle the embers. One of the woodstove brochures boasted that the radiant stove would hold a fire for twelve hours. Neighbors told Dan that it wouldn't hold longer than six. They were right.

Just in tending their woodstoves, the Palmers probably put fifty extra miles on their shoes in one winter. The stoves not only initiated the physical exercise but created an indoor climate that demanded it. Where the oil furnace had warmed the house to toasty if expensive consistency, the woodstoves put peaks and valleys in the temperature levels. When the fires died down, Dan was glad to drag in more wood because the trip itself warmed him up. Away from the radiant stove and up in the far corners of the bedroom, the temperature was always 15 degrees colder than it was near the burning wood. Occupants of Palmer's house were either buried under covers, sitting near the radiant stove, or ambulatory. (The circulating stove did keep two bedrooms reasonably warm.)

The little inconveniences and discomforts caused by woodstoves are sometimes called "lifestyle changes" by the people who sell the equipment, a description that tickles the imagination. Stacking logs in the backyard thereby becomes an advertising equivalent to jumping ship. I suppose the Palmers were not unaware of the theatrical possibilities of wood heat. Having woodstoves was part of spartan country virtue, the indoor equivalent of farming. Dan bought all his wood unsplit, which made it cheaper but also tougher to handle. In New York he could hardly switch on a light without calling the building super; now he flexed his muscles on axes and wedges. He spent hours splitting and stacking, and visitors were drawn into Lincolnesque competition.

Dan spent more hours talking wood with the locals, learning how to mix hardwoods and soft, how to dry and cure, how to tune a stove for a long, untended run. Wood became a major topic of conversation with old friends, supplanting even baseball, once Dan's first love. He once amused his guests by reciting the starting lineups of all twenty-six major-league teams. Now he could rattle off the BTU value of almost every known type of firewood.

At the end of the first woodburning winter, Dan added up his bills and found that he spent $600 on heating the house—$450 for wood plus $150 for back-up oil. I thought it was a bargain only if he didn't count the hundred or so hours it took to buy, split, stack, cure, move, tend, discuss, load, light, stroke, replenish, sweep, and contemplate the wood and its ashy residue. Dan and Rebecca didn't put their own time on the balance sheet because they considered woodstove chores to be entertainment. Wood gave them a common bond with the neighbors. It gave them a way to exhibit country skills to urban visitors. It gave them a physical link to the territory. It gave them something to do on soporific nights. The fact that woodstoves saved them $800 the first year was important, but not that important.

Dan could pay off his woodstoves in two heating seasons on the savings from oil he didn't use. I didn't know if the enthusiasm would last that long, but I figured that wood-tending would soon become a less self-conscious part of the Palmer routine. Woodburning was part of local tradition, and the Palmers wanted to share in that.

. . .

Now, the folly. Paul and Molly Falcone live in an urban brown-stone in Washington, D.C. Their woodstove sits right in the middle of a rather narrow living room, as a kind of ethical sculpture. They get more compliments on their woodstove, on their decision to do something about energy, than the Palmers, whose neighbors take woodstoves for granted.

The disturbing fact is that after they installed their woodstove shortly before the onset of the winter of 1980, the Falcones' natural gas bill went up. I went to investigate the anomaly, which Paul Falcone was convinced violated the physical laws of energy.

Falcone and Palmer had read the same woodstove books, but Washingtonians did not have the benefit of local savvy. My quick appraisal was that neither the house nor the location nor the occupants were suited to a woodstove. Unfortunately, the people who sold and installed the stove said nothing to Falcone earlier.

The house consists of five floors connected by an elaborate continuous stairwell. Falcone carefully measured the square footage of the house and picked up a huge woodstove that was supposed to heat that much area. But he didn't consider all the walls and obstructions that stand between people and the source of the heat. The installer didn't say anything about this either.

At one end of the living room is the sitting area, but the chairs and couches here were out of the woodstove's range. The dining room is separated from the woodstove by a half-wall, so it didn't get much wood heat. The kitchen is cut off from the rest of the first floor by a full wall, so it got no wood heat at all. The upstairs bedrooms are set back from the stairwell, so the stove's output couldn't get to them. Falcone's imposing cast-iron box, however, did an impressive job of heating the passageways that are never occupied. It also warmed the narrow part of the living room, which people use only as a corridor to get to the dining room, and it warmed the stairwell.

The inopportune woodstove placement still didn't explain Falcone's higher natural gas bills. They were caused, I decided, by the woodstove's proximity to the furnace thermostat. The natural gas furnace was working hard to heat the inhabited areas of the house. When the woodstove was fired up, the thermostat was fooled into thinking the house was too hot, so the furnace turned off. This drove temperatures in most parts of the house to such frigid levels that Paul or Molly would have to reset the thermostat to 75 or even 78 just to get the furnace operating again. When the woodstove died down, they would forget to reduce the thermostat setting, and the entire house would overheat. The overheating was expensive, and it probably produced the increases in the gas bill.

The Falcones remained eager to learn how to use more wood and less gas, and I was going to suggest that they move the furnace thermostat. I shelved that idea when Paul Falcone told me about recent changes in the way they obtained their wood. The original idea was that they would spend weekends out in rural Virginia with chain saws and axes, cutting wood and dragging it back to the city in their Datsun station wagon. These noble efforts had created a small stack of elm drying in the basement. "We aren't going to do that anymore," Paul said. "It's not convenient. One weekend we are about to make a wood run, and then somebody gives us tickets to the Bullets game. The next weekend Molly has to visit her mother in Maryland. I met this firewood dealer down on H Street who said he could supply us with split and dried wood for $135 a cord. That's a bargain when you consider that our time is worth something, too. We still save some money by getting our kindling and small pieces from dead oak trees in the park."

When I heard the price, I told Paul the best thing he could do with the woodstove was stuff rags in the flue pipe and use the cast-iron box as a coffee table. The elm he was buying for $135 had the same energy value as 20,000 cubic feet of natural gas, which he could get for $80. Falcone's gas furnace delivers not only cheaper heat but also cleaner and less troublesome heat. The flue pipe on the gas furnace doesn't have to be cleared of creosote every few weeks, and he doesn't need to put natural gas in his station wagon and then lug the gas into the basement to dry.

Paul and Molly Falcone made an all-too-typical gesture in the name of energy conservation. They spent $1,000 on a woodstove installation for the chance to burn fuel that was one-third more expensive than the fuel they already used. And, to make matters worse, they managed to burn the expensive fuel while consuming more of the cheaper gas than before. But their friends complimented and admired them.

There is no accurate way to determine how many of the estimated 5 million woodstove owners have replaced lower-priced utility-company heat with higher-priced wood heat. The Wood Energy Institute, a kind of woodburner's lobby, commissioned the Gallup poll to ask stove and fireplace owners a series of burning questions. Gallup concluded that 42 percent of the owners cut their own wood, while 36 percent decided, like Falcone, that it's easier to buy wood. Some in the 36 percent group are losing money, but wood is not always more expensive than competing fuels. I suspect that the losers are concentrated in urban areas, where neophyte stove owners are willing to pay a premium price for prepared stacks of logs. Based on information I got from Curtis Mildner, a wood specialist for the New England Regional Commission, I devised the tables on pages 175–176 that show any woodstove enthusiast whether he gains or loses on his woodburning, relative to consuming electricity, oil, or natural gas. The first table lays out the BTU value of various kinds of wood; the second, the equivalent amount of fossil fuel, or electricity, it takes to produce the same amount of heat. The third compares prices. If anything, these tables are too kind to wood because they assume that a woodstove burns its fuel as economically as a heater or furnace. In fact, woodstoves are 40 to 60 percent efficient (that is to say, they waste up to 60 percent of the heating value of the wood) while furnaces are 60 to 85 percent efficient.

From the third table, one can see where Falcone made his mistake. He was paying $135 a cord for medium-quality firewood, and his utility was charging only 30¢ per therm for natural gas. At that price, he should pay only $54 for the firewood. Even if gas prices increased to 75¢ per therm, Falcone would only break even on his $135 medium-quality firewood.

Firewood is a better investment relative to electricity, which is so expensive that almost any competing fuel is a bargain. But wood may or may not be a good investment relative to oil. Hundreds of thousands of log-splitting converts crowded the woodstove market in the late 1970s, bringing a dormant industry back to life. The vast percentage of these new woodstove converts lived in New England, where surging oil prices made wood immediately attractive. Before 1979, well-cured firewood of medium quality routinely sold for less than $60 a cord. Firewood companies are small, neighborhood outfits that

THE HEATING VALUE OF COMMON TYPES OF
FIREWOOD, MEASURED IN BTUS PER CORD

(This chart is based on the assumption that the wood is dry. If it is green, or incompletely cured, reduce heating values by 20 percent.)

Highest Heat Value. 28–30 million BTUs per cord.
Apple, black birch, black locust, hickory, hop hornbeam, white oak.

High Heat Value. 25–26 million BTUs per cord.
Ash, beech, red oak, sugar maple, yellow birch.

Medium Heat Value. 21–23 million BTUs per cord.
Black cherry, elm, gray birch, red maple, tamarack, white birch.

Low Heat Value. 13–17 million BTUs per cord.
Alder, balsam fir, basswood, cedar, hemlock, poplar, spruce, white pine.

SOURCE: New England Regional Commission

AMOUNTS OF OIL, GAS, OR ELECTRICITY IT TAKES
TO PRODUCE SAME AMOUNT OF HEAT AS WOOD

Highest Heat Value. One cord of wood equals:
  191 gallons of home heating oil
  228 therms of natural gas
5,020 kilowatt-hours of electricity

High Heat Value. One cord of wood equals:
  176 gallons of home heating oil
  211 therms of natural gas
4,600 kilowatt-hours of electricity

Medium Heat Value. One cord of wood equals:
  150 gallons of home heating oil
  180 cubic feet of natural gas
3,971 kilowatt-hours of electricity

Low Heat Value. One cord of wood equals:
  108 gallons of home heating oil
  129 therms of natural gas
2,800 kilowatt-hours of electricity

WHEN WOOD IS AND ISN'T A BARGAIN RELATIVE TO OIL, GAS, AND ELECTRIC HEAT

At the following prices for oil, gas, and electricity, you break even if you pay these corresponding prices for a cord of wood. If you pay less for wood, you gain; if you pay more, you lose.

	Heating Value of Wood			
	Highest	High	Medium	Low
Oil heat at $1 per gallon	$191 per cord	$176	$150	$108
$1.50 per gallon	$286	$264	$225	$162
$2 per gallon	$382	$352	$300	$216
Gas heat at 30¢ per therm	$68 per cord	$63	$54	$38
50¢ per therm	$114	$105	$90	$64
75¢ per therm	$171	$158	$135	$97
Electricity at 4¢ per kwh	$200 per cord	$184	$159	$112
7¢ per kwh	$351	$322	$277	$196
10¢ per kwh	$502	$402	$397	$280

are not supposed to behave like an oil cartel; the fragmented market of competing dealers was expected to keep prices down.

But according to Curtis Mildner, who investigated firewood prices for the New England Regional Commission, the expectation was ill founded. "Firewood," he says, "began to behave like international gold. Prices skyrocketed, especially in urban areas, after the 1979 oil price hikes. The extent of the increase surprised me. I talked to some of the firewood dealers. Even the unsophisticated ones knew exactly how much oil their firewood would replace. They were starting to peg the value of the firewood to the value of equivalent amounts of oil. OPEC price movements reached even those dealers wielding one chain saw in rural Massachusetts."

The demand for firewood slackened somewhat in 1980, and prices came down. Mildner predicts a volatile market, with short-term prices depending on whether firewood dealers overcut or undercut in anticipation of the demand for the next winter. In the long term he guesses that firewood prices will continue to track oil and other equivalent fuel prices. The Wood Energy Institute estimates that 1.2 million homeowners will buy woodstoves in the near future. If the current division between wood cutters and wood buyers holds up, about half of these new people will be lining up at the firewood dealer's door or truck. Fireplaces will also add to the pressure on wood supplies. They are popular items in new construction, even though they are big energy losers. By the end of the decade, the nation may contain more than 6 million woodstoves and 18 to 20 million fireplaces.

Many investors are buying up timberland, anticipating that wood demand will remain strong and that the natural resource will continue to increase in value faster than inflation. Mildner thinks the firewood industry will become more sophisticated and probably more centralized. Nobody doubts that supplies are available to meet demand, but the industry is not set up to exploit the resource. New recovery techniques will be needed as old firewood sources are depleted and firewood is hauled from harder-to-reach forest areas. A less fragmented industry would only put more upward pressure on prices.

So unless you are a Palmer and enjoy cutting wood to save money, you should investigate the local firewood market very carefully before concluding that wood is a bargain. Once you lose interest in the woodstove hobby, you may be tempted to avoid the work involved by paying for ready-to-burn wood, which is when you lose your advantage. The easier it is to get wood into the stove, the more the price of wood approaches that of oil.

If you still think you're more like Palmer than Falcone, here is the accumulated wisdom on buying and maintaining a woodstove:

1. Choosing a Woodstove. In *The Wood-Burning Stove Book* (Macmillan, 1977), Geri Harrigan writes: "It is not surprising that no spectacular changes have been made in stoves since our grandfathers." Actually it does seem surprising, after reading some of the new manufacturers' publicity brochures. Like solar water heater manufacturers, the makers of woodstoves have tried to take a simple, old-fashioned product and hype it with technical jargon about secondary combustion, extensive baffling, and complete burning of gases in the volatile stages. Woodburning is not like computer programming. It puts sap on the palms, soot on the floor, and creosote in the chimney, and its success depends on the intuition and a pioneering knack for controlling fires. Whatever anybody says, a woodstove performance depends more on the owner, less on the manufacturer.

There are four basic *types* of stoves, and the distinctions between them are worth careful attention. There are important differences in the amount of heat you get from each type, but not so much from the various brands within each type. The four types are:

A. Leaky Boxes. This category includes Franklin stoves, chunk stoves, potbellies, sheet-metal stoves, and parlor stoves. All of them tend to be loosely constructed, and you can often see the flames through cracks in the doors, even when the doors are closed. The leaks are necessary, because they provide air for combustion. Actually, they provide too much air for combustion, but there is no way to control and damp down the fire so that it burns cooler and longer. So much useful heat escapes up the chimney in these stoves that their overall efficiency is only 20 to 40 percent. That is twice as good as a regular fireplace, as we will see, but not as good as a tight woodstove.

Benjamin Franklin, who invented the type of open, leaky stove that carries his name, put his enormous intelligence to work trying to improve the stove's efficiency relative to the tight Scandinavian competitors. He failed. Scandinavian stoves and other tight wood-stoves still throw off the same heat for half the wood, just as they did in Franklin's day.

B. Tight Boxes. This category includes all the airtight stoves—Scandinavians; damper-controlled, U.S.-made stoves like the Fisher; thermostatically controlled stoves like the Ashley; downdraft stoves; and stoves with two heat chambers for secondary combustion. The airtights can be made of cast iron or plate steel, and they are manufactured in a variety of shapes and sizes by more than a hundred companies here and abroad. They share two important characteristics. They are radiant stoves—that is, the heat is given off directly from the metal box itself—and they are carefully constructed to eliminate air leaks. You can't see the fire through the cracks in the door, as you can in some Franklins. The only air that enters the firebox comes through the dampers, which are either manually or thermostatically operated.

Because the air intake can be regulated in tight stoves, the heat of the fire can also be controlled. A tight stove can burn for more hours on less wood than a leaky stove, and less heat is lost up the chimney or flue. The overall efficiency of airtight stoves falls in the 40 to 65 percent range.

As I mentioned, the performance of an airtight stove depends on the operator and his skill at putting in the right kinds of wood in the right amounts at the right time. Some sellers of stoves say that performance depends on some special feature that their brand of stove possesses. The favorite differentiating feature is called "secondary combustion."

In stoves with the feature, the wood isn't supposed to simply burn up in the metal box, sending smoke and exhaust gases up through the chimney. The exhaust gases are routed back through the stove where they too can be ignited. Theoretically, a great deal of extra heat can be generated from this form of secondary combustion. The trick is to get a stove at once hot enough to burn the excess gases (which requires more air) and cold enough to offer efficient, long-lasting fires (which requires less air).

Various stoves offer special baffles, extra passageways, double-decker heat chambers, or reverse heat flow patterns called down-drafts to produce superior secondary combustion. Mildner's personal response on the issue: "Manufacturers just guess about the nature of combustion and the extent of combustion. They express their guesses in sales brochures. Most are misleading, if not fraudulent, in claims about stoves. The bottom line is that there is not much difference in efficiency from one airtight stove to another."

Mildner also says the manufacturers make exaggerated claims about the length of time their stoves will burn without refueling. Some stoves supposedly burn for ten to twelve hours on a full load of wood. But to get that kind of performance, the damper has to be almost completely closed, so the fire burns at a very low temperature. Even in the unlikely event that a stove could hold a flame for twelve hours, the result is excessive creosote buildup in the flue pipe from inadequate combustion. Most airtights can burn from four to six hours without difficulty.

Another differentiating feature is the type of metal the stove is made of—cast iron or plate steel. Cast iron is heavy and holds heat very well, but it cracks easily if hit with a hard object. Plate steel is lighter and makes a more portable stove, but it doesn't retain heat as long as cast iron.

Mildner says both cast iron and plate steel give about the same range of efficiencies. The quality of welding and the workmanship in any stove is more important than the type of metal used.

The big difference in the various brands and models of airtight stoves is price. Some stoves cost from $300 to $400; other stoves of similar design cost from $400 to $600. The prices depend on whether the model is domestic or foreign, whether it has fancy drawings on the side of the box, and so forth. Higher prices do not mean that the stove will give you more heat on less wood.

C. Boxes within Boxes. These are the circulating stoves. They consist of an inner firebox surrounded by an air passage, so that a flow of air is created down one side of the stove, around the bottom, and up the other side. Circulating stoves look like regular gas space heaters, and their outer surfaces do not get red-hot like the surfaces of radiant airtight stoves. The fireboxes are also quite large, and they hold more wood and burn for a few hours longer than some airtights.

If you want greater reach from your stove, you will probably be more satisfied with the circulating type. Some have blowers to push the warm air even farther. Some have thermostats to regulate the air intake and the rate of combustion. The range of efficiencies for circulating stoves is about the same as for airtight radiant stoves. Again brand names and combustion features are not as important to fuel economy as how you operate the stove.

D. *Wood Furnaces*. These are forestry's answer to central heating. Wood furnaces have been around for a few years and are accepted in certain states, although fire codes in other states still prohibit their use. Wood furnaces do the same job as, say, an oil furnace in the basement. They can be connected to hot-water radiators or to warm-air ducts. The water or air is heated with wood, instead of oil, in a large firebox.

Wood furnaces, however, are much more trouble than oil heaters, requiring a hundred times as many trips to the basement. The fire must be fed, the ash box cleaned out, the heat exchanger scraped of creosote deposits. Existing wood furnaces do have thermostats, but they are certainly not fully automated. A load of wood may last as long as twelve hours, but not much longer.

The advantage of a small woodstove is that it allows you to spot-heat certain occupied areas of a house and let the rest stay cold. Since a central furnace heats the entire house, a central wood furnace will consume much more wood. You need to buy twice as much wood to feed one of these big fireboxes as you would for one or even two woodstoves. A careful price comparison with traditional fuels is even more important here. Obviously, a large supply of cheap wood is imperative.

A multifuel furnace can switch back and forth between oil or gas and wood, depending on what is cheaper in any given heating season or even in any given week. Such furnaces offer a certain amount of security in times when fuel shortages might occur. On the other hand, conversion from a standard oil or gas furnace to one of these multifuel types could cost several thousand dollars, and handling wood is still hard work.

2. Choosing the Wood. Some firewood dealers are honest. Others take advantage of the ignorance of new customers. They don't lie, they just exploit a semantic opportunity inherent in the word "cord."

A full cord of wood is 128 cubic feet, or a stack eight feet long, four feet high, and four feet wide. But when a dealer sells you a "cord of wood," he may be describing a face cord, which is also eight feet long and four feet high, but contains pieces of varying length. A face cord has less wood than a full cord, and accordingly should be priced less.

If the dealer is even less exacting, he will sell you "about a cord." About a cord can be anything from one-quarter to one-half of a full cord. About a cord is often delivered in a half-ton pick-up truck whose box can hold only 40 to 50 percent of a full cord.

"Dry wood" is another term with a variety of possible connotations. Dry wood might have been cut two weeks ago or six months ago, but the difference in heating value in the two instances can be substantial. It takes heat energy to burn off the moisture in wet wood, which is why wet wood provides only 80 percent of the heat of dry or seasoned wood. Wood should be aged for at least six months before it can reasonably be termed "dry."

Even if the wood is dry, it will give off varying amounts of heat depending on the type of tree it comes from (see the table on page 175). High-heat-value hardwoods should be more expensive by 40 to 50 percent than low-heat-value softwoods like pine, which not only provide less heat but also gum up the flue pipe with more creosote. The business of identifying trees from the characteristics of logs is quite esoteric. If you are a newcomer to all this, I suggest you find an old-time woodburner who can accompany you to the firewood dealer and advise you on what you are getting.

3. Choosing the Installer. Installation is critical to efficient wood-stove performance, not to mention safe woodstove operation. Flue pipes must be properly sized, and they must extend a certain number of feet above the roof line. Then, too, the walls and floor around the stove have to be fireproofed. Some insurance companies see new woodstove installations as potentially so dangerous that they refuse to insure houses that acquire them. You should talk to your local insurance agent before you spend money on a woodstove, because you could lose some of your fuel savings in the higher insurance rates.

In any event, the chances of fire are greatly reduced when the stove is correctly installed. Palmer found an installer with many years of experience, recommended by the neighbors who had woodstoves. I would not rely on intuition and the Yellow Pages to find a person to do the job.

4. Choosing a Source of Supply. Nobody knows how many fireplaces and woodstoves the country could support, though the saturation point certainly hasn't been approached. Just a hundred years ago, the country got 75 percent of its heat energy from wood. Now, wood provides only about 1 percent.

Woodburning enthusiasts say that the national demand for firewood can be met with small trees, fallen trees, and scrub lumber that should be thinned out of forests, anyway. They say all the woodstoves and fireplaces can be supplied without the cutting of any big trees used in building construction.

The experience in New England, where most of the woodstoves are located, indicates that the problem lies not in the theoretical but in the practical supply. The increase in the demand for wood in New England over the last three years caused spot shortages in certain areas, and as with oil, these shortages put upward pressure on wood prices.

Small firewood dealers do not always have access to large expanses of timberland, either public or private. Various state and local governments have tried to open up new lands to spot-cutting and thinning for firewood through cut-a-cord programs and through monetary incentives to timberland owners. The results have been encouraging, but the programs are still small.

I'm not suggesting that the nation will run out of firewood, but availability in any area depends on the structure of the firewood industry and its access to woodland. Before you buy a woodstove, check with your state or local energy office to see if they have done an inventory on wood supply sources. Ask the people who sell firewood where they get it and what they see as future supplies. Ask other woodstove owners whether they have had problems obtaining firewood, and if prices fluctuate wildly as local supplies expand and contract. Supply-demand ratios in your area will have considerable bearing on whether wood is priced competitively with oil, gas, or electricity.

5. Avoid Contagious Fantasy. If you decide to buy a woodstove and cut your own wood, based on fantastic results reported by neighbors, you may be headed for a big disappointment. People who brag that they have saved $500 on one year's operation of a woodstove tend to leave out some important expenses—such as the cost of extra insurance for the house, the smoke detector, the two visits from the chimney sweep, the repair on the chain saw, the gas for the chain saw, the axe-sharpening, the cradle for the wood, the fireplace tools, the gas for the car on wood foraging trips, and so forth. Such expenses can make or break a woodstove investment. Make sure you get a full accounting, especially if the proselytizers are recent woodstove converts who, like Palmer, have fallen deeply in love with the log pile.

Fireplace Folly

Eighteen million open fireplaces are proof of America's continuing fascination with visible flame. Even in Benjamin Franklin's day, the Europeans knew that a fireplace was a hopelessly wasteful way to make heat. Franklin tried to cross European woodstove efficiency (they didn't have as much wood to burn over there) with the New World campfire fetish by inventing a woodstove with folding doors. The resulting device, mentioned before, was the Franklin stove.

Most Americans even then were unwilling to compromise, and their descendants still like their open fireplaces, wasteful or not. My parents have a large masonry fireplace in their house in North Georgia. My father is tired of cutting twelve cords of wood every year to feed it, and he knows that a woodstove would reduce his burden by half. My mother, however, refuses to give up the aesthetics of the roaring fire at any cost.

I have been quietly sending my father information to bolster his side of the argument. Fireplaces have never been famous for energy economy, their fatal defect being that they draw up to ten times more air than is needed to keep the wood burning. That huge draft sends 80 to 85 percent of the wood heat up the chimney. Without the chimney losses, a standard fireplace could serve as the solitary heat source in most houses. The heat output from wood is about 100,000 BTUs an hour, which is equal to the output from most gas or oil furnaces. But as I say, 80 to 85 percent of the heat goes up the chimney to warm the great outdoors.

A 15 to 20 percent overall efficiency is bad enough. A recent study by the Lawrence Berkeley Laboratory says that fireplace performance is really even worse than that. The lab found a way to measure the secondary losses from fireplaces. The fireplace exhausts huge quantities of air up one stack. The resulting draft creates a low-pressure system in the house, a miniature version of what you see on weather maps. That area of low pressure, which is to say the inside of your house, attracts more cold air, which enters your dwelling through the now-familiar cracks around windows and doors and through other leaky places. The fireplace thus helps to engender infiltration and therefore creates more work for the furnace.

When you add the infiltration losses into already dismal fireplace performance, real efficiency drops to 5 to 6 percent of the heating value of the wood, according to Lawrence Berkeley. Without the cooling effect of the onrushing air, a fireplace may send 20,000 BTUs an hour into the living room; with the cooling effect, which adds about 15,000 BTUs an hour to the heating burden, the net contribution of the fireplace is 5,000 BTUs an hour. The fireplace is therefore the most wasteful heating device on the American market.

There is more bad news. Unless the damper is very tightly closed when the fireplace is not in use (most dampers are leaky even in the closed position), even the paltry 5 percent fireplace contribution may be wiped out. A leaky damper can rob the furnace or air conditioner of enough BTUs to turn the fireplace into an annual energy loser. So in addition to all the wood he buys, a fireplace owner is paying more in heating and air conditioning bills with his hearth than without it.

My father used these arguments in a renewed plea to plug up the fireplace and make the chimney hole into the flue pipe of a 50 percent efficient woodstove. My mother insisted that any person with a sense of beauty would never substitute an ugly, black metal box for a fireplace. My parents searched for a point of compromise. Like thousands of other families facing the same dilemma, they settled on glass doors. In fact, there is an entire industry built on the idea that you

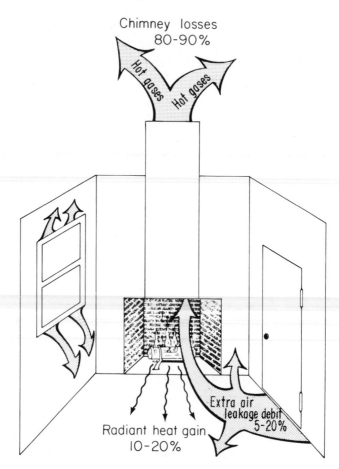

can salvage the open fireplace and make it pay—with special grates, blowers, and glass doors that enclose the flame but don't obscure it.

My parents bought their glass doors before the winter of 1980. The result was that my father still cut twelve cords of wood, the same amount as before.

My suspicions aroused, I contacted Lawrence Berkeley and also Dr. Jay Shelton of Shelton Energy Research, one of the few academics who have done extensive studies on fireplace performance. Shelton and Berkeley essentially agreed with each other—and with my father. Glass doors don't do much for fireplaces. Neither do those tubular, heat-boosting grates.

"It seems unlikely," says Shelton in a publication called *Measured*

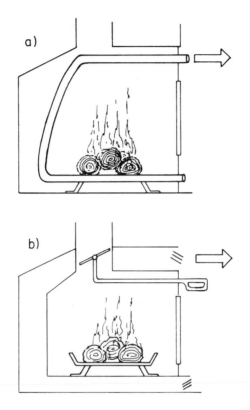

Combination Fireplace Accessories:
a) C-shaped Convector with Glass Doors
b) Shell-within-a-Shell Convector with Glass Doors and Adjustable Damper

Performance of Fireplaces and Fireplace Accessories, "that use of any glass doors on any operating plain masonry fireplace would result in an increase in net energy efficiency. . . . The reduction in heat output is far greater than the energy saved by reducing air flow up the chimney."

Lawrence Berkeley tested a glass-door addition to a fireplace and concluded that such doors add very little on to the fireplace's poor efficiency. Perhaps they improve the fuel utilization by 3 percent. In other words, for every $100 worth of firewood you buy, you get $6 worth of usable heat without the glass doors and $9 worth of heat with them. Glass doors do stop some of the warm indoor air from flowing up the chimney. This is especially useful at night, when the

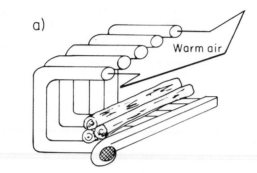

a)

Warm air

b)

c)

Warm air

Fireplace Accessories:
a) C-shaped Convector
b) Glass Doors
c) Horizontal Tube Convector

fire is dying. Unfortunately, they also prevent some of the fireplace heat from flowing into the room, which makes for a kind of thermal standoff.

The Lawrence Berkeley scientists also looked at some varieties of tubular grates, those C-shaped metal frames that are inserted into a fireplace. Some manufacturers of such grates claim big energy savings. The tubes that comprise the structure of the grate are hollow, with the fire built on top of the tubes in the middle of the grate. Cold room air enters the tube openings below, is heated by the fire, and is then forced out the tube openings above into the room. The natural convection supposedly adds to the supply of usable heat. But in the Lawrence Berkeley tests, the grates contributed only 1 to 2 percent to the fireplace's efficiency. In other words, they will save you about $1 or $2 for every $100 worth of wood burned.

Grates are also sold with blowers, or extensions that presumably push even more warm air into a room. Lawrence Berkeley says the blowers boost the grate's performance by perhaps an extra 3 to 4 percent. A more elaborate grate with an extension can save you about $7 for every $100 worth of wood bought and burned.

Glass doors and tubular grates are not very effective, Lawrence Berkeley says, because each attacks only half a problem. The grates may send more hot air into the house, but they don't keep the cold air from escaping out the chimney; the glass doors create the reverse effect.

The two products can be fused together in a single device, and the grate-and-glass combinations come in two designs. One is a C-shaped grate with glass doors at the open end, and the other is a special insert firebox that makes a shell within the shell of the fireplace (see the illustration on page 187). In both, the glass doors serve as a barrier to heat flowing out of the house. Meanwhile, cold air can still reach the fire either through the hollow tubes or through a passageway in the second metal shell. Heated air returns to the room from the top of the tubes or the top of the shell.

The combination devices cost as much as $600. Lawrence Berkeley tests show that they routinely improve fireplace efficiency by 10 to 12 percent, and therefore save $10 to $12 for every $100 spent on wood. That's a slight improvement over an open fireplace, but it still doesn't approach woodstove efficiency.

One shell-within-a-shell arrangement, with a damper, got a 31 percent efficiency rating from the lab. That is the best of any of the grates, glass doors, or combinations. But even with this modification, a fireplace gives you worse fuel economy than the worst oil heater, 100 percent worse than the standard oil or gas heater, while burning twice as much wood as the standard woodstove. If a woodstove is only marginally competitive, anyway, you can imagine how expensive wood gets when used in a fireplace that puts only 30 percent of the heat produced into your house. Consider the case of my friend Palmer. With oil at $1 a gallon, he can break even with his woodstove when wood is priced at $150 a cord. If he had a 30 percent efficient fireplace, he would lose money using it with wood at $75 a cord.

Other experts might quibble over the numbers, but the bottom line here is that people who modify fireplaces to save wood and to preserve the sight of dancing flames are fighting a losing battle. My father is now convinced that no point of compromise exists between the aesthetic and the economic position. He will continue to cut twelve cords until his complaints about an aching back overmatch the pleasure my mother takes in open fires.

A fireplace, in other words, is a luxury—an energy-guzzling luxury, like a big car. If you want to burn wood for economy or for spartan virtue, burn it in a woodstove. If you want to burn wood for

FIREPLACE PERFORMANCE CHART

Device	For Every $100 Spent on Wood, How Much Heat Gets into the House?
Untreated fireplace (masonry, prefab metal, brick, etc.)	$5–6
Fireplace with glass doors	$6–10
Fireplace with simple grates (tubular grates, radiant grates, other energy-saving grates)	$6–10
Fireplace with extended grates or grates with blowers	$8–13
Fireplace with combination grate and glass doors	$10–18
Fireplace with shell-within-shell modification, including damper	$30
Woodstove	$40–60

SOURCE: Lawrence Berkeley Laboratory

the thrill of a roaring fire, make sure you enjoy the view. You are paying for it with a vengeance.

Burning Coal

Anthracite coal, a low-sulfur, clean-burning solid fuel, is enjoying a household revival. Its appeal is price. Anthracite can be bought for $70 to $110 a ton, depending on how far it has to be shipped from the coalfields, most of which are located in eastern Pennsylvania. A ton of this coal is equivalent to at least a cord of good firewood, which now costs as much as $150. Even at $100 a ton, a price that many residential coal customers paid last year, anthracite makes cheaper heat than wood, oil, electricity, and possibly natural gas.

One can apply the BTU yardstick for a more definitive local comparison. Since 25 million BTUs of heat is generated from a ton of anthracite, the cost of 1 million BTUs can be calculated by dividing the price of a ton by 25. For instance, coal at $100 a ton produces 1 million BTUs for $4. That's a bargain relative to oil at $1.20 a gallon (or $8.60 for a million BTUs), to electricity at 6¢ per kilowatt-hour ($17.58 for a million BTUs), or to natural gas at 60¢ a therm ($6 for a million BTUs). In the Northeast last year, you could keep warm on anthracite for half the money it took to keep warm on oil.

Bituminous coal, the softer and sootier kind, is even cheaper than anthracite and is generally more available. But bituminous is a notorious pollutant, and although it is used for residential stoves and furnaces in some parts of the country, it is not recommended as a source of home heat. Even with its modest recent increase in popularity, coal is already facing opposition from environmentalists. Some state and local governments are considering pollution control standards that would restrict or prohibit the burning of the dirtier coal. Unless new stoves or furnaces are manufactured to take care of the pollutants internally, anthracite is the coal that people with neighbors should choose.

But what happened to last year's anthracite supply after consumers learned of the cost advantage is a sobering reminder that too many takers can spoil a bargain. There is plenty of anthracite coal in the ground—17 billion tons of it by some estimates—but coal companies have stopped mining it in great quantities and they don't keep a reserve supply. Last winter the sellers were unprepared for the surge in demand, especially for the "chestnut" and "stove" sizes of coal that fit into residential furnaces and stoves. Some homeowners who converted to coal (100,000 to 300,000 coal-burning stoves and furnaces were sold in 1979, according to various estimates) got caught in the shortfall and were forced to find other sources of heat. Anthracite was unavailable in some parts of the Northeast at any price, and where there was coal, the price tended to increase. The coal rush of 1980 is sadly reminiscent of the wood rush of 1979, when high demand and a clumsy delivery system drove the price of that popular fuel so high that incipient woodburners began to think about switching to coal.

The supply-demand situation is something of a Catch 22. As reported in the December 1980 issue of *Wood 'n' Energy,* a professional solid-fuel journal, the big coal companies are wary of investing the capital necessary to revive the anthracite market until they are sure that homeowners will respond. Some of the coal companies lost money after the oil embargo in 1973 by preparing for a coal revival that didn't occur. But homeowners who learned of last winter's shortages aren't likely to run out to buy expensive coal furnaces until they are convinced that the industry will increase supply. Each side may cannily wait for the other to move.

The anthracite supply problem is compounded by the fact that it is impossible to mine only those sizes of coal that are used in stoves and furnaces. For every ton of "chestnut" coal that comes out of the mine, four tons of smaller nuggets are also scooped up. Coal companies have to find a market for these extra four tons before their efforts become very profitable, which means that expansion in the residential market may depend on increased coal demand from utilities and heavy industries that can use the smaller chunks.

So the first rule of residential coal-burning, given this tricky supply situation, is don't buy the furnace before you find an assured source of coal to put in it. Investigate the local suppliers carefully to determine if they have a plentiful source, and ask what steps have been taken to avoid shortages in the future.

Second, make sure that no prohibitions on coal-burning are being contemplated in your state or locality. It would be frustrating to invest in all that new equipment and then be told you couldn't use it.

Third, find a competent source of advice, preferably from a stove company that has been in business for a number of years and has a reliable history of serving local customers. The parallels with the woodstove business are instructive. The recent coal revival has created dozens of new coal-burning stove and furnace companies that make small stoves, add-on furnaces, and central units. The characteristics of each type of furnace and stove are different: a good anthracite-burning model will not work well with bituminous fuel, and vice versa. Coal stoves are potentially more hazardous than woodstoves because coal burns hotter and because the smoke and gases released in the exhaust can be very poisonous. Coal stoves require heavier fireboxes made of cast iron; if a lighter metal is used, the fireboxes must be lined with brick or some other material that keeps heat away from the metal surfaces. The chimney or flue systems have to be constructed of insulated pipe, and getting just the right amount of draft is even more important with coal than it is with wood. It is possible to make a woodstove into a coal stove, but only certain types of woodstoves can burn coal safely. You have to find an installer with adequate training and experience or else you can burn yourself up.

Like some of the manufacturers of woodstoves, a number of sellers of coal-burning equipment try to survive in a competitive market by making unsubstantiated claims of efficiency. One common claim is that a coal stove or furnace is 90 percent efficient, as opposed to a woodstove, which is presumed to be only about 50 percent efficient. C. H. Anthony, a fuel combustion engineer who writes for *Wood 'n' Energy*, distrusts the 90 percent figure: "to the best of the author's experience and knowledge, no U.S.-made coal stove has yet been tested for efficiency in a laboratory qualified to do this testing. Figures in advertisements have indicated efficiencies of up to 90 percent. There is no basis in fact for these figures."

Many of the new coal customers are making only a partial commitment to that fuel, using it as an auxiliary or backup to wood or oil. They burn their coal in woodstoves that have been adapted for the cheaper solid fuel, or in add-on devices that attach to large wood or oil furnaces. The dual-fuel capability is important insurance, especially where there are doubts about future supply. But this insurance can also bring some sacrifice in efficiency of the furnace or stove involved. Anthony points out that it is impossible to design a stove or furnace to burn coal and wood equally well, so when one buys a dual-purpose heater, one may not be getting the most for one's money out of either fuel that the heater consumes.

Burning coal in a small stove can also be messy and irksome. Bagged coal, wood chips, and compressed coal logs are beginning to be sold as convenience items for people who are exasperated with the real stuff, but this packaged or processed coal is uniformly more expensive than oil or gas, which brings us back to the woodstove paradox. Some people who cut their own wood for the price break have turned to precut wood for the convenience, and as a result they spend more money than they would have if they had stuck to the conventional fuels. The same thing can happen with coal.

The most sensible way to use coal seems to be in the fully automated central heating systems that are coming back into style. Such systems were installed in millions of American homes up until the 1950s, so there is no doubt that they work. The idea is to feed the coal into the furnace automatically from the coal bin, so that human hands never come into contact with the sooty stuff. There are automated central coal heaters for bituminous and anthracite, and the ones that burn the latter coal also shake and process the ashes automatically. With bituminous coal, the unburned chunks, or clinkers, must be removed manually with tongs.

For coal use to increase significantly, industry people believe, the public has to start buying big basement coal furnaces in preference to oil or gas furnaces. Then homeowners can purchase bulk coal in enough quantity to keep a winter's supply in the basement and to get a good price. But until the production problems are resolved, one can give coal-burning at best a lukewarm endorsement.

Part Seven

HOW TO BUY
A HOUSE
FOR
ENERGY

Real estate people tell me there are two ways the smart buyers protect themselves after they have fallen in love with a house and before the deal is closed. They can ask for three kinds of inspections —termite, roof, and appliances, to determine whether the place is safe and sound. Then they can ask for a list of expenses—taxes, mortgage, insurance, closing costs—to find out if they can afford to live there.

Energy is left out of the formalities, and information sheets that real estate agents hand out don't commonly include any category like "annual energy costs." Yet energy is the biggest operating expense after the mortgage, and also one that varies wildly from house to house. A buyer could ask all the standard questions about two 1,500-square-foot houses in the suburbs of Chicago, both of which are in similar condition. He would still not know that House A, which has R-19 in the ceiling and R-7 in the walls and double-glazed windows (the seller calls this an energy saver) is twice as expensive to heat and cool as House B, which has an R-38 ceiling and R-11 walls and is also called an energy saver.

House A produced a $1,300 energy bill in 1980, while House B was run for $675. Even if you project energy prices conservatively, the difference pulls $20,000 more out of the pocketbook of the owner of House A over twenty years, or $20,000 wasted. The additional expenditure of course brings no comfort or added value to the house.

While few people are willing to throw away $20,000 on anything else, they do it routinely in buying houses. In this instance, House A and House B were sold for the same price. The new owner of A has to either upgrade the energy efficiency, a proposition that will cost money, or accept the long-term penalty.

Some prospective buyers and sellers are beginning to sense that energy is a useful sales point. The results of recent surveys by Dow Chemical Company show that: (1) 78 percent of the real estate appraisers believe that a well-insulated house can now bring more money in the market; (2) 66 percent of real estate salespeople say the same; and (3) 83 percent of homeowners think that energy-saving features will add to the resale value of a property. These new attitudes, however, don't mean much unless they are connected to real numbers on appraisal forms or in the negotiations between buyer, lender, and seller. That is happening in the secondary mortgage market. Both the Federal Home Loan Mortgage Corporation and the Federal National Mortgage Association have revised their appraisal forms so that the appraiser must at least mention energy efficiency or the lack of it. The Federal Home Loan Mortgage Corporation has taken the more radical step of changing its purchasing guidelines to allow bigger loans for people who borrow on energy-efficient houses. The theory is that a family with lower energy bills will have more money to pay off the mortgage and will therefore constitute a better credit risk.

At the homeowner level, when the energy issue is brought up as an informal adjunct to the negotiations, it is sometimes handled by what I call the "one-feature finagle." I mean that some real estate agents can find a reason to call all of their houses energy savers, usually on the strength of one characteristic. In California or Florida, a hot little dwelling with enormous air conditioning bills can be sold as an energy saver because it has a solar water heater on the roof. In Minnesota or Massachusetts, a drafty old Victorian can be deemed "renovated for energy" because the owner put six inches of extra insulation in the attic. In Chicago or Portland, a house with most of its windows on the frigid north side can and will be described as energy efficient because the windows have double panes of glass. In Maine or Pittsburgh, a twenty-year-old furnace with leaky ducts may be advertised as "modified to save energy" because it has a vent damper.

The one-feature finagle is not necessarily a deliberate or cynical ploy. The lack of better information creates it. Buyers and sellers alike have no rating system to measure the energy performance of houses, and have no way to pin down elusive but consequential factors like the design of a house or its placement on the lot. So they concentrate on features, especially the insulation levels, since insulation is the most heavily promoted conservation product. It is as if there were no EPA mileage ratings for cars, and regular consumers had to guess the energy economy of the various models by comparing the carburetors and pistons.

Some sellers also attempt to prove the worth of their favorite energy features with a casual, offhanded, often low estimate of the yearly utility bill. Such estimates are as unreliable as the one-feature finagle, with people minimizing household energy consumption just as they do their physical weight. I was along on an audit where the customer lied to the auditor about his annual fuel bill. The homeowner later recanted when the auditor insisted that the figure was impossible in a big Massachusetts house with an old furnace. The customer's "about $500" estimate actually turned out to be $1,150. He said he had been too embarrassed to admit the real amount, even though it was critical to the auditor's calculations.

If home energy costs are occasionally understated to auditors, they are frequently understated to potential buyers of houses. An energy hog can easily be disguised behind one or two conservation features and some sloppy guesswork about the real costs of heating and cooling. The fact is that energy information, as currently presented in the real estate market, deceives as many buyers as it enlightens.

So what do you do if you're the buyer? There is a simple rating system that can be used in conjunction with the features-and-guess-work approach, and it's called dollars per square foot, the housing equivalent to miles per gallon. This rating takes the emphasis off the characteristics of a house and puts it on the annual energy performance, as shown in the actual utility bills, thereby making it possible to rate houses of different shapes and sizes by reducing total energy costs to dollars per square foot. Dollars per square foot is one energy yardstick touted in *The Realtor ®'s Guide to Residential Energy Efficiency*, an excellent manual produced by the Department of Energy in cooperation with the National Association of Realtors®.

"Now that the guidebook has been adopted," says Linda Schuck, a former Department of Energy official who directed the project, "we expect the dollars-per-square-foot idea to catch on." Norman Kaido, a New Jersey realtor and chairman of the association's energy committee, told me that "as many as 100,000 real estate salespeople are being trained to make intelligent judgments about the energy efficiency of houses," adding that dollars per square foot will be one of the measures that they use.

The beauty of dollars per square foot is that it is easy to compute. All you do is add up the energy bills for a house during any twelve-month period and then divide the total by the size of the house. For example, a 1,500-square-foot house with a gas heater and electric appliances that produced a twelve-month electric bill of $500 and a heating bill of $1,000 would have a rating of $1 per square foot. To get an accurate rating, it is important to include fuel bills from all sources of energy—electricity, gas, oil, propane, kerosene for auxiliary heaters, and wood for the fireplace. It is equally important to calculate the square footage only on the basis of the conditioned space of the house, the part artificially heated or cooled. Garages, unheated basements, and carports don't count, and would distort the ratings if included.

Dollars per square foot has one major defect, which is that it is tied to prices. This year's ratings will be different from next year's, since energy prices are certain to rise. But as long as energy costs are compared only for the same twelve-month period, the rating system has some practical advantage over the more technical alternative, BTUs per square foot. For one thing, many people don't know what a BTU is; for another, the dollar rating reflects the fact that an all-gas house is cheaper to operate than an all-electric. The BTU standard doesn't differentiate between types of fuel and does not take fuel costs into account.

A real estate agent can help you collect energy cost information from one or several sellers, and if the sellers haven't kept records, the information can usually be obtained from the utilities involved. With utility bills in hand, you can compute the annual energy costs. If you do enough houses, you can get a general sense of the range of efficiencies in your area; if you do only two or three, you will at least discover which of these is the most economical. You may want to measure the dollars-per-square-foot rating of a house you want to buy against the rating in the house you now occupy. That way, you will learn if you are moving up or down in energy efficiency.

Energy ratings can be further refined with some detective work about the former owner's thermostat habits. An inherently economi-

ZIP CODES AND CLIMATE ZONES

If your zip code begins with these three numbers,
your climate zone is:

010 7	060 7	118 5	165 7	215 6
011 7	061 7	119 5	166 7	216 4
012 8	062 7	120 7	167 7	217 5
013 7	063 6	121 7	168 7	218 4
014 7	064 7	122 7	169 7	219 5
015 7	065 7	123 8	170 6	220 5
016 7	066 6	124 7	171 6	221 5
017 7	067 7	125 6	172 6	222 5
018 6	068 6	126 6	173 6	223 5
019 6	069 6	127 7	174 6	224 4
020 6	070 6	128 8	175 6	225 4
021 6	071 6	129 8	176 6	226 5
022 6	072 6	130 7	177 6	227 5
023 6	073 6	131 7	178 6	228 5
024 6	074 6	132 7	179 6	229 4
025 6	075 6	133 7	180 6	230 4
026 6	076 6	134 7	181 6	231 4
027 6	077 6	135 7	182 7	232 4
028 7	078 7	136 8	183 6	233 3
029 7	079 6	137 8	184 7	234 3
030 7	080 5	138 8	185 7	235 3
031 7	081 5	139 8	186 7	236 3
032 8	082 5	140 7	187 7	237 3
033 8	083 5	141 7	188 7	238 4
034 8	084 5	142 7	189 7	239 4
035 8	085 6	143 8	190 6	240 4
036 8	086 6	144 7	191 5	241 4
037 8	087 6	145 7	193 5	242 5
038 8	088 6	146 7	194 5	243 4
040 8	089 6	147 7	195 6	244 4
041 8	090 6	148 7	196 6	245 4
042 8	100 6	149 7	197 5	246 6
043 8	103 5	150 6	198 5	247 6
044 8	104 5	151 6	199 5	248 6
045 7	105 6	152 6	200 4	249 6
046 7	106 6	153 6	202 4	250 4
047 8	107 5	154 6	203 4	251 4
048 7	108 6	155 7	204 4	252 4
049 8	109 6	156 6	205 4	253 4
050 8	110 5	157 6	206 4	254 4
051 8	111 5	158 8	207 4	255 4
052 8	112 5	159 6	208 4	256 4
053 8	113 5	160 6	209 4	257 4
054 8	114 5	161 6	210 5	258 6
056 8	115 5	162 6	211 5	259 6
057 8	116 5	163 7	212 5	260 6
058 8	117 5	164 7	214 4	261 5

ZIP CODES AND CLIMATE ZONES—*continued*

262 6	314 2	378 4	433 6	486 8
263 6	315 2	379 4	434 7	487 8
264 6	316 2	380 3	435 7	488 7
265 6	317 2	381 3	436 7	489 7
266 5	318 2	382 4	437 6	490 7
267 6	319 2	383 3	438 6	491 7
268 5	320 2	384 3	439 6	492 7
269 5	322 2	385 4	440 7	493 8
270 4	323 2	386 3	441 7	494 8
271 4	324 2	387 3	442 7	495 8
272 4	325 2	388 3	443 7	496 8
273 4	326 1	389 3	444 7	497 8
274 4	327 1	390 2	445 7	498 8
275 3	328 1	391 2	446 7	499 8
276 3	329 1	392 2	447 7	500 7
277 3	330 1	393 2	448 6	501 7
278 3	331 1	394 2	449 6	502 7
279 3	333 1	395 2	450 6	503 7
280 3	334 1	396 2	451 6	504 8
281 3	335 1	397 3	452 6	505 7
282 3	336 1	400 4	453 6	506 8
283 3	337 1	401 4	454 6	507 8
284 2	338 1	402 4	455 6	508 7
285 3	339 1	403 5	456 6	510 8
286 3	350 3	404 5	457 5	511 8
287 4	351 3	405 5	458 6	512 8
288 4	352 3	406 4	460 6	513 8
289 4	353 3	407 4	461 6	514 7
290 2	354 3	408 4	462 6	515 7
291 2	355 3	409 4	463 7	516 6
292 2	356 3	410 5	464 7	520 8
293 3	357 3	411 5	465 7	521 8
294 2	358 3	412 5	466 7	522 7
295 3	359 3	413 4	467 7	523 7
296 3	360 2	414 4	468 7	524 7
297 3	361 2	415 5	469 6	525 7
298 2	362 3	416 5	470 5	526 7
299 2	363 2	417 4	471 5	527 7
300 3	364 2	418 4	472 6	528 7
301 3	365 2	419 4	473 6	530 8
302 3	366 2	420 4	474 5	531 8
303 3	367 2	421 4	475 5	532 8
304 2	368 2	422 4	476 4	534 7
305 3	369 2	423 4	477 4	535 8
306 3	370 4	424 4	478 6	537 8
307 3	371 4	425 4	479 6	538 8
308 2	372 4	426 4	480 7	539 8
309 2	373 3	427 4	481 7	540 8
310 2	374 3	430 6	482 7	541 8
312 2	376 5	431 6	484 8	542 8
313 2	377 4	432 6	485 8	543 8

544	8	603	7	665	6	728	3	787	2
545	8	604	7	666	6	729	3	788	2
546	8	605	7	667	4	730	4	790	4
547	8	606	7	668	5	731	4	791	4
548	8	609	6	669	6	734	3	792	3
549	8	610	7	670	5	735	3	793	4
550	8	611	7	671	5	736	4	794	4
551	8	612	7	672	5	737	4	795	3
552	8	613	6	673	4	738	4	796	3
553	8	614	7	674	5	739	5	797	3
554	8	615	7	675	5	740	4	798	3
556	8	616	7	676	6	741	4	799	3
557	8	617	6	677	6	743	4	800	7
558	8	618	6	678	6	744	4	801	7
559	8	619	6	679	5	745	3	802	7
560	8	620	5	680	7	746	4	803	6
561	8	622	5	681	7	747	3	804	8
562	8	623	6	683	7	748	3	805	8
563	8	624	5	684	7	749	3	806	7
564	8	625	6	685	7	750	2	807	7
565	8	626	6	686	7	751	2	808	7
566	8	627	6	687	8	752	2	809	7
567	8	628	5	688	7	754	2	810	6
570	8	629	4	689	6	755	2	811	8
571	8	630	5	690	6	756	2	812	8
572	8	631	5	691	7	757	2	813	8
573	8	633	5	692	8	758	2	814	8
574	8	634	6	693	7	759	2	815	6
575	8	635	6	700	2	760	2	816	8
576	8	636	5	701	2	761	2	820	8
577	8	637	4	703	2	762	3	822	7
580	8	638	4	704	2	763	3	823	8
581	8	639	4	705	2	764	2	824	8
582	8	640	5	706	2	765	2	825	8
583	8	641	5	707	2	766	2	826	8
584	8	644	6	708	2	767	2	827	8
585	8	645	6	710	2	768	2	828	8
586	8	646	5	711	2	769	2	829	8
587	8	647	5	712	2	770	2	830	8
588	8	648	4	713	2	773	2	831	8
590	8	650	5	714	2	774	2	832	7
591	8	651	5	716	3	775	2	833	8
592	8	652	6	717	3	776	2	834	8
593	8	653	5	718	3	777	2	835	6
594	8	654	5	719	3	778	2	836	6
595	8	655	5	720	3	779	2	837	6
596	8	656	5	721	3	780	1	838	7
597	8	657	5	722	3	781	2	840	6
598	8	658	5	723	3	782	2	841	6
599	8	660	5	724	4	783	1	843	6
600	8	661	5	725	3	784	2	844	6
601	7	662	5	726	4	785	1	845	6
602	7	664	6	727	4	786	2	846	8

ZIP CODES AND CLIMATE ZONES—*continued*

847	7	884	4	918	2	945	3	976	7
850	2	890	2	920	2	946	3	977	7
852	2	891	2	921	2	947	3	978	6
853	2	893	8	922	2	948	3	979	6
855	3	894	7	923	2	949	3	980	4
856	2	895	7	924	2	950	2	981	4
857	2	897	7	925	3	951	2	982	6
859	6	898	8	926	2	952	3	983	5
860	8	900	2	927	2	953	3	984	5
863	5	902	2	928	2	954	3	985	6
864	3	903	2	930	2	955	5	986	7
865	6	904	2	931	2	956	3	988	7
870	4	905	2	932	2	957	3	989	6
871	4	906	2	933	2	958	3	990	7
873	6	907	2	934	2	959	2	991	7
874	6	908	2	935	2	960	4	992	7
875	7	910	2	936	3	961	7	993	6
877	7	911	2	937	3	970	5	994	6
878	6	912	2	939	2	971	5	995	8
879	4	913	2	940	3	972	5	996	8
880	4	914	2	941	3	973	5	997	8
881	4	915	2	943	3	974	5	998	8
882	3	916	2	944	3	975	5	999	8
883	5	917	2						

SOURCE: This material was taken from *Realtor®'s Guide to Residential Energy Efficiency,* a publication of the National Association of Realtors®.

cal structure can get bad dollars-per-square-foot marks because the occupants set the winter thermostat at 74. A poorly insulated and leaky structure can receive a good rating because the inhabitants set the winter thermostat at 55. At Princeton, the researchers discovered that one family might produce a dollars-per-square-foot rating of 50¢ while another family living in an identical house next door might produce a rating of $1.

So before you can be confident with the rating system, you have to make an intuitive judgment as to whether the occupants of the houses involved are profligate or careful with energy. Questions such as "Where do you set the thermostat in winter?" and "How much air conditioning do you need?" will give you clues enough to put the people in a guzzler or conserver category. If guzzlers live in a house with a very good dollars-per-square-foot rating, it means that the house is even more efficient than you may have thought; if compulsive conservers live in a house with a very poor rating, it means that

ENERGY COSTS PER SQUARE FOOT FOR HOUSE
(INCLUDES HOT WATER, HEATING, AND AIR CONDITIONING)

	With Electric Heat and Hot Water	With Gas Heat and Hot Water	With Oil Heat and Hot Water
Zone 1:			
Unreformed house*	$1.00	76¢	89¢
House with minimal energy features†	79¢	60¢	71¢
House with average energy features‡	62¢	47¢	56¢
House with excellent energy features§	41¢	29¢	38¢
Zone 2:			
Unreformed house	$1.36	69¢	90¢
House with minimal energy features	97¢	49¢	61¢
House with average energy features	66¢	34¢	41¢
House with excellent energy features	32¢	19¢	24¢
Zone 3:			
Unreformed house	$1.64	71¢	$1.13
House with minimal energy features	$1.20	53¢	83¢
House with average energy features	78¢	38¢	58¢
House with excellent energy features	27¢	23¢	41¢
Zone 4:			
Unreformed house	$1.97	76¢	$1.30
House with minimal energy features	$1.42	55¢	94¢
House with average energy features	91¢	40¢	67¢
House with excellent energy features	19¢	24¢	44¢
Zone 5:			
Unreformed house	$2.30	83¢	$1.34
House with minimal energy features	$1.67	61¢	$1.11
House with average energy features	$1.09	41¢	74¢

*No insulation or energy features.

†R-11 ceiling insulation, some caulking and weatherstripping.

‡R-19 ceiling insulation, R-7 walls, double-glazed windows, insulated ducts.

§R-38 ceiling insulation, R-19 walls, heat pump (if electric heat), double-glazed windows, insulated ducts.

	With Electric Heat and Hot Water	With Gas Heat and Hot Water	With Oil Heat and Hot Water
Zone 5:			
House with excellent energy features	58¢	31¢	60¢
Zone 6:			
Unreformed house	$2.56	89¢	$1.67
House with minimal energy features	$1.84	63¢	$1.17
House with average energy features	$1.21	44¢	82¢
House with excellent energy features	61¢	34¢	66¢
Zone 7:			
Unreformed house	$2.82	93¢	$1.80
House with minimal energy features	$2.02	65¢	$1.26
House with average energy features	$1.30	39¢	73¢
House with excellent energy features	69¢	35¢	70¢
Zone 8:			
Unreformed house	$3.44	$1.09	$2.18
House with minimal energy features	$2.46	78¢	$1.57
House with average energy features	$1.58	51¢	$1.02
House with excellent energy features	89¢	39¢	80¢

the house is less efficient than the numbers would imply. You have to use your own fudge factors on the utility bills you collect.

THE ENERGY AUDIT

Dollars-per-square-foot ratings work best in conjunction with an energy audit. Since auditors are now readily available, I'd get one before buying any house. Utilities, as I've said before, are required to perform audits at a homeowner's request, and a prospective buyer can encourage the seller to request one. Remember that simple termite inspections are just as expensive as what you pay out-of-pocket for a utility-sponsored energy audit, and termite damage may not be as costly over the long haul as an energy problem uncovered in a routine audit.

In fact, I can't think of a better way to organize a general structural review of a house. A good energy audit takes in the building from basement to attic. In other words, the audit will point you toward the trouble spots that may need fixing before you'd want to close any deal. It will also help you to determine whether the house's energy rating is what it is because of design, structure, or habits of the occupants.

Of course the audit, along with dollars per square foot, can strengthen your position in bargaining for a house, a prospect I alluded to earlier. This is, remember, new territory, but it is promising. Let's say you have evidence that a certain house is an energy guzzler. Even though the occupants leave the thermostat at reasonable levels and last year's winter was a mild one, the house produced a per-square-foot rating twice as high as anything else you have found in the area. Still, you can't resist buying the place. You get an energy audit, which shows that insulation levels are half what is recommended for new construction, and that $2,500 worth of improvements would cut energy consumption by 50 percent. That reduction would bring the per-square-foot rating into line with other ratings in the area.

Who will pay for such improvements? If the house needed repair on the roof or foundation, and the seller was anxious to sell, he might volunteer to bring the house up to standard. Or he might cut the purchase price by the cost of the work and let the new owner do it. Such arrangements are routine in existing real estate transactions. Why shouldn't similar arrangements apply to energy saving? Doesn't an uninsulated basement or an oil-guzzling furnace make for a less-than-attractive housing buy? A few municipalities, notably in the Pacific Northwest, now require that houses be upgraded for energy efficiency before they are sold. You may have to meet such standards by the time you sell. So shouldn't the owner from whom you want to buy pay for some of the needed work now?

There are no rules here, and what I'm suggesting is not routine procedure. But I have a hunch it will become routine soon enough.

If it is impossible to get an audit—utilities don't have to do the same house twice—you can at least perform your own informal energy inspection on the premises. This is also something you should do when you don't have the time or inclination to collect the utility bills and compute dollars per square foot. Here are the things to look for and the things to ignore:

1. Orientation and External Factors. Twenty-five to 50 percent of the heating and cooling energy is saved or lost here. Every house either fights the climate or uses it to some advantage, and its placement on the lot determines which. A house with inadequate insulation protected from the wind by a hill or some other natural obstruction may in some cases produce a better energy rating than an adequately insulated house naked to the elements. Even in the same apartment building, a California study shows, a unit facing south can have 30 percent higher cooling bills than a unit facing north.

The details and refinements of orientation are too numerous to reproduce here. There are no formulas or things to measure. But to have an economical relationship with climate, a house should have the following characteristics:

Northern Climates. The emphasis here should be on protection from the elements. The less wall surface exposed to the north side, the better. The best arrangement is one in which the north side of the house is bermed, or built into a hill. Next best, the north side is shielded from the wind by a hill, another building, a man-made windbreak, or trees.

There should be few windows on the north side of the house, and more on the south. Winter sun should reach these south-facing windows without obstruction. The south-facing windows should be shaded from the sun in summer. Deciduous trees here are a solution: sunlight can penetrate through the bare branches in winter, and the trees' foliage provides shading in summer.

Southern Climates. The emphasis should be on shade and breeze. In very warm climates, a house should be exposed to the wind as much as possible, so natural breezes can substitute for air conditioning at certain times. Protecting the north side of a house is not as crucial here, of course, but winter sun should still reach the south-facing windows. Summer shading is of prime importance.

2. The Shape of the House. Square or rectangular houses are easier to heat than L-shaped houses or than other designs having many extensions and protuberances. The greater the exposed wall surface, in relation to the floor area, the higher the energy bills per square foot. Overhangs, gables, and other architectural flourishes may be hard to insulate.

Townhouses and other buildings that share common walls may produce lower heating bills, since the heat from one apartment or unit can seep into the next. If the common walls, however, are constructed of unfilled concrete block, cold air can travel up through the holes and create huge and costly bypasses.

3. Attic Insulation. First I would check to see what kind it is, and how thick. Don't take the seller's estimate on faith. Many people really don't know what insulation they actually have.

In an unfinished attic, the insulation is usually found on the floor. In a partially finished attic, it may be found under the floorboards or overhead in the rafters. In a finished attic, it may be hidden under the floorboards or behind a dropped ceiling. In these latter instances, unless the owner is willing to remove a floorboard or a ceiling panel, you cannot determine whether the insulation exists.

But in most cases, the insulation will be visible; it comes in blanket form or as loose fill. Either way, it could be fiberglass (white, yellow, or pink shiny fibers), rock wool (white or gray dull fibers), or cellulose (shredded newspaper).

Once you determine the type of insulation in the attic, you can measure the thickness with a ruler and estimate the R-value from the chart on page 53.

I would also inspect the quality of the insulation coverage, as described earlier. Also check for moisture damage in the attic resulting from insufficient ventilation.

4. Wall Insulation. There are two ways to check the seller's claim that he has wall insulation. One is to remove the faceplate on an electrical outlet (turn off the power to the outlet first) and probe around the sides of the outlet to feel what's in the wall cavity. If the hole is big enough, you can see into the wall cavity with a flashlight. The other is to ask the owner to drill a small hole into the wall in an inconspicuous place and to pull out a small sample of the insulation. Auditors drill holes when the owner isn't sure what kind of insulation has been installed.

I give superior marks to a house that has rigid styrofoam insulation sheathing in addition to the insulation between the wall studs. Sheathing goes on the outside of the house, beneath the final siding. More houses have some type of sheathing, but tongue-in-groove styrofoam panels are especially effective in cutting down air leaks as well as increasing the R-value of the wall. Sometimes there are strips of "beadboard" insulation attached to aluminum siding. These strips are not connected to the shell of the house directly, and they are not particularly useful because cold air can get in behind them.

If insulation has been blown into the walls after construction, you can check the coverage by looking for the small wooden plugs around the outside walls of the house. The placement of plugs depends on how the house is constructed, but in standard houses, you should find a plug every 16 inches. (These plugs are often painted over, but you can see them if you look carefully at the bottom or top of the walls.)

5. Basement Insulation. This is the best place to test the overall quality of the house's insulation job. Inspect the band-joist area, as described on page 60.

6. Windows and Panes. Most newer houses have double-glazed windows, and some even triple-glazed windows. I'd give extra points for houses with the triple glazing or with the special insulated shutters or shades described earlier. Double-paned windows or single panes with storms are adequate in some climate zones, but no one should brag about them as energy savers.

7. Caulking and Weatherstripping. Check the condition of caulk around windows and weatherstripping around doors. If the materials appear to be old, chipped, torn, or dried out, the owner hasn't taken the effort very seriously. But it is simple enough to replace caulk, so this isn't a big money issue. Ask the owner if he has caulked behind baseboards or around recessed bathroom cabinets and light fixtures or in the other places described earlier. If not, it's a day's work for you or a day's pay for a laborer.

8. Furnaces and Heaters. Again, the owner may want to point out features—"this furnace has an energy-saving vent damper," or "this furnace has pilotless ignition." You want to get a measure of steady-state efficiency, and an estimate of seasonal efficiency given by an accredited furnace technician.

Gas and oil furnaces (when I say "furnace," I mean both forced-air and hot-water systems) in the 40 to 70 percent seasonal efficiency range are guzzlers, furnaces in the 70 to 80 percent range are moderately efficient, and furnaces above 80 percent are excellent. Escalating fuel prices will probably force you to trade in anything below "excellent" in a matter of years, so don't be thrilled by a brand-new furnace exhibiting 70 percent efficiency.

9. Solar Equipment. I wouldn't buy a house with a solar collector system without getting it checked over by a solar contractor, for reasons gone into in "The Fashionable Alternatives."

10. Woodstoves. Get a competent person to review the installation. Woodstoves can be dangerous if they aren't placed at a proper distance from the adjoining wall, if the adjoining wall is not properly insulated, and if the flue pipe is the wrong diameter. You should also have the stove checked for creosote buildup before you use it.

11. Air Conditioners. A sales pitch has it that central air conditioners are more economical than room air conditioners, but don't believe it. What central air conditioners gain in a kind of economy of scale, they lose in cooling the entire house when only spot-cooling may be required.

In warm climates, any house with cooling flexibility has energy advantages. A dwelling with a whole-house fan or other mechanism that reduces the need for air conditioning is preferable to a house that locks people into an expensive dependence.

12. Other Appliances. It is tempting for tract builders and condominium builders to cut costs by installing cheap appliances that often have poor energy ratings. In fact, this is one good reason to keep government appliance efficiency standards, which have come under recent attack. Consumers can make self-interested choices when they buy their own appliances, but in a secondary market where the builders make purchasing decisions, consumers can get stuck with a lifetime of higher energy costs, with builders getting a short-term advantage.

As an individual buyer, you can probably do little about this, except to demand that fuel-stingy furnaces and appliances be installed in any apartment or condominium still under construction that you might buy. If appliances are already in place, you can perhaps haggle for some last-minute replacements, depending on how anxious you are to buy and they are to sell.

TAKING IT TO THE BANK

Your energy inspection may be cursory or thorough, but it should enable you to put a house into one of four general categories, as defined in the realtor's guide. A house may have many attractive energy features and high fuel bills. In that case, its energy efficiency is ambiguous.

Or a house may have few notable energy features and low fuel bills. Again, the situation is ambiguous. Either the former owners were willing to shiver in winter and swelter in summer to hold the energy costs down, or else the house has some special advantage (passive solar, perhaps) that didn't show up in the inspection. Again, a conversation with the owners will be revealing. Were they away a great deal of the time?

A house may lack laudable energy features and produce high fuel bills. This is a house where extra money will have to be spent either on energy renovation or on continually punishing energy costs.

Finally, a house may contain many good energy features and have low fuel bills. This is the kind of house that needs no further attention.

Money is the key element. I haven't said much about the banks, because until recently not many of them have gotten involved in energy evaluation. This is changing. Lenders are worried that energy bills may imperil people's ability to make mortgage payments, which, as I said, has already changed the appraisal procedures in the secondary markets. Some lending institutions are also considering energy efficiency to evaluate how large a loan to give prospective buyers of a house. Daniel Yergin has identified a hundred savings and loans that now offer financial incentives to buyers or sellers of energy-efficient homes. You should ask your local lending sources whether any of them use a loan-to-income formula that takes energy into account. If you find a bank or savings and loan that does, and you have chosen to buy a low-fuel house, you might get the benefit of a larger loan for your income level.

Energy investigating may seem irrelevant, since it is not yet a part of the selling and lending rituals. But people who pay attention to energy in their search for a home are a step ahead of the game, which is a good place to be during inflationary times.

RATING YOUR HOUSE AGAINST THE COMPETITION

Until the realtors begin to collect more dollars-per-square-foot numbers, it's hard to measure the performance of any one house against a local, regional, or national average. But as a rough point of comparison, we can use some national estimates that come from a computer simulation run at Lawrence Berkeley Laboratory. You can figure out the dollars-per-square-foot rating for your own house or for a house you want to buy, and then see how it stacks up on the chart of your own climate zone (see pages 205–206). The Lawrence Berkeley computer shows that the dollars-per-square-foot ratings vary from as low as 7¢ to as high as $3.44, depending on type of house, type of heating fuel, and location.

The charts don't take into account the energy used in lights, televisions, and small appliances, so the ratings are probably understated by about 20 percent. In any case, the calculations are based on the following fuel prices—natural gas at 35¢ a therm, oil at $1 a gallon, and electricity at 6¢ a kilowatt-hour.

These estimates should not be taken as gospel. They may be too high on the high end or too low on the low end for some or even all the climate zones. But they do show the tremendous relative savings that come from owning a house at the low end of the ratings. They also show that the type of fuel in the furnace can affect energy costs as much as the amount of insulation in the attic. And they show the impact of location on energy consumption: an energy hog in Zone

1 is cheaper to operate than a very efficient house in Zone 8.

As long as you don't take these computer estimates too seriously, you can get a general sense of whether your house is a guzzler or an economy model. For instance, if you happen to live in a 1,500-square-foot house in Zone 4, you heat with gas, and you pay an annual energy bill of $900, then your energy rating is 48¢ per square foot. ($900 minus the 20 percent for lights and appliances is $720, which when divided by the 1,500 square feet makes 48¢.) That puts your house somewhere in the average range between the 76¢ energy hog and the 24¢ energy miser.

If you want to know more about your house's relative energy economy, it is useful to sit down with friends and neighbors and compare square-foot ratings between your house and theirs. These sessions can produce some useful ideas about why one house might be cheaper to operate than the others, and what adjustments might be made to bring the others into the high-mileage realm.

Part Eight

SIDE EFFECTS

At a meeting of energy experts last year in Santa Cruz, California, an entire evening was devoted to a discussion of indoor pollutants that have become the unhappy surprises of the house-tightening movement. This was no light-hearted event. Many of the experts had never imagined that any harm could come from building fuel-efficient houses. Now they find that at least in certain houses designed to be "super-tight" the pollutants are not flushed out and unhealthy conditions may result.

The speaker was Craig Hollowell of the Lawrence Berkeley Laboratory. Hollowell's office is located just down the hall from those of other scientists who work to seal houses down to below .5 air changes per hour; by zipping up a house as if it were a freezer bag, they cut heating and cooling energy use by as much as 40 percent. Hollowell, meanwhile, is researching the unintended consequences of this very energy-saving technique.

Hollowell and others have identified the big five indoor contaminants. They include: radon gas, which is emitted from the soil or from concrete and breaks down into radioactive particles; formaldehyde gas, released from plywood, certain types of paneling, and foam insulation; nitrogen dioxide, given off by unvented gas appliances; carbon monoxide, from the same source as nitrogen dioxide; and cigarette smoke. Nobody blames the existence of these contaminants on energy conservation, except perhaps for the formaldehyde in the foam insulation. In the past twenty years, we have enveloped ourselves in strange new chemicals from sprays, dyes, paint, glue, and building materials. Radon, which is emitted from concrete, stone, or the ground itself, has been trapped in buildings for as long as man has put them up. But we are just finding out what its effects are.

There may be no cause to ring the national alarm bell about all this, but Hollowell is especially concerned about the high pollution readings in his colleagues' test houses, some of which exceed federal standards for outdoor air in smoggy cities. He suspects that the old leaky houses, the ones that waste energy, may have at least one advantage—flushing out some of the pollutants that hang in the air of low-infiltration experimental models.

One low-infiltration model Hollowell discussed was a house in San Jose. It was a demonstration project of the Pacific Gas and Electric Company, along with a few California organizations involved in residential construction. PG and E, a progressive utility when it comes to conservation, wanted to show that regular-looking houses could be built to use less energy. The San Jose house, completed in 1977, employs what is called a solar-assisted heat pump. On sunny days during the winter, the solar energy does most of the heating, and when that isn't enough, a heat pump takes over. Warm air is delivered to the house through a unique plenum system that uses part of the crawl space beneath the floor as a heating duct.

The San Jose house is well insulated and also very tightly sealed. While most homes get a complete change of fresh air once an hour through all the incidental cracks and gaps around doors, walls, and windows, this house flushes its air only once every five hours.

John Hailey, the PG and E representative directing the San Jose project, was sitting next to me during Hollowell's speech. He was more than a casual observer. PG and E had gotten on to radioactive radon derivatives very quickly through a bizarre set of circumstances that Hailey described:

"We ran the San Jose house as a walk-in demonstration model for about a year," he said. "Then we sold it. The buyers were a retired couple who loved the house. Part of our agreement with them was that we be allowed to continue to monitor it.

"The people at Lawrence Berkeley Laboratory called PG and E and asked if we had any houses that could be tested for air leakage. We told them about the one in San Jose. We thought it was a very tight house, which is what Lawrence Berkeley was looking for. They also said they would be taking some indoor air pollution measurements. It didn't sound very important at the time. None of us had even heard about radon.

"When Hollowell informed us what he had found in his pollution grab samples of the house, we were completely taken aback. I had to sit down with the owners of the house and tell them the results of the tests. 'The good news,' I said, 'is that you have a tight house, only .2 air changes per hour. Very few houses are this well sealed. The bad news is that you may have high concentrations of indoor pollutants, especially radon particles. We don't know how dangerous this might be as yet, but we are going to find out. If it is a problem, we will do something about it.'

"The owners, Ervin and Gladys Rohe, took this discussion very calmly."

Hollowell's samples indicated that the Rohes were living with radiation levels halfway between what is accepted as safe and what is found in uranium mines. The radiation comes from radon gas. The gas itself is not dangerous, but it breaks down into tiny decay products, called "mutant daughters," that are radioactive. The radon is the most sinister of the indoor pollutants because it cannot be smelled or otherwise detected by the homeowner and because long-term exposure may increase one's chances of getting lung cancer.

The cancer issue is still speculative, since indoor air quality is such a new topic for investigation. Nobody can yet make a direct connection between the amounts of radon found in certain houses and a higher incidence of cancer. What has Hollowell worried is that his indoor measurements of radon sometimes exceed those levels acceptable to the Environmental Protection Agency for outdoor air.

The amount of radon that seeps into any single house depends on how the house is constructed, what it is made of (concrete floors and walls emit radon), and where it is located. One house may sit on a radon concentration ten times greater than what is found under neighboring houses, or than what is found in the next city or town. In areas with greater concentrations, an old, leaky house may also be a dangerous place to live. That's why Hollowell is proposing a nationwide program to measure radon levels in thousands or perhaps millions of houses.

The specific cause for alarm in the super-tight houses comes from direct measurements taken not only at San Jose but also in a number of other places. The National Association of Home Builders, for instance, has its own version of the San Jose house in Mount Airy, Maryland. This house doesn't have a solar-assisted heat pump, but it breathes as infrequently as the San Jose house, or about .2 air changes per hour. The Mount Airy house got all kinds of good reviews for its advanced design and its low fuel bills. But when the pollution researchers moved in with detection equipment, they found excessive amounts of formaldehyde gas, and radioactivity that was a hundred times greater than normal background levels.

The Mount Airy house differed from the San Jose house in one important respect. In San Jose, there were no visible signs of the indoor pollution or lack of ventilation, but at Mount Airy the occupants found slime and mold around the windows.

The connection between air changes and indoor pollution was firmly established at Mount Airy. When the house was opened up and allowed to breathe, all the pollutants diminished to safe levels, and the slime and mold disappeared. Maybe there was some wisdom in the lackadaisical and traditional construction that left enough cracks and gaps to ventilate the houses.

The question is: How tight is too tight? A standard house gets about .75 air changes per hour, according to Princeton and Lawrence Berkeley. The leak-plugging techniques of the house doctors can bring that level down to .5 air changes per hour or less. A super-tight house that is sealed up during construction breathes in the .2 air changes region, and that is where the indoor pollutants have been noticeable. Luckily, it takes meticulous attention to get a house this tight, and all of your caulking and leak-plugging won't get your existing house below .5 air changes.

But that doesn't mean that one should feel threatened at .2 and safe at .5. None of the experts is willing to advance a cutoff point, because the research is embryonic and because the concentration of pollutants varies so much from house to house. They suggest only that gas appliances be properly vented, that houses be opened up as much as possible during nonwinter seasons when there is no energy penalty, and that weekend caulkers and leak pluggers probably have little to worry about.

Meanwhile, PG and E has fixed the San Jose house, where the Rohes still live. I had a long conversation with Ervin Rohe, a retired heavy-duty truck salesman who had three heart operations prior to moving into the house. Although Rohe says he was "surprised when they told us about the air quality," he is still very pleased with the house:

"It's one of the most comfortable houses you'll ever come into," he said. "There is no feeling of overheating or drafts in either winter or summer. I used to be a cigar smoker, but I gave that up after my heart trouble, so there isn't much smoke in the air unless we have visitors. In fact this house seems sterile. I mean that in a good way. I think it may even have helped my health."

Rohe says he and his wife had to compensate for the lack of natural air flow into the bedroom at night. "We are basically a fresh-air family. We don't like to be sealed in. During the winter we close off our bedroom from the rest of the house and then open a window. In the summer we keep windows open most of the time."

An open window may add something to the fuel bills, but it also exhausts some of the pollutants that may accumulate, including the radon derivatives. The Rohes were happy with the trade-off. Even with the nightly dose of fresh air, Rohe reports that winter fuel bills have never exceeded $38 a month.

While the Rohes were taking the radon news philosophically ("Nothing has been proven," Rohe told me), the utility company was eager to do something about it. PG and E still isn't sure if the health threat is real or imagined, but the utility didn't ignore Hollowell's warnings.

PG and E corrected the overtight situation with a device called an air-to-air heat exchanger. It's unfortunate that American energy experts didn't discover this device earlier. The exchangers are routinely used in parts of Europe, particularly Sweden, where supertight houses are now produced in quantity. The Swedes take the indoor pollution threat very seriously, with many of them having the foresight to install air-to-air heat exchangers while their houses are still under construction.

An air-to-air heat exchanger can be nothing more elaborate than a box with a couple of fans to move air back and forth, and some type of paper or plastic core to absorb the heat as the air blows by. This creates the best of both worlds—plenty of fresh air and lower fuel bills. In the winter an exchanger can trap about 75 percent of the heat in the air it is flushing out of the house, and transfer that heat to the air it is blowing back into the house. In the summer the process is reversed.

There are two basic types of air-to-air heat exchangers: window units that are installed like small room air conditioners, and elaborate central systems that require ducts and registers. Hollowell is convinced that the exchangers represent the technical solution to unhealthy dwellings. He is heartened by experiments like the one done at Mount Airy, where the air-to-air heat exchanger immediately brought pollution levels down from the danger zone. As long as people use the devices, Hollowell says, they can tighten their houses as much as they want, without fear.

The big question is whether people will accept the new product, especially when the heat exchanger is marketed as an afterthought. PG and E had to go back to the Rohes, clear its corporate throat, and say: (1) there's this little problem we didn't tell you about; (2) we didn't tell you because we didn't know; (3) we thought tightening a house would be good for your budget, but now we have to loosen it for your health; and (4) all this will cost money.

The Rohes welcomed the modifications because they believe in PG and E's good-faith efforts and because PG and E paid for the heat exchanger. In the private market, the pollution protection will alter the economics of energy conservation. Let's say a family is willing to spend $400 extra to get a low-infiltration house that will save it $2,000 in fuel bills over twenty years. Now, they face the additional expense of a couple of $400 heat exchanger window units, or perhaps a central ventilation system that could cost as much as $2,000. In any case, no real domestic market for air-to-air heat exchangers exists at the moment. Most units have to be imported (see the list of U.S. and Canadian distributors on page 223) and they are expensive.

Hollowell says that further pollution research will determine how widely heat exchangers will be adopted. If unhealthy houses, especially those with high radon levels, turn out to be a tiny percentage of the total housing stock, people probably won't worry about polluting the great indoors. But if radon is proven to be a national health menace, people will be happy to buy air-to-air heat exchangers at whatever the cost.

U.S. AND CANADIAN DISTRIBUTORS OF
RESIDENTIAL AIR-TO-AIR HEAT EXCHANGERS

Manufacturer	*Approximate Cost*
Automated Controls and Systems ATTN.: Ray Kollock 500 East Higgins Road Elkgrove, IL 60007 (312) 860-6860	Call for quotation; wide range of prices
D.C. Heat Exchangers Rural Route 3 Saskatoon Saskatchewan, Canada (306) 384-0208	$425 (Canadian)
Des Champs Labs Incorporated ATTN.: Nicholas Des Champs P.O. Box 348 East Hanover, NJ 07936 (201) 884-1460	$350–$450
Enercon Projects Ltd. ATTN.: Dennis D. Rogoza 3813 Regina Avenue Regina, Saskatchewan S4S OH8 (306) 585-0022	$795 (Canadian)
Flakt Products Incorporated (for Svenska Flakt Fabriken) ATTN.: Fulton M. Cooke P.O. Box 21500 Fort Lauderdale, FL 33335 (305) 524-6521	$600–$1000
Mitsubishi Electric Sales America, Inc. ATTN.: Mike Thomas 3030 East Victoria Street Compton, CA 90221 (213) 537-7132 (800) 421-1132	$200–$700

Manufacturer	Approximate Cost
Q-Dot Corporation	call for quotation
ATTN.: Axel Bucher	
726 Regal Row	
Dallas, TX 75247	
(214) 630-1224	

In the meantime, what constitutes the prudent course of action? The best research now suggests the following:

1. It is almost impossible to tighten existing standard houses beyond .5 air changes per hour. You can caulk, weatherstrip, and seal attic bypasses to cut energy bills without much concern.

2. Gas appliances that are poorly vented may be more dangerous than most people think, although research on this point is inconclusive. In the Lawrence Berkeley test house at Walnut Creek, California, Hollowell found that nitrogen oxide concentrations around the gas stove exceeded federal outdoor pollution standards. The suspicion exists that excessive nitrogen oxide in the air can cause bronchitis and respiratory problems.

Hollowell suggests using the kitchen exhaust vents or opening nearby windows whenever one cooks with a gas stove.

3. The dangers of indoor pollutants such as radon particles are long-term and cumulative. Tight houses present less risk if they are opened up whenever artificial heating or cooling is not needed.

4. Some indoor pollutants are easily detectable. The formaldehyde used in building materials, and especially in urea formaldehyde insulation, has caused headaches and skin irritation. Complaints of formaldehyde contamination are not confined to tight houses. Enough people have reported symptoms that the state of Massachusetts has banned urea formaldehyde insulation, and federal agencies have considered doing the same.

5. If you have bought a house advertised as super-tight and have observed some of the consequences described in this section (mold on the windows, general stuffiness of the air, occupants complaining of headaches and skin irritation), you want to look into an air-to-air heat exchanger. Maybe you can convince the builder that he is responsible for part of such a purchase.

6. If you are designing a house, you should resist the challenge to

make it as tight as possible. There are other ways to save energy and still get adequate ventilation. If your builder or architect seems to be selling the no-leak, freezer-bag approach, show him this part of the book.

Craig Hollowell at the Lawrence Berkeley Laboratory is looking for more low-infiltration houses to monitor and for people who have had problems with indoor pollution. Any questions or comments can be addressed to him at Energy and Environment Division, Lawrence Berkeley Laboratory, University of California, Berkeley, California 94720.

INSULATING THE ATTIC

While Craig Hollowell lives in Berkeley worrying about polluted indoor air, Gautam Dutt sits in Princeton worrying about rotten attics. The problem is not as threatening, but it is more prevalent. Dutt says that if we are not careful, we will create a nationful of overhead decay as a legacy of saving energy.

Dutt has seen enough attics to know. As part of Princeton's house doctor program, he has crawled into hundreds of them. He is usually looking for air leaks, or bypasses, but he often finds moisture. Dutt guesses that 25 percent of the attics in America may not be properly ventilated. That means the moisture from the house below can seep through the insulation, collect in the attic, and condense on the rafters and other wood surfaces. Over the years, the condensation can rot the wood.

Dutt's estimates on improper attic ventilation may even be conservative. In the Massachusetts Building Code Commission survey of eighty homes in 1978, only 50 percent of those homes were found to have any such ventilation. In the Dynatech study of home insulation, out of one sample of fifteen attics, nine had minimal venting, two average venting, and four had no venting at all. These numbers suggest that the need for ventilation is not understood by the public or by some of the insulation professionals, which is why you should check the work overhead.

Attics may require more ventilation when the insulation is thickened. Extra insulation on the attic floor makes the attic colder, since less heat is getting through from the warm house beneath the attic. A colder attic accelerates the process of condensation, and the additional ventilation may be needed to exhaust the moisture.

A number of contractors even install the insulation wrong side up, according to the Massachusetts survey: out of eighty attics, the vapor barriers—the plastic, aluminum foil, or paper backing on the insulation—were upside down in twenty-five of them. The vapor barrier is supposed to stand between the house and the insulation. If the attic is insulated from above, the vapor barriers should be visible. If the attic is insulated at the floor level, the vapor barriers should be hidden beneath the insulation. When vapor barriers are turned the wrong way, moisture gets trapped inside the insulation.

The symptoms of excess moisture in an attic are obvious: green slime or mold on the rafters, or small pools of water in the corners of the attic, or droplets of water forming on the rafters like dew on the lawn. Soggy or wet insulation is another sign that the attic doesn't get enough ventilation, assuming the vapor barriers are facing the right direction.

The cure for an upside-down vapor barrier on the floor of the attic is to remove all the insulation and reverse it (a time-consuming process) or to slash the vapor barrier every few inches with a knife. This allows moisture to pass through the insulation and out the attic. The slash cure will undo some of the leak-plugging efforts described earlier, but in this situation, having a dry attic is more important than stopping all the little heat leaks.

The solution to the general attic moisture problem is to enlarge the total area of the vents. A builder's rule of thumb is that attics should have one square foot of ventilation for every 150 square feet of attic. Ventilation can come through openings in the vertical walls at the ends, or gables, of the attic; through openings in the overhang of the roof called soffit vents; or through mushroom-type protrusions on the roof called roof vents. Sometimes these vents are blocked or clogged, especially when they are cut into the overhang of the roof. Loose-fill insulation on the floor of an attic can drift and cover up the vents. Before you spend money to enlarge the vents, make sure the existing ones are clear of obstructions.

If you have to increase the ventilation, the cheapest way is usually to put bigger holes in the end walls of the attic. You can discuss all the possibilities with a carpenter or with the attic insulation contractor. I would first call the insulation contractor, who should be pressured to correct the problem. Allowing for proper ventilation is part of the attic insulation job.

Fire Damage in Attics. Some house fires have been blamed on attic insulation, although the numbers here are small. Fires occur when insulation comes into direct contact with such heat sources as recessed light fixtures, flue pipes, or chimneys. The Denver District Attorney's Office investigated the hazards of insulation and pointed to cellulose and recessed light fixtures as a potentially dangerous combination.

Since cellulose is installed loose, it can drift over a recessed light fixture. If the cellulose is not treated with enough fire-retardant chemical, this is where the smoldering begins. Recessed light fixtures covered over with insulation can produce very high temperatures, since the heat inside has no avenue of escape.

Cellulose now carries a government or industry seal of approval, but if you bought the stuff several years ago, you can't check the old bags to ensure that you got a properly manufactured batch. The best fire prevention in such a case is to keep the cellulose away from the attic heat sources. One method is to push the material back from the light fixtures or chimneys, leaving a few inches of air space between insulation and heat.

A more permanent solution is a buffer zone of fiberglass insulation around every hot spot in the attic. Fiberglass with no vapor barrier backing (you can buy it like this in the hardware store) has a better flame rating than cellulose. The fiberglass can be stuffed around the perimeter of a light fixture or chimney pipe so that it blocks the cellulose from coming into contact with the heat. Again, it is important not to smother the top of a recessed light fixture, even with the fiberglass, but it is all right for the fiberglass to touch the sides of the fixture.

ADDING STORM WINDOWS

The pre-energy-crisis storm windows were made loose so that moist air couldn't get trapped in the space between the original window and the storm addition. Even when a house had leaky windows, the warm indoor air that might otherwise condense on the storm panels found a way around the storms and outside.

But since all air leakage from a house adds to the fuel bills, the storm window manufacturers have been tightening their product so that less air gets through. This is good for energy conservation, but when a tight storm window is installed over a leaky original window, the result can be condensation on the inside of the storm. Over time, the condensation can damage some of the wood surfaces around the edges of the window.

The condensation problem is even more acute when energy-saving shutters or panels are put over the windows inside the house. When these interior shutters don't make a tight seal with the window casing, moisture can get around the shutters and collect on the window frames and sills. The water can be especially troublesome, because it attacks finished surfaces on the lived-in side of the house. People who cover up windows with large insulated boards until spring are sometimes greeted with puddles of water on the window-sills, and repainting jobs that cost more than the amount of energy saved by the insulated boards in the first place.

Such consequences are easy to avert. Interior shutters can be built with rubber gaskets or weatherstripping around the edges so that moist indoor air cannot get through to the window. It is also advisable to remove the shutters every once in a while to see if moisture has collected around the window casings before any damage is done.

The condensation on the outdoor storm windows will disappear once the interior windows are made less leaky with caulking and/or weatherstripping.

INSULATING THE WALLS

Blown-in wall insulation has been the source of great controversy. It has been accused of rotting out the framing of the house from inside (urea formaldehyde and cellulose), corroding the electrical fixtures through chemical action (urea and cellulose), sending unpleasant and/or unhealthy gases into the house (urea), and causing fires (cellulose). The evidence from a few wall insulation experiments suggests that the dangers are not as great as has been believed.

The moisture and wall rot criticism is disproved by the wall insulation studies I know about, including the Dynatech study in Minnesota and the National Bureau of Standards study of insulation jobs in eight states. In each case, samples were taken from various walls that had been filled with blown-in insulation. The verdict was unanimous. "Project results," said the Dynatech report, "indicate that moisture buildup is not a serious problem." The National Bureau of Standards said: "No observations were recorded for the thirty-nine homes which indicated that the retrofitting of side walls had adversely affected the conditions of the wall components. [There was] no visible evidence of excessive moisture accumulation."

Wall insulation also isn't corroding many electrical outlets, according to Dynatech, which found no evidence that the chemicals in cellulose had damaged the wires or pipes that run through the walls.

ACTIVE SOLAR WATER HEATERS, SPACE HEATERS, POOL HEATERS

We have already discussed the number of things that can go wrong here, especially with rooftop equipment. Your best protection is a strong guarantee from a solid solar company and a professional installer who has done good work before.

WOODSTOVES

Unless you are very confident about the placement of the stove, the insulation around it, and the design and location of the flue pipes, call the local fire department or fire marshal to check the installation for safety. Make sure the flue or chimney is cleaned regularly, because creosote buildup is a major cause of house fires from wood-burning equipment.

Part Nine

HEATING A HOUSE ON A DOLLAR A WEEK

S askatoon, Canada, is a very cold place in the winter, but a line-up of fourteen houses on Christopher Street shares a remarkable indifference to the weather. The winter heating bills in these houses reach appalling levels like $6 or $8 or $3 a month, undercutting the normal bills up here by 85 to 90 percent. The light bills in these houses are higher than the heating bills by a factor of three, and the monthly energy costs, appliances and all, settle in at around $60.

Not only are these Canadian houses economical beyond what are considered the usual boundaries of possibility, but they are in most respects conventional subdivision houses—or routine-looking rectangles. I am more fascinated by the results produced by the Canadian government project than I am by the scattered triumphs of cave houses, yurts, bermed houses, glass houses, solar houses, and adobe esoterics. The numbers in Saskatoon prove that you don't have to stray very far from routine construction to eliminate any need for artificial heat in houses built in the United States. The cost of the energy-saving extras in Saskatoon varied from about $4,000 to $8,000 per house.

Success up there involved doing the routine things, only more of them. Insulation levels—and we are talking about new-house construction here—are as high as R-60 in the attics and R-40 in the walls and one has to build a double-thick wall to accommodate that much fiberglass. Instead of double or triple glass on the windows, several of these houses have quad glazing, or four layers of glass, bringing the window R-values to around 4, or as high as an uninsulated wall.

These houses are also meticulously sealed for air leaks, with continuous plastic vapor barriers under the attic insulation and inside all the walls. In fact, recessed light fixtures are not put into these

233

walls just so they won't disturb the seal, which is an indication of how seriously the builders are taking the air leaks. The Canadians are also one step ahead of the game in giving the tight houses air-to-air heat exchangers, which allow a homeowner to control air flow through the house without a big energy penalty.

A few of the Saskatoon houses have passive solar features such as Trombe walls or large expanses of glass on the south side that can be insulated at night. The following three pages contain a description of one of the Saskatoon houses—which as you can see is conventional in design and layout—and also an estimate of the monthly savings that will accrue to the owner over time.

I'm not arguing for a specific design here; each of the fourteen houses is slightly different. You can write to the Office of Energy Conservation, Saskatchewan Mineral Resources, 1914 Hamilton Street, Regina, Saskatchewan, S4 4V4 for details. The lesson is that you can hardly go wrong if you strike a balance between insulation, tightness, and passive solar.

Saskatoon is the culmination of a decade of experience with three different approaches to energy economy, and the results suggest that its better to combine them than to get caught up in one. In the early 1970s an energy-saving house was simply a reasonably well insulated house with double-paned windows. In the middle 1970s research outfits like Princeton discovered the importance of infiltration, which is just beginning to be understood in the building trade. Meanwhile, passive solar has come along, which opens up a house to sunlight. Some trade-offs present themselves, especially in southern climates. One theory is to zip a house up and isolate it from the elements. A house with few windows, thick insulation, and low infiltration rates will be easy to heat and cool. Another theory is to use the elements, particularly sunlight, to most advantage, thereby eliminating the need for artificial heating and cooling. The ultimate energy-saving house in Florida may be a house that has wide overhangs, ceiling fans, and so many windows that air conditioners are not needed. On the other hand, if you put an air conditioner in such a house, the electric bill would be very high.

So how does one build a house for maximum savings and maximum comfort? Doub Balcomb, the passive solar expert, argues for what he calls balanced design. You can go too far with the routine

426 Christopher Road
120 square metres (1,292 sq. ft.)
bungalow
featuring:
3 bedroom
½ bath off master bedroom
formal dining-room
valence lighting kitchen counter

Energy Showcase consists of 14 new homes located on Christopher Road in Saskatoon's Lakeview subdivision.

These homes have been designed so that they require only one-third of the energy needed to heat conventional homes. And, at today's prices, this translates to a heating bill of about $100 or less per year for an average 100m² bungalow.

The showcase is a joint venture sponsored by the governments of Canada and Saskatchewan, the Saskatoon branch of HUDAC and the city of Saskatoon.

MAJOR ENERGY EFFICIENT FEATURES

1. **DOUBLE WALL SYSTEM -** this features a high density of wall insulation equivalent to R-60 with the vapour barrier located in the wall.

2. **HOT WATER HEAT -** space heat from the service hot water heater is delivered through a fan coil unit.

3. **QUAD GLAZING -** this builder has introduced window units which are completed sealed and incorporate four panes of glass per unit.

4. **CHIMNEY VENT -** the hot water tank chimney vents through the foundation wall as opposed to the normal roof mount.

5. **WALL MOUNTED ELECTRICAL FIXTURES -** to avoid potential damage to the vapour barrier, fixtures mounted on ceiling have been eliminated.

Engineered Homes

Registered Builder Member
NEW HOME CERTIFICATION PROGRAM OF SASKATCHEWAN

HILTON HOMES LTD.
501 - 45th Street West
Saskatoon, Saskatchewan.
Telephone (244-4410)

INSULATION VALUES

Ceiling	Walls	South Windows	Non South Windows	Doors	Basem Above	Basement Below Grade	Basement Floors
RSI Value 10.6	RSI Value 10.6	RSI Value .776	RSI Value .776	RSI Value 4.2	RSI Value 4.5	RSI Value 3.5	RSI Value 0
R Value 60.	R Value 60.	R Value 4.4	R Value 4.4	R Value 24.	R Value 26.	R Value 20.	R Value 0

Insulation values given are for insulation material only and do not include vapour barriers or siding.

FLOOR PLAN

2. **Energy Requirements Analysis**

Annual Energy Requirement

	Reference House	Low Energy House	% Reduction
Appliances & Lighting	8040 KWH	7500 KWH	7%
Space Heating	174 Mcf	17 Mcf	90%
Water Heating	48 Mcf	36 Mcf	25%

3. Cost Analysis

(i) Mortgage Specifications

	Reference House	Low Energy House
downpayment rate*	—	25%
interest rate	14%	14%
term	25 Yr.	25 Yr.
incremental house cost	$0	$3484
incremental downpayment	$0	$871
incremental PI	$0	$31/Month

* effective rate required on incremental value.

(ii) Total Monthly Payment Comparison

YEAR	PI Reference House (base)	PI Low Energy House (Incremental)	Appliances & Light Reference House	Appliances & Light Low Energy House	Space Heat Reference House	Space Heat Low Energy House	Water Heat Reference House	Water Heat Low Energy House	Total Reference House	Total Low Energy House
1980	$0	$31	$22	$20	$30	$3	$8	$6	$60	$60
1981	$0	$31	$24	$23	$33	$3	$9	$7	$66	$64
1982	$0	$31	$27	$26	$37	$4	$10	$8	$74	$69
1983	$0	$31	$31	$29	$42	$4	$12	$9	$85	$73
1984	$0	$31	$34	$32	$47	$5	$13	$10	$94	$78
1985	$0	$31	$38	$36	$53	$5	$15	$11	$106	$82
1986	$0	$31	$43	$40	$59	$6	$17	$12	$119	$88
1987	$0	$31	$48	$45	$67	$6	$19	$14	$134	$95
1988	$0	$31	$53	$50	$74	$7	$21	$15	$148	$102
1989	$0	$31	$60	$57	$83	$8	$24	$17	$167	$112
1990	$0	$31	$68	$63	$93	$9	$26	$19	$187	$121
1995	$0	$31	$119	$111	$163	$16	$45	$34	$327	$192
2000	$0	$31	$209	$195	$287	$28	$79	$60	$575	$314

of insulation and leak-stopping and create a house that is stuffy, unpleasant, and overly dependent on furnaces and air conditioners. Or you can go too far in the solar direction and create a house that gets too much sunlight or shade, one that is too hot during the day and too cold at night.

A good architect can strike the right balance between shade and sun, thermal storage and insulation, air flow and tightness; the important thing is to find one who understands the passive/conservation compromise, one who can quantify the intangibles with a technique called design load calculation. He or she can determine the optimal mix between glass area, thermal storage, insulation, shading, and siting. If I were building a new house, I would seek out an architect capable of making design load calculations, because the capacity indicates familiarity with the fine points of energy.

You should be able to come out of the collaboration, like the people in Saskatoon, with a house that requires almost no artificial heating in the North; and either very efficient air conditioning or no air conditioning in the South. Don't settle for less. The building code requirements for such things as insulation levels are far below what is cost-effective in most areas, given the price trends. The projected budgets in Saskatoon (see page 237) show what happens to a family in an average house, or reference house, as opposed to the family that spent an extra $3,484 for the energy-saving package.

The family in the Saskatoon energy project house is paying an additional $31 on the mortgage to finance the cost of the improvements. The house, a 1,292-square-foot bungalow at 426 Christopher Road, has an energy package that includes R-60 walls, an R-60 ceiling, quadruple-glazed windows, and no interruptions in the vapor barrier. Even with the extra $31 carrying cost, the total monthly payments of the occupants continue to shrink, as shown on the chart, relative to the family in the standard dwelling.

A passive solar scorecard (see page 239), derived from the Solar Energy Research Institute (SERI), also shows the kinds of savings people are getting in this country from various passive solar techniques.

PASSIVE SOLAR SCORECARD

Location	Size of House (square feet)	Passive Solar Features and Cost	Value of Energy Produced by Passive Solar, Compared to Traditional Fuels at Average 1980 Prices
Sommersworth, NH	2,388	295 square feet of south-facing glass. $1,500.	37 million BTUs, worth: $542 in electricity $240 in oil $111 in gas
Ames, IA	2,200	500 square feet of south-facing glass, with concrete floor as heat absorber. $6,000. Also movable insulation panels for windows.	35 million BTUs, worth: $512 in electricity $105 in gas $226 in oil
Prescott, AZ	1,400	South-facing greenhouse, Trombe wall, rock-bed for heat absorber. $3,400.	58 million BTUs, worth: $850 in electricity $174 in gas $375 in oil

PASSIVE SOLAR SCORECARD—*continued*

Location	*Size of House (square feet)*	*Passive Solar Features and Cost*	*Value of Energy Produced by Passive Solar, Compared to Traditional Fuels at Average 1980 Prices*
Royal Oak, MD	1,300	460 square feet of south-facing glass. $2,500.	55 million BTUs, worth: $805 in electricity $165 in gas $356 in oil
Atascadero, CA	1,100	Roof pond. House 100 percent solar heated. $1,815.	32 million BTUs, worth: $468 in electricity $96 in gas $207 in oil
Santa Fe, NM	2,300	409 square feet of south-facing glass, greenhouse, rock bed for heat absorber. Almost 100 percent solar heated. $3,450.	66 million BTUs, worth: $967 in electricity $198 in gas $428 in oil

Bozeman, MT	2,200	470 square feet water wall. $7,920.	76 million BTUs, worth: $1,113 in electricity $228 in gas $492 in oil
Yakima, WA	1,728	378 square feet south-facing glass. Triple-paned windows in house.	20 million BTUs, worth: $293 in electricity $60 in gas $130 in oil
East Pepperell, MA	1,200	100 square feet south-facing glass. Super insulated.	6 million BTUs, worth: $87.9 in electricity $18 in gas $38.8 in oil

SOURCE: Solar Energy Research Institute

A Final Word

What has been provided in these pages is a solution to a problem that the American people know all too well—rising home energy costs.

A decade ago, the bills for heating, cooling, and powering a house were so low that they almost did not matter. But the situation has changed dramatically. Since 1970 the average cost of electricity has tripled; natural gas is five times higher; home heating oil, seven times higher. (It's well worth another look at the table on page 8.)

These bills will continue to rise in the 1980s. Natural gas, which currently is less expensive than oil, will increase in large steps over the next few years, as it approaches "equivalence" with oil. Indeed, a vigorous campaign has already begun in Washington to accelerate decontrol, now scheduled for 1985. We can certainly expect more international crises that will send the price of oil ever higher in the world market, as occurred in 1973–74 and 1979–80.

Thus, the smart homeowner should move quickly to batten down the hatches because, insofar as home energy costs are concerned, the next several years are going to constitute a very stormy season.

The big obstacle has been the knowledge gap. *Stop Burning Your Money* goes a long way toward helping close that gap.

This book has rightly stressed self-interest as the motivation for action on home energy use. Still, it is worth a moment to reflect on the larger context, and to recognize that what we are talking about is really enlightened self-interest. For what is good for the individual also happens to be good for the nation. The benefits to the United States of a substantial reduction in energy use are considerable. The residential sector uses about 20 percent of the energy used in this country—roughly equivalent to our total oil imports. Reducing energy use in homes that burn oil would mean less oil imports. Using less energy in other homes would free up other energy sources, such as natural gas, that could be used to replace imported oil in other parts of our economy.

The result?

The United States would import less oil, saving tens of billions of dollars a year. This would mean less pressure on our balance of payments, and on our political and even military security. Lower demand in the United States would mean less opportunity for foreign producers to continue to push up the price of oil—and less vulnerability for the United States to disruption in the world oil market. Lower demand would in general mean less strain on supplies, and so fewer upward price pressures. There would be less need for electric utilities to build expensive new generating capacity. We would have more time and greater flexibility as a nation to manage the trade-offs between energy, environment, and cost, and we would stretch out our own domestic energy supplies.

Last, but in no way least, a reduction in energy use in homes would be one of the principal counterattacks against inflation. Greater energy efficiency in the home is the "least cost" energy strategy, which makes it an anti-inflation strategy.

This is the context that makes home energy efficiency so valuable to the nation. But, obviously, most people will act for a very practical reason—their own wallets. A great deal of money can be saved. In other words, you do have a choice: Go on wasting money for levels of energy use you don't need. Or invest a little time and money now to reduce the growing outflow of dollars in the future. And you may not have to invest much money if you pay attention to the low cost/no cost strategies in this book, as well as to the questions posed for the more expensive investments. If you act on this book, your standard of living will go up, not down. For you will still have the same level of physical comfort—perhaps an even better one—with more dollars left over for other purposes.

The need is there. The American people are ready. The public has finally and correctly decided that the energy problem is not going to go away, that costs are going to continue to rise, and that we all ought to do something about it. A poll done for the Alliance to Save Energy found that the majority of Americans now believes that *not* to become more energy efficient will lead to a decline in our standard of living!

Moreover, the tools are now at hand. A great deal has been learned in the last few years about what to do—and what not to do—to save energy in the home. Many utilities are now willing and, in some instances, are even eager to provide a valuable helping hand to reduce energy use.

Financing has become more available in one form or another, both from federal and state programs, and from banks and savings-and-loan associations, and even from utilities.

But the big question has remained: What to do?

Homeowners still need a sensible, informed guide through the maze. This book is such a guide. It will enable all of us to become more "economic" in the original sense—to manage our households wisely at a time when home energy prices have become a constant pressure and, for some, a constant pain.

This need not be the case. Because, now that you've read this book, you really are ready to stop burning your money.

—DANIEL YERGIN

Index

About the Authors

JOHN ROTHCHILD is the nation's most broadly informed home energy expert, having developed for the Department of Energy the entire "no cost/low cost" approach to household conservation. He lives in Miami Beach, Florida, with his wife and three children. DANIEL YERGIN is co-editor of *Energy Future: Report of the Energy Project at the Harvard Business School,* and a Lecturer at the Energy and Environmental Policy Center, Kennedy School of Government, Harvard University.